CW00690174

LOTUS

The

SPORTS·RACING

C · A · R · S

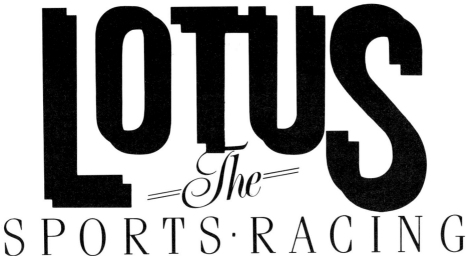

LOTUS
The
SPORTS·RACING
C·A·R·S

DESIGN·DEVELOPMENT·RACING HISTORIES

ANTHONY PRITCHARD

PSL

Patrick Stephens, Wellingborough

© Anthony Pritchard 1987

All rights reserved. No part of this publication may be reproduced, stored in a retrieval system or transmitted, in any form or by any means, electronic, mechanical, photocopying, recording or otherwise, without prior permission in writing from Patrick Stephens Limited.

First published in 1987

British Library Cataloguing in Publication Data

Pritchard, Anthony
    Lotus: the sports-racing cars.
    1. Lotus automobile — History
    I. Title
    629.2'28   TL215.L67

    ISBN 0-85059-795-9

*Patrick Stephens Limited is part of the
Thorsons Publishing Group*

Printed in Great Britain by
Butler & Tanner Ltd, Frome and London

Contents

Introduction

There was a magic and mystique about the growth of Lotus. During the 1950s British power in motor racing rose in a gradual crescendo, through the victories of Jaguar at Le Mans, the two seasons of brilliant success in Grand Prix racing enjoyed by Vanwall and Cooper's World Championship victories in 1959 and 1960. While Cooper's single-seaters were dominant in Formula One, Lotus had proved overwhelmingly successful in short-distance sports car events, but unable to achieve reliability from the over-complex front engined 12 and 16 *monopostos*. It was not until Colin Chapman switched to a rear-engine layout that Lotus, from 1960 onwards, enjoyed success in Formula One.

Just as the 1950s provided immense scope for success in International motor racing, so the period was one of economic growth and there was the opportunity to build a business in a financial climate much less harsh than the traumatic 1980s. Chapman combined enthusiasm and dedication for motor racing with engineering and design skills and business acumen that has been unmatched in the world of motoring.

He also possessed to a remarkable extent the ability to win and keep the enthusiasm and loyalty of others. In 1954 when Chapman went motor racing seriously with the Mark 8 he was surrounded by a dedicated band of enthusiasts who worked impossibly long hours to ensure that SAR 5 arrived at the circuit: Mike Costin who became technical director until he left in August 1962 to devote his energies full-time to Cosworth, a company that he had founded with Keith Duckworth in 1959; Fred Bushell who eventually became Deputy Managing Director and, for a short while after Colin's death, Managing Director; Colin Bennett who in 1953 coined the name 'Team Lotus' and between 1957 and 1960 was Lotus sales manager; Tony McKusker, a schoolteacher and dedicated AC enthusiast whom I met in 1954 through the AC Owners' Club. These were just a few of the enthusiasts whose support Chapman won and kept.

Since Colin Chapman died in late 1982, his reputation tainted by his involvement with De Lorean, it has become fashionable to discredit his integrity and stories to Chapman's detriment are legion. To me at least there can be no greater tribute to Colin Chapman than his ability to win—and to keep—his friends.

From a builder of 'specials' Chapman rapidly progressed to a serious competition car manufacturer and Lotus production figures during the years 1955-60 completely eclipsed all of his rivals. Nor can Chapman's ability as a driver be under-rated—in sports car events he raced on level terms (and frequently beat) such well-known names as Mike Hawthorn and Roy Salvadori. Only the need to concentrate on the business and management of Team Lotus cut short his racing activities. As late as 1960 Chapman turned in a magnificent 'one off' drive to win the saloon car race at the British Grand Prix meeting with a Jaguar 3.8.

Following the introduction of the Lotus Elite as a production GT car Lotus rapidly developed as a serious manufacturer (the full, troubled story of the Elite is told by Dennis Ortenburger in *The Original Lotus Elite* published by the Newport Press in 1977). The company moved from the cramped Hornsey premises to Chesunt in Hertfordshire in 1959 and to the present premises at Hethel at the end of 1966. Over the years Lotus has competed in vitually every category of motor racing and produced an immensely wide range of competition and road-going cars. It was not until the early 1970s that Lotus ceased to build competition cars for sale and whilst Team Lotus concentrated solely on Formula One, the Lotus public company built the production road-going cars.

This book is devoted solely to the sports-racing cars of the 1950s and 1960s and they represent the era in Chapman's brilliant career when he was an enthusiast amongst enthusiasts, struggling hard to make a success of his cars and his career. As a young enthusiast I was always drawn to Team Lotus in the paddock (unless of course my beloved works D-types were running!) and I admired Chapman's ambition, design ability and driving skill. That admiration has not diminished with the passing of the years.

Chapter 1

The Early Cars

Not a great deal needs be said about the earliest Lotus cars in this book; apart from the fact that they have been fully documented elsewhere, they were not sports-racing cars. The first Lotus was a trials car built by Colin Chapman whilst he was an undergraduate reading engineering at London University. It was based on a 1930 Austin Seven fabric-bodied saloon rebuilt with the chassis boxed and plywood body with three bulkheads and alloy skin. This car, named the Lotus and subsequently designated the Mark 1, was completed in the early part of 1948 and that spring Colin drove it in two trials, winning awards in both events.

No sooner had he finished the first Lotus than Chapman planned its successor, the Mark 2, also basically a trials car. He had barely started construction when he joined the Royal Air Force on a short term engagement. Work continued during his stint in the services and the Mark 2 emerged in 1949 as a Ford 8 hp-powered car, still based on an Austin Seven chassis, with Austin four-speed gearbox, Ford front axle and brakes and Austin back axle. When the car was completed Chapman realized that the engine was not powerful enough and a Ford 10 hp was soon substituted. During 1949 the car was modified with shapely nose cowling incorporating twin headlamps behind the grille that turned with the steering. By this time Chapman had decided that the RAF was not for him and he was out of the services and working for a constructional engineering company.

During 1950 the Mark 2 was gradually developed and Chapman tackled a full season of competition work, including speed trials and club races. He won a sixteen-lap race at the Eight Clubs meeting at Silverstone after a fantastically close battle with Dudley Gahagan's Bugatti Type 37 (and finished third in a handicap race) and at the end of the year sold both cars, Mark 1 and Mark 2 — the latter to Mike Lawson who drove it with great success in Trials.

Chapman had now started to build a car for the 750 Motor Club's 750 Formula for Austin Seven-based cars and so successful was this new project that the club was compelled to change the rules! To build the new car Chapman teamed up with Michael and Nigel Allen and the original intention was to build three 750 Formula Mark 3 cars so that each of the partners had his own car. Based on the Austin Seven chassis, with wheelbase of 6 ft 9 in, the Mark 3 featured a Ford 8 hp front axle divided to provide independent swing axles and suspended on a transverse leaf spring, giving a track of 4 ft 0 in, an Austin Seven rear axle, Austin 'Nippy' gearbox with remote control change and an Austin Seven steering box positioned on its side ahead of the

Above *An epic struggle at the Eight Clubs, Silverstone meeting, 1950 with Chapman (Lotus Mark 2) on the inside and Gahagan (Bugatti) on the outside. (Guy Griffiths.)*

Below *On the starting grid at the Eight Clubs meeting, with, from left to right, Gahagan (Bugatti), a Morgan, Chapman with the Mark 2 and an MG. (Guy Griffiths.)*

axle. Lockheed hydraulic brakes were fitted front and rear. The neat two-seater aluminium body featured a full-length undershield, properly upholstered seats and a practicable hood.

What made the Lotus so different from its rivals was the engine. Originally the Mark 3 was powered by a two-bearing Austin Seven engine, but there were problems with the con-rods and so at an early stage Chapman substituted a three-bearing engine. Chapman revolutionized the performance of this side-valve unit with twin inlet ports; he successfully 'de-siamezed' the ports by opening up the inlet ports and used special manifolds built up from welded sheet steel with a vertical steel strip in the centre of the manifold extending into the ports. A Stromberg twin-choke downdraught carburettor was used and the result was the same as if the Austin cylinder head had a twin carburettor induction system.

During 1951 the Mark 3 enjoyed a fantastic run of success driven by Chapman, the Allen brothers and Hazel Williams (who did not become Hazel Chapman until October 1954). So much time was needed preparing and developing Chapman's car that the other two were never finished. By the end of the season Chapman was so obsessed by motor racing and car construction that he knew clearly where his future lay. On 1 January 1952 the Lotus Engineering Company was formed with Chapman

Colin Chapman with the Lotus Mark 2 at Great Auclum hill climb in Berkshire in July 1950. (Guy Griffiths.)

and Michael Allen as partners. The initial arrangement was that Michael Allen worked full-time for Lotus, whilst Chapman continued his job with British Aluminium (in fact he did not give up his employment until the end of 1954). The new firm had two immediate projects, the completion of one of the Mark 3 chassis as the Mark 3B for Adam Currie, who enjoyed a good season of success, and building a new trials car, the Mark 4, for Mike Lawson. The designation Mark 5 was reserved for a new Austin Seven-powered car derived from the Mark 3, but this was never built. Whilst Lotus intended to concentrate their efforts on the Mark 6, development of this was interrupted by the construction of a new sports-racing car chassis for the Clairmonte brothers.

Initially designated the Mark 7 (although in fact this 'mark' was later alotted to a much more famous design), the new car raced as the Clairmonte featured a multi-tubular space-frame chassis, front suspension by double wishbones and inboard-mounted coil spring/damper units (a very advanced feature for 1952), de Dion rear axle and final drive with quick-change ratios. A stark two-seater body with cycle wings was fitted. Apparently it was intended that the Clairmonte should be powered by an ERA 2-litre supercharged engine. It is said that this was wrecked before it was installed (it is not clear how) and the car was raced with a Lea-Francis unit enlarged to 1,960 cc—which implies that it incorporated more than a few Connaught components. Painted black, the Clairmonte made an impressive sight—and equally impressive sound—I remember watching it at the North Staffs MC Silverstone meeting in October 1954 where it displayed a very considerable turn of speed.

Whilst the Mark 6 was a very basic, very simple car that was equally suitable for road use or club competition work (depending on the state of tune and equipment fitted) it was also a very sophisticated design compared with most of its rivals. There was always a great deal of discussion as to whether Derek Buckler or Colin Chapman built the first British car with a multi-tubular space-frame, but I am certainly a supporter of the Lotus camp in this particular argument.

The chassis of the Mark 6 formed the basis of a very long line of later Lotus chassis all the way through to the 15 of 1958 onwards. The main lower chassis tubes were in 1⅛ in 18 swg with 1 in round and square upper tubes, fully triangulated, forming a main, very rigid box-shaped structure with additional rigidity provided by the riveted stressed aluminium panels of the floor scuttle and sides of the chassis. The bare chassis weighed only 55 lb and when the stressed panels and various mounting brackets are included, the figure was still only 90 lb.

At the front Chapman again relied on independent swing-axle suspension with steeply inclined coil spring/damper units and located by radius arms—because of the skimpy front wings these coil springs were one of the most prominent 'recognition points' of the Mark 6. At the rear there was a Ford 10 axle suspended on coil springs with lateral location by a Panhard rod. A normal Ford steering box and column was laid on its side and there were the usual Ford-type Girling cable-operated brakes. To power the first car Chapman used the newly-introduced Ford Consul engine, acquired by an energetic tour of Ford dealers to acquire enough spares to build up an engine, as the Consul unit was too new for Ford to make any available. The capacity of the Consul engine was reduced from 1,508 cc to just under 1,500 cc and a special

Above *The Mark 3 built to the 750 Motor Club's 750 Formula with Chapman at the wheel at the Eight Clubs meeting at Silverstone in June 1951. Because of big-end problems in practice, with piston and connecting rod removed, Chapman raced the car on three cylinders, pulling out an enormous lead until the crankshaft broke. Note the 'snorkel' on the left-hand side of the bonnet which some rivals mistakenly thought was the secret of the Mark 3's speed. (Guy Griffiths.)*

Below *Fast special – the Clairmonte with Lea Francis engine in action at Silverstone in 1953. (Guy Griffiths.)*

Michael Allen at the wheel of the prototype Mark 6 Lotus on its debut at the MG Car Club race meeting at Silverstone in July 1952. (Guy Griffiths.)

manifold with twin SU carburettors was fitted. The body was the work of Williams and Pritchard Ltd of Edmonton who were destined to enjoy a long relationship with Lotus. Apart from the very first car, all early Mark 6s were characterized by very bulbous, rounded rear wings that formed a full vallance over the wheel.

In fact the first Mark 6 produced was built as a trials car for Sinclair Sweeney and featured a rigid front axle, much greater ground clearance and very skimpy wings front and rear. The works prototype, registered XML 6, first ran at the MG Car Club race meeting on 5 July 1952 and scored two second places, both with Chapman at the wheel, in a handicap and also in a team race. The car was also driven at this meeting by Michael Allen. After another outing at the Aston Martin Owners' Club meeting at Silverstone, the Lotus was entered in the 100 mile race at the International Boreham meeting in August and although the Mark 6 practised it did not race as it was written off in a road accident with Nigel Allen at the wheel on the morning of the race. The accident was no fault of Allen's, but it brought the small firm to its knees and wrecked the year's racing plans.

Early in 1953 Michael Allen decided to withdraw from Lotus and so in February 1953 Chapman formed Lotus Engineering Company Limited. He decided to lay down a line of eight production Mark 6s. The specification was finalized with a wheelbase of 7 ft 3½ in, front track of 4 ft 1 in and rear track of 3 ft 9 in. Early purchasers included P. A. Desoutter who raced his car in the 'standard' form with

Ford 1,172 cc side-valve engine and three-speed gearbox and Fred Hill who ran a business called Empire Garages and whose Lotus, fitted with 746 cc supercharged MG engine was known as the 'Empire Special'. It later passed to Austen Nurse who raced it throughout 1954 before moving on to the prototype Mark 8, then to Lister cars who then sold it to David Piper, who had first raced a 746 cc supercharged MG in 1954 and later achieved fame as driver/entrant of private Ferraris. Another, very successful, owner was Peter Gammon, but more will be said of his successes with his Mark 6 later. Another early purchaser was Nigel Allen who also used the Ford 1,172 cc side-valve engine.

During 1953 Colin Chapman met Mike Costin and Costin built the ninth Mark 6 before joining the small company. This car, registered 1161H, was raced by both Chapman and Costin. Its specification included a Ford 1,172 cc engine reduced in capacity to 1,099 cc and with twin 1¼ in SU carburettors it was said to have a power output of 40 bhp at 6,000 rpm. It was Chapman's incredibly quick drive with this car at the Crystal Palace in September 1953 that brought Lotus a great deal of publicity and 1161H was subsequently road-tested by John Bolster for *Autosport*. Bolster was full of praise for the Mark 6: "'My' Lotus had a Ford 10 engine which had been

A view of the engine compartment of the prototype Mark 6 with Ford Consul engine and showing the special manifold with twin SU carburettors devised by Chapman. This photograph was taken on the car's debut at the MG Car Club meeting at Silverstone in 1952. (Guy Griffiths.)

warmed up as far as the "1,172 Formula" allows. It had an aluminium cylinder head, raised compression ratio, larger inlet valves than standard, and double valve springs. It had twin SU carburettors mounted on a flexible induction system, to avoid frothing of the fuel from vibration. Two separate exhaust manifolds paired cylinders 1 and 4, 2 and 3, as is correct practice.

'The three-speed Ford gearbox was converted to close ratios by the use of Buckler C-type gears. A remote control was mounted on top of the propeller shaft tunnel, which was of considerable height, due to the general low build. The rear axle had been fitted with a 4.4 to 1 final drive.

'On the road, the performance just didn't make sense! I have driven many Ford 10-engined cars—in fact I own one myself—but this was an entirely different experience. At the very bottom end, it had not perhaps quite the "stepaway" of the standard job, and the tickover was a little lumpy. Once on the move, however, the little thing screamed away at apparently unlimited revs. I would say that the unit peaked around 6,000 rpm, but the owner told me that I could exceed "seven thou" if I felt like it. As that would be equivalent to 84 mph in second gear, it will be realized that this is quite a car!

'The total weight of only 8½ cwts gives the willing power unit every chance to show its paces. The acceleration is even better than the figures in the data panel indicate*, for the very high bottom gear makes considerable slipping of the clutch essential on get-away. However, that component seemed to have no objection to such rough treatment, in spite of the many standing starts that are entailed when taking the average of a number of runs in both directions. The mean maximum speed was 88 mph, and I frequently exceeded 90 mph under favourable conditions. After all that, I had to have another look under the bonnet and, yes, it really was a side-valve.

'In close-ratio form the Ford gearbox gave a very easy change between top and second, the synchromesh operating well. First speed was a little less easy to engage, and one had to judge the relative speeds fairly accurately if noiseless meshing of the pinions was to be secured. By pressing the lever to the right, the shift from bottom to second went through in one quick, clean movement.

'The suspension was fairly firm without being in any way harsh, and the ride was level and free from pitching. The springing was by helical springs all round, with telescopic hydraulic dampers. At the rear, lateral location of the axle was by a Panhard rod, and alternative holes were provided for its brackets, so that the roll centre could be raised or lowered to choice. In front, the divided axle automatically gave a high roll centre, and certainly the machine remained on an even keel while cornering.

'To begin with, the steering felt a little unusual. The Burman box gave a light operation and a moderate degree of caster return action but, at low speeds only, one felt that there was a slight tendency to wander. As soon as one became used to the general "feel" of the car, that tendency entirely disappeared, and one was free to enjoy the very exceptional cornering powers provided. The car has just enough under-steer for stability, and no more. What is so uncanny is the exemplary behaviour of the rear end. Thus, although a corner may be taken with the back wheels definitely sliding, a complete breakaway does not occur. Once one has

Above *Peter Gammon (in white shirt) and helpers load his Mark 6 after the International Trophy meeting at Silverstone in May 1954. (T. C. March.)*

Below *Peter Gammon on his way to second place with UPE 9 in the 1,500 cc sports car race at the Grand Prix meeting at Silverstone in July 1954. Note the enormous vallanced rear wings which identify this Mark 6 as part of the first production run. (T. C. March.)*

Bottom *Mike Anthony's immaculate Mark 6 at Silverstone in July 1956. Apart from the rear wings, Anthony's car differs from Gammon's car in a number of respects including the exhaust system and the wheels (Gammon's car had non-standard wheels).*

The 'Empire Special' Lotus Mark 6 driven by Austen Nurse at the Aston Martin Owners Club meeting at Silverstone in July 1954. Again the rear wings identify this car as one of the first production batch. (LAT.)

learned that the machine will not "swop ends", the curves may be swerved with a very great degree of abandon indeed.

'The standard Ford brakes are comparatively enormous, having regard to the weight to be stopped. More elaborate equipment is available, but I would regard the present arrangement as entirely adequate for any type of competition. The brakes may be applied at maximum speed without inducing any deviation or patter; that comes from the positive location of the axles.

'The very low seating position was comfortable, and the steering wheel was ideally placed for "doing a Farina". At the outset, the pedal department seemed rather full of feet, but I soon became accustomed to the fairly narrow space. The weather protection, with hood and side flaps in position, was much better than one would expect, even though a slight defect in the body allowed some water to enter my right shoe during heavy rain.' The complete road test report is reproduced in Appendix I (p 131-2).

*Acceleration 0-50 mph 9⁴/₅ sec
0-60 mph 12³/₅ sec
0-70 mph 16³/₅ sec

John Bolster's sheer enthusiasm bubbled through everything that he wrote and the test reads as fresh as if it was written yesterday after a long testing session last week!

By 1954 the Mark 6 was in considerable demand and by the end of 1955, when production finally ceased, slightly more than a hundred had been built. One of the most famous Mark 6 cars was Peter Gammon's, one of the original batch of eight registered UPE 9, but not raced until 1954 when it was fitted with the engine and gearbox from Gammon's outstandingly successful MG. During 1954 Gammon, who

With this Lotus Super Seven, Coventry Climax-powered, and with BMC B-type gearbox, Graham Hill drove magnificently in the wet to win an 1,100 cc sports car race at Brands Hatch on Boxing Day 1958. (LAT.)

raced as a member of Team Lotus, entered seventeen events, taking fourteen first places, two seconds and a third. Apart from defeating Chapman with the Mark 8 on more than one occasion, Gammon took third place in the British Empire Trophy at Oulton Park (the first occasion on which it was run on the Cheshire circuit) and he was second to Chapman in the 1,500 cc sports car race at the British Grand Prix meeting in July, beating the works Porsche 550 of Hans Herrmann and John Coombs's Lotus Mark 8-Connaught.

Another outstanding Mark 6 was Mike Anthony's car, superbly constructed and finished, painted superbly in British racing green and also run as a member of Team Lotus. Anthony was remarkable more for his lurid press-on driving style than his successes, but he finished ninth at the British Grand Prix meeting, thereby ensuring that Lotus won the team prize. Bill Perkins fitted his Mark 6 with a pre-war BMW 2-litre engine (necessitating a large bulge in the bonnet), Fred Marriott raced a car with Coventry Climax FWA engine and John Harris's Mark 6 featured both the FWA engine and a de Dion rear axle. The majority of Mark 6s were however Ford-powered and in this form they dominated the 750 Motor Club's 1,172 Formula for cars powered by Ford side-valve engines.

After an interval of two years, at the 1957 Earls Court Show, Chapman produced the successor to the Mark 6, the much-loved Seven that has remained in production by Caterham Cars up until the present time and is likely to be available for many years to come. It has appeared in a whole host of different forms, including with Coventry Climax FWA engine, and it has proved immensely successful in club racing. It does not however form part of the mainstream of Lotus sports-racing cars and by the end of 1953 Chapman was ready to progress his advanced ideas a stage further.

Chapter 2

The Mark 8, 1954

Without doubt the Mark 8 represented a major turning point in Chapman's career as a constructor of competition cars. After the success enjoyed by the Mark 6 in Club racing during 1952-53, Chapman was seeking to build a car that would be a radical advance on what had been basically a very simple design. His aim was to combine maximum rigidity of chassis construction with outstanding road holding, on a basis of readily available components, coupled with exceptionally low weight and good aerodynamics to combat the low output of the only suitable available engine for 1,500 cc sports car racing, the MG XPAG engine, enlarged to 1,467 cc. The result was a radical improvement on anything seen at that time in British racing for most constructors were still content to build cars with ladder-type chassis based on two main tubes and cloaked in a simple all-enveloping body of no great distinction, Where the constructor had chosen to follow a more adventurous course in body styling, such as the Tojeiro-Bristol raced by Cliff Davis or the Cooper-Bristols built by Alan Brown, then the body was merely imitative of contemporary Italian styles.

The chassis, constructed in 1¼ in 18 and 20 gauge steel tubing weighed only 35 lb. In concept it was a very simple, exceptionally light and very stiff chassis. From a triangulated central bulkhead there ran to the front of the car the forward section, triangular in plan view, and consisting of upper and lower tubes running to form the apex of the triangle and in themselves triangulated. Near to the apex of the triangle formed by the front tubes a further triangular frame of sheet steel mounted the front suspension. Behind the central bulkhead were further tubular sections on either side forming a triangle in side elevation and with the apex of the two sides linked by a further tubular structure at the rear of the car.

At the front the suspension design was derived from that used on the Mark 6 and consisted of a divided Ford 10 axle to provide swing-axles and coil spring/damper units. These coil spring/damper units were inclined at an angle and were linked at their top end to the front triangular sheet steel member. It has to be accepted that Chapman's front suspension design was less than innovative, for the split swing axle front suspension layout had been pioneered by L. M. Ballamy and was used by a number of other constructors and manufacturers, including, of course, Allard. One writer recently has drawn a comparison between the early Lotus sports-racing cars and the contemporary Allard J2R. The same writer made the point that whilst the Allard was powered by a large capacity American engine and built, hopefully, for outright victory at Le Mans, the aim of Chapman was to achieve the lowest possible weight. However the differences are so much greater and the only real area of comparison in design between the two cars lies in the front suspension. Within a very short space of time Chapman had abandoned the swing axle front suspension in favour of a layout of wishbones and coil spring/damper units.

At the rear Chapman chose a de Dion layout, with the tube located longitudinally by tubular radius arms and vertically by ball-race moving within a steel channel. There was a single transverse coil spring in a rubber sleeve linked to hydraulic dampers. Hydraulic brakes were fitted front and rear with 10 in by 1½ in Alfin drums and mounted inboard at the rear on either side of the final drive unit.

The bodywork had been designed by Frank Costin, former de Havilland aerodynamicist. Relying on his considerable experience of aircraft aerodynamics and also tests carried out by the Lotus team to prove the efficiency of his ideas, he produced an exceptionally graceful and low body design with extended front wings tapering to points, the passenger side of the cockpit fully enclosed by a metal tonneau, valances over the rear wheels and twin tail fins. This body, which was fully stressed, was mounted on light alloy sheet bulkheads. Only the front section of the bodywork could be removed and the remainder of the body was riveted to the supporting sheet alloy.

As has been mentioned previously, the engine was the four-cylinder push rod MG XPAG unit enlarged to 1,467 cc (72 mm x 90 mm) fitted with twin 1¾ in SU carburettors and developing approximately 85 bhp at 6,200 rpm. The engine was installed in such a manner that loads could be reacted directly through the front suspension and accordingly there was a very complicated mounting for the engine consisting of a tubular pyramid of four thick-wall single tubes at the front of the engine. The rear mounting was taken from the usual MG position on the gearbox and loads were taken out into the stressed skin propeller shaft tunnel.

Once initial teething troubles had been resolved during the early part of the 1954 season, Chapman enjoyed an immense run of success with the car, but it soon became evident that there were many problems with running it which arose directly from the design. Because of the front triangular layout of the space-frame chassis, the cylinder heads, manifolds, oil pump, water pump, distributor, front mounting, starter and dynamo had to be removed before the engine would pass through the narrow opening in the space-frame. One inevitable result was that once the engine had been installed in the chassis and reassembled, its power out proved to be less than that achieved during bench tests. It must be remembered however that Chapman was quick to learn from the shortcomings in design of the new car, registered SAR 5, and that subsequent production Mark 8s built in 1954 used a simpler means of construction that facilitated access and maintenance.

The 1954 Racing Season

Whilst Colin Chapman was the driving force and inspiration behind Lotus, he was of course still in full-time employment, and apart from the fact that he was very much

Overleaf *Extract from the May 1954 issue of* Motor Racing *showing the Mark 8 in original, unpainted form before its first race, the British Empire Trophy at Oulton Park in April.*

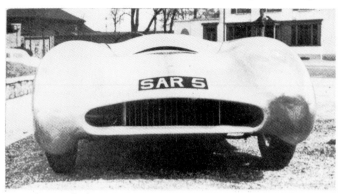

Impressive head-on view reveals detachable-tube radiator and small frontal area and low (2 ft 4 in) overall height. Air reaches carburetters through inlet in bonnet leading-edge.

A NEW LOTUS

CHAPMAN'S PROMISING NEW CAR

THE Lotus takes on a futuristic shape to enter the 1954 season. In this latest product of that near-genius Colin Chapman we have, it would seem, a serious British challenger for *voiturette* races.

For some two seasons Lotus sports cars driven by Chapman, Gammon, Desoutter, Allen and Hill, have carried away the awards at club meetings. The cars have been steadily improved until last year the Mark VI, with its light, stressed-skin frame, Ford 10 engine and suspension components as well, seemed to have reached the ultimate in its class. Colin Chapman thought so too so decided that a wind-cheating body was needed to maintain winning form.

The first of a team of three aerodynamically developed prototype Mark VIII Lotus cars is now complete. Owner Michael Costin and designer constructor Colin Chapman will drive this in 1954 sports-car events. Owner drivers of the other two cars now under construction remain unannounced.

The impressive truly aerodynamic body fits also the stand Mark VI Lotus frame and is already separately obtainable, but the complete Mark VIII car is not to be made generally available just yet.

The full-width shape was developed from a model handed over to an expert aerodynamist. He made so many alterations that Chapman decided to design a completely new car and so take advantage of

With front cowling removed. Note suspension units, brakes, radiator air-scoop, and body framework. A heat-exchanger is fitted behind the radiator, which is in fact an oil-cooler mounted around the water circuit and ensures rapid warming of the oil, then a constant temperature.

De Dion rear-suspension layout with the fabricated "diff" housing and ball-race axle beam location. The cable and levers control handbrake actuation.

Transverse coil-spring and rear-suspension. Part of the spring is invisible due to its encasement in a rubber sleeve. The strengthened shock-absorber arms which transmit the spring movement can be clearly seen.

Side-view of the advanced body design. The aim has been to keep a clean, rising line from front to rear. If the panelling drops away below the angle of the " rising-air " an eddy is formed with consequent loss in aerodynamic efficiency.

all that the perfect shape had to offer. For racing purposes it seemed pointless merely to fit this new body to a frame which had to be panelled to achieve its stiffness.

The new chassis takes the form of a triangulated space frame, built up of 1⅛ inch, 20 gauge, 45 ton steel tubing providing the minimum but most rigid structure, additional tubes would increase weight but not the strength.

Front suspension is basically similar to the Mark VI, coil-spring/damper units connected to the divided (and lightened) Ford 10 axle, but the brakes are now hydraulic with 10-in. x 1¼-in. Alfin drums with two-leading-shoe actuation at the front.

Rear suspension is De Dion with the axle tube located by a ball-race travelling vertically within a steel channel lined with chromium strips to defeat rapid wear. Additional location is provided by longitudinally mounted tubular radius arms. Springing is supplied through a single transverse coil spring in tension and transmitted to the rear wheels through links and suitably braced hydraulic dampers.

The differential housing on the prototype has been built-up from sheet steel, but subsequent housings will probably be cast. The differential gear and final-drive unit are Austin A70, which provides a ratio of 4.125 to 1, but an A90 unit may later be used to provide a higher ratio. Inboard brake drums are mounted on the " diff " housing.

In the interests of long-distance racing, a 12-gallon rear fuel tank has been fitted, but for short-distance events a smaller sponson tank can be mounted in the nearside " wing." The strap-secured rear tank shares the tail with a 12-volt battery and spare wheel, and can be removed in less than three minutes. Access to all three items is gained by removing a Dzus-fastened panel.

The light-alloy Wynne radiator, with removable rubber-mounted tubes has proved to be a boon during tests since over-cooling was experienced initially. The remedy merely entailed removing several tubes, saving weight, water, and metal, and lessening wind-resistance.

Another feature which illustrates the thought that Chapman puts into weight re-

duction is in the seating accommodation. A light-alloy " pan " is shaped into the body structure where the seat cushion would normally be, and a rubber-sprayed felt pad fits into it. This in turn is trimmed with a light-weight nylon material. The backrest consists of rubber bungee cords transversely attached by hooks to a recessed section of the body panelling which again is covered with nylon material. Total weight of seating accommodation is 7 lb compared with 24 lb on the Mark VI Lotus. A full-length fully stressed under-tray is fitted beneath the body.

In spite of the fact that the car is fully aerodynamic it weighs only 9 cwt. less than most non-streamlined competition cars of similar engine capacity. By wind-tunnel tests the Lotus fitted with an 85 bhp. 1500 cc " TC " MG engine should reach a maximum speed of 138 mph.

At the time of going to press, the car was being prepared for the British Empire Trophy at Oulton Park on April 10th to make its competition début.

MOTOR RACING *Classified Advertisements*

RATES : 4d. per word. Minimum charge for each insertion 5s. All advertisements must be prepaid unless by pre-arrangement. CHEQUES AND POSTAL ORDERS must be made payable to Pearl, Cooper Ltd. and instructions addressed to : Classified Advertisement Department, "Motor Racing," 2-3, Norfolk Street, Strand, W.C.2.

PRESS DATE : 4th of each month.

THE PUBLISHERS reserve the right to refuse or withdraw advertisements at their discretion and although every care is taken to avoid mistakes, they cannot hold themselves responsible for clerical or printers' errors.

BOX NUMBERS : Private advertisers wishing to have replies sent care of " Motor Racing " may do so for the payment of 1s. to cover the cost of booking and postage. The words Box —— must be added and paid for.

FOR SALE

NORTON double-knocker £185, single-knocker £90. Both Beart tuned.—Gill, East Meon, Hants. Tel. : 74.

ROOTS SUPERCHARGER with S.U. carburetter, almost new Exford 8 will fit up to 2,000 c.c. £25, o.n.o.—Box 180.

10 CWT. FORD engine with clutch, genuine works reconditioned, not yet run in. Also gearbox and rear axle.—H. R. Martindale Ltd., 14, Harrison Street, Leeds, 1.

H.E. SIX 1927 2/4-seater Corsica touring car. Engine rebuilt by Burtonwood, chassis rebuilt, new electrical apparatus, 1,000 miles ago. Second complete car for spares. A rare car in first-class order. 200 guineas. Photograph and particulars.—Box 181.

SEMMENCE SPECIAL. Sprint car, 1991-c.c. A.C engine, with single-seater Frazer-Nash chassis. Big overhaul just completed, new crankshaft, pistons, con-rods, shock-absorbers, and tyres. Offered complete with new load trailer at £350 or thereabouts.—Jennings, 16, Poyle Road, Guildford.

1941 (first regd.) Mercédès Cabriolet, similar to 500.K with 3.8-litre engine, super-charged L/H drive, black and polychromatic grey with red leather, really beautiful specimen, £435.—Pantiles Service Garage, London Road, Guildford. Tel. : Guildford 5326.

COOPER body and chassis frame, 1951 model, good condition, £45, or near offer.—R. Gowers, 84, Orchard Grove, Edgware, Middx.

1949 H.R.G. 1500, telecontrol, shock-absorbers, good tyres, 27,000 miles only. £425.—L. F. Ward Ltd., Grange Road Garage, Thornton Heath. Tel. : 3347.

1935 AUSTIN 10 Cabriolet in sound mechanical condition. Engine recently overhauled. 35 m.p.g. £95. —D. Parker, 17, Verdayne Gardens, Upper Warlingham, Surrey. Tel. : Upper Warlingham 2363.

BUGATTI, Type 35B, in sprint trim with lightweight fuel tank, radiator, etc. Ready for the 1954 season. This car has been consistently reliable. Full history known. With valuable spares and transport trailer. Photo, trial run. £550 or part exchange, small modern saloon.—Hukins, New House, Biddenden, Kent. Tel. : 319.

JAGUAR-engined 2-seater racing sports car. Aluminium body. Detachable hood and screen. £250, or offer.—Douglas, 15, Westfield Crescent, Riddlesden, Keighley.

SINGER LE MANS 1935 2 4-seater. New battery, hood, oversize rear wheels, slab tank, crank reground, new pistons, rebore, bearing and ends remetalled, new king-pins, brakes relined, new C W P. chrome, paint good. Nice looking, good runner. Reliable. £125, o.n.o.—68, Hatherley Road, Sidcup. Tel. : FOOtscray 6342.

VALE fitted Coventry Climax engine, £70 overhaul 7,000 ago, good tyres, paintwork, etc. (B R G) enthusiast maintained. £185—Fenton, Upper Warlingham, 96.

MARENDAZ Special, 1936, scarlet, open 2 4-seater 2-litre, Coventry Climax, 85 m.p.h. third, 24 m.p.g on 3 S.U.s. Engine recently reconditioned. New maroon silk mohair hood, side screens and tonneau cover. New king-pins, total mileage 29,000. Whole car in excellent condition. Spare available. £325 or thereabouts.—Jacobs, Heanton Close, Braunton, N. Devon. Tel. : Braunton 322, evenings.

dependent on his willing team of unpaid helpers, all the work that he put into the project was in the evenings and at weekends. In these circumstances it is hardly surprising that there was a tremendous battle against time to get the new Lotus ready for its first race of the season. It was scheduled to make its debut in the British Empire Trophy at Oulton Park on 10 April, the first time that this race had been held at the Cheshire circuit after a long history of races in the Isle of Man. For Team Lotus the race proved an unmitigated disaster. The events of the day make the Mark 8 look a typical unreliable but rather spectacular 'special' which in effect helped to delude the opposition into believing that the Mark 8 was nothing significant for them to worry about.

It was only after three full nights of work that the Mark 8 set off on the then very inadequate A roads of the time from Hornsey to Cheshire. Initially Chapman took the wheel, but later Mike Costin was the driver. Not long after Costin had taken the wheel he was forced to outpace a police car whilst passing through a 30 mph built-up area at around 70 mph and not long afterward failed to see a roundabout and ploughed straight through the centre. The car was very badly damaged and it was only by dint of extensive work from the following team that the Mark 8 was repaired in time to start the race.

On the Friday Chapman covered three laps of the Cheshire circuit at the wheel of Mike Anthony's Mark 6 Lotus and in a special session laid on for the Saturday morning (an arrangement made not to help Chapman but rather to assist Ken Wharton who had taken over the Lister-MG from the banned Archie Scott-Brown) he was able to drive on the circuit with the Mark 8. The Saturday morning practice times did not count for places on the grid, but by virtue of his lapping in the Mark 6 Chapman, with a time of 2 min 8 sec, took a place on the grid alongside Ted Lund (MG) and Jones (Kieft) with only the untimed Wharton behind him. Chapman worked his way through to hold fifth place in his heat, but after setting joint fastest lap with Peter Gammon's Mark 6 in 1 min 56 sec, he retired with a blown cylinder head gasket.

Nine days later Chapman and the Mark 8 were in action at the Easter Goodwood meeting, running in the Second Easter handicap, but retiring when the MG engine went on to three cylinders. At this stage Team Lotus were suffering very badly from the problems of having to install the MG engine into the car in still stripped-down form. Next came the International Trophy Meeting at Silverstone on 15 May. The sports car race was an unlimited capacity event with class awards for smaller cars. Opposition in the 1,500 cc class came from the Connaughts of John Coombs and Ken McAlpine as well as the Mark 6 Lotus entries of Peter Gammon and Mike Anthony. Now the Mark 8 came good and Chapman finished fifteenth overall to win the class, beating such larger capacity opposition as Joe Kelly's C-type Jaguar. It was the turning point in the Mark 8's fortunes.

The following weekend Chapman had entered the Mark 8 in the Eifelrennen over the tortuous Nürburgring circuit in the Eifel mountains. Inevitably, and over-enthusiastically, Chapman had arranged an almost impossible schedule, driving the car to work and parking all day in St James's Square before he and Mike Costin drove on the Friday night to the Channel to take a ferry and then embark upon a long drive to the German circuit. The reasons why Chapman did not race the car himself are somewhat shrouded in mystery; it has always been said that the organizers would not allow Colin to drive the car because of his lack of racing experience, but it is more likely that the car arrived too late at the circuit to run in official practice; Chapman was allowed to run the car provided that it was driven by a more experienced driver and he negotiated with Erwin Bauer of Stutgart to handle the Lotus. In this 71 mile event, by 1954 a very parochial German event, despite its International status, the Borgwards of Günther Bechem and Hans Hugo Hartmann took first two places from the Osca of Giardini, with the Lotus in fourth place. Admittedly Bauer was nearly three minutes behind the winner, but of course he was unfamiliar with the car and it was a very worthwhile performance from which Chapman learned a great deal. Needless to say Chapman and Costin drove the car straight back to England after the race, arriving just before the start of business on Monday morning and once more leaving the car in St James's Square throughout the day.

Now the season was in full swing and race succeeded race, mainly with success for Team Lotus, but not always. At Aintree on 29 May Chapman left the road at Bechers and the Lotus was bent enough to require substantial panel beating. At Goodwood on Whit Monday Chapman won the 1,500 cc class of the sports car race, taking sixth place overall. On 19 June Chapman drove the Mark 8 at Crystal Palace, that delightful road circuit in the South London suburbs, now sadly long closed. In the sports car race Chapman swept through into the lead on the second lap, heading the 2 litre Cooper-Bristol of Alan Brown and Roy Salvadori's Maserati. Only two laps later the Lotus was out of the race because of a broken drive-shaft. Although Chapman set a new lap record at Brands Hatch on 4 July, he was beaten into second place in both 1,500 cc sports car races by Peter Gammon with the Mark 6 Lotus-MG, but it must be remembered that in those days Brands Hatch was a short 1.2 mile circuit, slow and tortuous and a circuit on which the Mark 8's aerodynamics showed no advantage. At this race, for the first time, Colin Chapman's Mark 8, together with the Mark 6s of Gammon and Mike Anthony all ran as Team Lotus.

A significant race for the team was the 1,500 cc sports car race at Silverstone on 17 July, the day of the British Grand Prix. Most of the entry consisted of the usual rather motley collection of British sports-racing cars, but Porsche had entered two of the new 550 Spyders in the name of AFN Ltd driven by Hans Herrmann and von Hanstein (the latter's car was in 1,100 cc form). Although the Lotus was specifically designed for the British short circuit events, and the Porsche entries were much heavier, they were also much more powerful. Herrmann was fastest in practice, but Gammon took the lead at the start of the race, Chapman came through to take the lead on lap four and at the end of the seventeen-lap race Chapman led Gammon across the line with the Porsche of Herrmann in third place. A week later Chapman won the 1,500 cc sports car race at the Fairwood Aerodrome circuit near Swansea and finished second in the race for cars up to 2,500 cc behind Scott-Brown's Lister-Bristol. Chapman also ran in the race for unlimited capacity sports cars, but unfortunately the very special MG engine of the Mark 8 with welded cylinder liners, special pistons and Laystall-Lucas cylinder head put a con-rod through the side of the crankcase, completely wrecking the engine.

There was now a frantic rush by Chapman and his still enthusiastic helpers to get the Mark 8 sorted out for the races over the August Bank Holiday weekend. It was vital, if Lotus was to succeed, that Chapman should not only successfully race the Mark 8, but that private owners should wish to buy it. The first private owner to take delivery of a Mark 8 had been John Coombs who had taken delivery of his car in time to drive it into fourth place at the Silverstone Grand Prix meeting. Coombs' car was fitted with the 1,484 cc Connaught engine. Now the next two private purchasers, Nigel Allen and Dan Margulies had taken delivery of their MG-powered Mark 8s in time for the August Bank Holiday weekend. They had entered their cars in the sports car race at the Nürburgring, but Chapman himself had entered this race and also the sports car races at the Crystal Palace and Brands Hatch on Bank Holiday Monday. It was enthusiasm gone mad!

During Thursday's practice at the Nürburgring Nigel Allen's Lotus had blown up the engine, but it was repaired in time for the start of the race. In fact all three Mark 8s performed very badly and none finished. Chapman retired because of a broken de Dion tube which had to be welded up before his drive back to the coast. He was back in time to run at Brands Hatch, but could only finish in fourth in his heat of the 1,500 cc sports car race. Immediately after this heat he drove on the road to the Crystal Palace, but retired on the second lap because of carburation problems. Chapman returned to Brands Hatch where he borrowed Nigel Allen's Mark 8, but he retired early in the second heat of the 1,500 sports car race with a very sick-sounding engine.

At Snetterton on 14 August another private owner, Dickie Steed, appeared with a Mark 9. This however was different from its predecessors in that it was the first Lotus (and indeed the first car other than an Kieft) to be fitted with the Coventry Climax FWA 1,098 cc single-cam engine. Others to take delivery of Mark 8s during 1954 included Brian Naylor and T. Cunane, but both of these cars were fitted with the usual 1,467 cc MG engines.

At Castle Combe on 28 August Chapman was in action once more, finishing third in the unlimited capacity sports car race and winning the event for 1,500 cc sports cars from John Coombs with his Connaught-powered car. Coombs won the 1500 cc sports car race at Brands Hatch on 5 September and finished third in the event for sports cars up to 2,000 cc. In September Chapman and Costin drove SAR 5 in the Tourist Trophy on the Dundrod circuit in Northern Ireland. Also running under the Team Lotus banner was Nigel Allen partnered by Mike Anthony. It was a short race for both Lotus entries, for Chapman went off the road on lap 31 as a result of a wheel stud failure and only six laps later the other Lotus was eliminated by a damaged track rod. Dickie Steed also entered his Climax-powered car for himself and Peter Scott-Russell, but this was also retired because of 'damaged wheel studs'. No time was recorded for the Chapman/Costin car through the flying kilometre, but the Allen/Anthony car, allegedly entered in this race with a 1,308 cc engine, was timed at 108.5 mph and the Climax-powered Mark 8 at 107.9 mph. These speeds were not particularly impressive as according to the time keepers the fastest 1,500 cc car in the class was the Gordini of Raymond Gallagher and Don Beauman which was said to have achieved a speed of 116.1 mph.

Later in September Chapman won the Anerley Trophy race for 1,500 cc sports

Above *Chapman and the Mark 8 on their way to first place in the 1,500 cc sports car race at Snetterton on 9 October. (LAT.)*

Right *Colin Chapman and the Mark 8 on their way to victory in the 1,500 cc sports car race at Castle Combe on 28 August 1954. Note the spectators in front of the fence and so close to the track. (LAT.)*

Below *This view of John Coombs' Connaught-powered Mark 8, which finished second in the 1,500 cc race at Snetterton, shows off the excellent lines of the early streamlined Lotus and the unusual colour scheme adopted by Coombs. (LAT)*

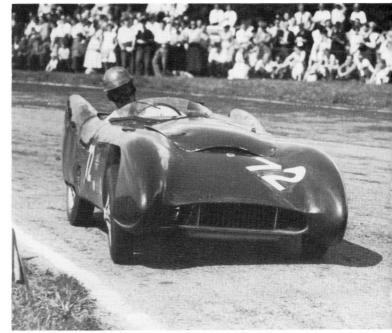

AERODYNAMIC LOTUS Mk. 8

This is the car that has been raced with considerable success by Colin Chapman throughout this season, and is without doubt the fastest 1½-litre car in the country. It has won numerous events including the following of major importance :—

1st 1500 class BRDC SILVERSTONE 15th May

4th EIFELRENNEN, NURBURGRING

1st 1500 class Johnson's Memorial Trophy, Goodwood

1st 1500 Sports car race, BRDC SILVERSTONE, 17th July

and including 1500 c.c. Lap Records at the following circuits :— Oulton Park, Goodwood, Brands Hatch, Silverstone, Crystal Palace, Castle Combe.

This car has just had a complete rebuild and all major mechanical components renewed in preparation for the T.T. It will be offered for delivery immediately after this event if required or alternatively at the end of the season after an additional final checkover.

Price, including numerous spares, ten spare wheels and tyres, etc.

£1,500

Apply:

LOTUS ENGINEERING CO. LTD.

7 Tottenham Lane, Hornsey, N.8.   MOUntview 8353

Left *Advert for SAR 5 that appeared in* Autosport *in September 1954.*

Right *John Higham straddles the road after spinning his Mark 8 at the International Silverstone meeting in May 1956.* (T. C. March.)

Below *An unusual photograph— Peter Gammon at the wheel of Nigel Allen's Mark 8 at Silverstone in May 1956. This photograph was taken in practice and Gammon non-started in the race.* (T. C. March.)

cars at the Crystal Palace and he finished sixth in the 2,000 cc sports car race at Goodwood (first 1,500 cc car across the line). On 2 October he finished second to Ken McAlpine's Connaught in the 1,500 cc race at Aintree. On 9 October Chapman raced the Lotus once more at Snetterton, winning the race for sports cars up to 1,500 cc from Coombs' Lotus-Connaught, but in a five lap handicap at the end of the day lost control on the fast Coram curve and collided with Scott-Brown's Lister. The Lotus was very badly damaged but fortunately it did not have to race again in 1954.

After it had been repaired it was tested by John Bolster for *Autosport* (see Appendix 1) and thereafter sold to Austen Nurse who raced it throughout 1955. In 1955 Brian Naylor raced John Coombs' Connaught-powered Mark 8. now re-registered JBN 1, selling his own MG-powered Mark 8 to John Higham, while Dickie Steed's Climax-powered car, HUD 139 was sold without engine to David Kelsey. Kelsey raced the car with a Ford 10 engine. In 1956 Austen Nurse graduated to a Lister-Bristol and sold the ex-works car SAR 5 to Roy and Jean Bloxham. After an accident at Mallory Park it reappeared with truncated rear end without fins and painted maroon.

By the end of 1954 Colin Chapman's fertile mind was already considering developed versions of the Mark 8 concept but certainly the Mark 8 had left its mark on the racing scene, particularly so far as the bodywork was concerned and the adoption of tail fins became a vogue seen, amongst other cars, on the 1955 Lister-Bristols.

Chapter 3

The Mark 9, 1955

In March 1955 Colin Chapman revealed to the press his 1955 car which represented an improvement over the Mark 8 in almost every respect. The new Mark 9, at 11 ft 8 in, was 8 in longer than its 1954 predecessor, but it in fact looked shorter, principally because it was 5 in lower, the frontal area was less and the tail fins were smaller in length but higher. At the front there was improved air flow and cooling for the larger 11 in brakes, the bodywork curved behind the front wheels so that these were more exposed and there were no rear valances. On the driver's side there was a drop-hinged door and the whole of the front section of the aluminium bodywork was removable so that there was now first class access to the engine, front suspension and to the rear of the instrument panel. There was still a panel in the bonnet, so as to give access to the engine for minor maintenance and to allow the stork-mounted headlamps to be raised. The plastic windscreen was lower and now wrapped closely round the driver both on the right-hand side and on the left where it was attached to the metal tonneau cover. There was also a removable panel at the rear to give access to the rear axle and inboard-mounted brakes.

Whilst the basic chassis construction remained unchanged, there had been a number of alterations in tube sizes which resulted in a reduction in weight. An important change was the adoption of coil spring/damper units at the rear in place of the former single horizontal coil spring. The Coventry Climax FWA 1,098 cc engine was now the standard installation mated to an MG TC-type gearbox. Because of the lower weight of this engine, to achieve balance the fuel tank was transferred from the rear of the car to the nearside of the bodywork and, according to the length of race in which the car was entered, the tank could be of 7, 12 or 19 gallon size. Centre-lock wire wheels replaced the former bolt-on wheels.

The 1955 Racing Season

The first two cars were built for American owners to race in the Sebring 12 Hours race in March. Frank Miller co-drove his car with George Rabe, while Norman Scott entered his car with Samuelson as co-driver. Despite some cynicism as to whether the Mark 9s were tough enough to survive the 12 hour race, both cars ran exceptionally well, leading the 1,100 cc class. However success eluded them, because the Scott/Samuelson car was eliminated by a holed sump after Samuelson had gone off the road, whilst the Miller/Rabe car was delayed by defective lights damaged when Miller hit a straw bale lining the circuit; after a pit stop for the damage to be checked, the engine would not fire and at the end of the race Miller pushed the car up to the finishing line, crossing on the starter motor, only to be disqualified.

The plan was that two cars would be entered by Team Lotus in 1955. The first was an MG-powered car for Colin Chapman and because it was lighter than the standard MG's box, the pre-war J2 MG gearbox was fitted to this car. The second car was to be powered by the 1,098 cc Coventry Climax FWA engine and was to be driven by Peter Jopp.

The year 1955 was to be the turning point in the 1,100 cc and 1,500 cc classes in British sports car racing. In the 1,500 cc category the Lotus Mark 9 faced opposition from the works Connaught of Kenneth McAlpine and the private car owned by Peter Bell and driven by Les Leston (this was Coombs' 1954 car which had been rebodied and of course fitted with a new engine now that the original engine was in a Lotus chassis). Apart from Coombs, who raced his Mark 8 with Connaught engine early in the year and a Mark 9 with flattened tail fins later, another Connaught-powered car

A view of the multi-tubular space-frame of the Mark 9.

was the Cooper run by Tommy Sopwith's Équipe Endeavour and usually driven by Reg Parnell. These Connaught engines were said to cost £850 apiece and with a power output of 115 bhp, they were considerably more powerful than the MG engines fitted to Lotus cars. There is no weight figure available for the works streamlined Connaught, but there is little doubt that it weighed rather more than the 9 cwt of the Lotus Mark 9 MG. The works car driven by McAlpine and the private car of Leston provided Chapman with formidable opposition in the 1,500 cc class and the cars were very closely matched, the extra power of the Connaught being offset by its greater weight.

Coventry Climax were now making the 1,098 cc FWA single-cam engine available in substantial quantities (for an account of Coventry Climax engines, see Appendix 2) and apart from its use by Lotus in the Mark 9 both in works and production forms, the engine was adopted by Cooper who were racing and selling their new rear-engined Manx-tailed sports car. This, especially when entered by the works, proved formidable opposition to the Lotus entries during the year. Other users of Climax engines were Eric Brandon in his Halseylec sports cars, Francis Beart in the Beart-Rodger-Climax and Elva. The 1,100 cc category soon however became dominated by Lotus and Cooper.

It was only at the beginning of 1955 that Chapman had begun to work full time in the Lotus business and inevitably he was still trying to do far too much, with far too little money and resources. There was the inevitable frantic rush to get the MG-powered car, registered 9 EHX to run in the British Empire Trophy at Oulton Park in April, it arrived late still painted in primer and as Chapman missed official practice, he was forced to start from the back of the grid. By the third lap of the 1,500 cc heat, Chapman had carved his way through the field to hold fourth place behind the Connaughts of Leston and McAlpine and the old Mark 8 driven by Nurse. Three laps later he was out of the race with a badly overheated engine. Another retirement, because of engine trouble, followed at the Easter Goodwood meeting. At the Ibsley circuit Chapman set fastest lap at nearly 83 mph, but was eliminated by accident damage. Quite what happened is not clear, but, in the words of the report of the time, 'getting on to the grass in passing another car, the ultra-low Lotus struck a concrete projection, doing its underparts no good at all!' Another failure followed at the International meeting at Silverstone on 7 May and Chapman retired in the sports car race with a broken crankshaft.

By the Whitsun weekend the Lotus-MG was racing with a completely rebuilt MG engine with dry sump lubrication and an oil tank positioned in the passenger foot well. In this form the Mark 9 proved vastly more reliable and began to achieve the level of success which had been expected all season. On Whit Saturday Chapman won the 1,500 cc sports car race at Snetterton and on Whit Monday he won the 1,500 cc race at Goodwood from Parnell with the Connaught-powered Cooper and McAlpine's Connaught. The main race of the day at Goodwood was the Johnson's Trophy Race for the successful qualifiers from the earlier races. Chapman retired early in this race after being hit up the rear by another car. Over the Whitsun weekend the MG-powered Lotus had also been driven by Peter Jopp, still awaiting his Climax-powered car, at Brands Hatch where he had finished second in the 1,500 cc Fawkham Trophy Sports Car race behind Leston's Connaught and ahead of Naylor's Mark 8 Lotus.

All Lotus efforts were now concentrated on preparing the Climax-powered car for the Le Mans 24 Hours race and it was not to be raced by Jopp until after that event. This new car, registered XPE 6, was to be driven at Le Mans by Chapman and Ron Flockhart, who had been brought into the team because of his considerable racing experience. There were a number of changes made to the basic Mark 9 design for this race including heavier constuction and body panelling in 22 gauge aluminium for additional strength, Girling disc brakes (which became standard wear on works Lotus cars after Le Mans) and conventionally mounted headlamps under perspex covers in the wings. Team Manager at Le Mans was John Eason Gibson, then editor of the distinguished quarterly *Autocourse* under the *non de plume* Robert Neil. The Team chose as a base the Auberge de St Nicholas at Mayet, 18 miles south of Le Mans on the Tours road.

The scrutineers objected to the retractable spot lights which on the Le Mans entry only supplemented the normal headlamps in the wings and as a result Team Lotus were obliged to mount spot lights within the air intake opening. Jopp was also present at the circuit and covered quite a distance in practice. The Lotus was not without its troubles during practice because, apart from the fact that it was shunted up the rear by a Porsche, the team was plagued by oil from the engine penetrating the clutch, a persistant fault on early Climax FWA engines. This latter problem was solved by Mike Costin who rigged a suitable breather system for the engine.

In the race the Lotus went incredibly well and initially Chapman led the 1,500 cc class from the Porsche 550 of Duntov/Veuillet. As the race progressed, the Lotus developed clutch slip and it lost time in the pits after Chapman had bent the nearside front wing against the bank at Arnage. The 1955 Le Mans race was of course the horrific event in which Pierre Levegh's Mercedes crashed into the spectator area causing numerous casualites. A result of this was that the organizers became over-sensitive to any breach of the regulations in the very difficult atmosphere in which the race was now being run. Shortly after 10 pm, about three and a half hours after the terrible accident, Chapman slid off the road at Arnage and reversed back on to the track without awaiting a signal from the marshall. The result was that the organizers immediately disqualified the Lotus and no pleading with them could change their decision. Accordingly Chapman was black-flagged and the Lotus came into the pits.

It was only after Le Mans that Lotus Engineering started to build Mark 9s for customers. Lotus offered the choice of two models. The 'Le Mans' with the Climax FWA engine was very much in accord with the specification described earlier in this chapter. In this form an assembled car was offered at £1,150, plus, of course, purchase tax. Lotus also offered the 'Club' model which was a much simpler car with Ford 10 engine and gearbox, together with a modified Ford 10 back axle suspended on coil spring/damper units and with standard Ford drum brakes. In fact most Lotus cars were supplied in component form, not only because this resulted in the saving of purchase tax, but simply because Lotus Engineering lacked the facilities and space to assemble cars to meet customers' demands.

Because private owners were assembling these cars, often with very limited

Colin Chapman with the Climax-powered Mark 9 follows the Triumph TR2 of Brooke/Morris-Goodall and the Panhard Monopole of the Chancel brothers through the Esses at Le Mans in 1955. (T. C. March.)

workshop facilities, quite a number of new Mark 9s did not make their racing debut until the 1956 season. One private owner, G. B. Hewitt, described his experiences with his car, registered XPJ 932, which he had finished in the latter part of 1955, in the October 1956 issue of *Motor Sport*: 'Then came the fabulous Lotus Mark 9. These are supplied as kits of parts, some of which one can purchase direct from the manufacturers, such as Ford axles, MG gearboxes, lights etc. But due to non-availability when required and other snags, all the parts are not obtainable at once, and when they do arrive they do not just go together like a Meccano set, as I had fondly imagined. The result is many hours of filing, drilling, sawing, fitting and changing about before the car finally becomes roadworthy. But when it does, what a thrill! My first time out, I carried as tools, one fire-extinguisher, and one screw-driver to open up the bonnet to see why it stopped, if it did. Then, with my wife as passenger and half-a-gallon of petrol, we tried it out and came home again without trouble. A few days later I drove it to Lotus Engineering to collect various items and was advised by Colin Chapman to run it in at 4,000 rpm. With my car, fitted at that time with 4.125 to 1 back axle, that meant around 70 in top. As is also well known, the exhaust on these cars are not as quiet as that of the Rolls and I just daren't do 4,000 in any gears for fear of having the Police on my tail. It is quite possible to drive it through built-up areas with a light throttle foot, reserving the heavier foot for open road and the race track, however . . .

'My car was only completed at the beginning of August [1955], so I have so far had only two months racing with it and that has been confined to club events, which had netted me one win (Oulton Park), two seconds and a third at Silverstone and a fifth at Goodwood. However, I have made the mistake of trying to do the job too cheaply by fitting the standard Ford brakes. These would fade almost completely in about three laps of Silverstone Club circuit and on examination after five club meetings the special Ferodo linings had worn half-way through the rivets on the front leading-edge

Chapman yet again, this time with the MG-powered Mark 9, 9 EHX, on his way to victory at the Crystal Palace on 30 July 1955. (LAT.)

shoes. I said then I would not race again until I had some proper brakes and around Motor Show time I ordered Girling disc brakes. Unfortunately, due to production difficulties, these did not materialize until June and so I missed the first half of the 1956 season.' Hewitt was the first private owner to fit disc brakes to his Mark 9.

With Le Mans behind them Team Lotus were back contesting the British circuits from the beginning of July onwards. At Brands Hatch on 10 July Chapman dead-heated with Ivor Bueb (Cooper-Climax) in a race for up to 1,200 cc sports cars but in the race for up to 1,500 cc sports cars Jopp, with the MG-powered car, was beaten into fourth place by a trio of Cooper-Climax cars. Of course Brands Hatch at this time was a very tortuous 1.2 mile circuit and the lithe and diminutive Coopers had an undoubted advantage. At the British Grand Prix meeting at Aintree on 16 July the MG-powered Lotus Mark 9 was driven by Chapman in the unlimited capacity sports car race and he finished ninth overall, on the same lap as the winning Aston Martin of Roy Salvadori. Team Lotus was in action again over the August Bank Holiday weekend. At the Crystal Palace on the Saturday Chapman won the event for up to 1,200 cc sports cars with the MG-powered Mark 9 from a pair of Cooper-Climax cars driven by Bueb and Sopwith. On the Monday at Brands Hatch Chapman won again, in the Air Kruise Trophy for 1,500 cc sports cars from the Cooper of Russell and the Beart-Rodger-Climax of Leston. Jopp was fifth with the Climax-powered works Lotus.

Team Lotus now concentrated its efforts on the preparation of cars for the Goodwood 9 Hours race, a short-lived but very entertaining endurance race that started at 3 pm on the Saturday afternoon and finished at midnight. It was the only British event of which part took place during the hours of darkness. Team Lotus entered the MG-powered car to be driven by Chapman and Jopp, while the Climax-powered Mark 9 was handled by Ron Flockhart and Cliff Allison. Other Lotus entries were Coombs' Connaught-powered Mark 9 driven by himself and John Young and a new, unpainted Mark 9 entered by Emeryson Cars and driven by Paul Emery and Tony Page. Lotus preparation for this race had been meticulous and the Chapman/Jopp car ran with larger fuel tank so that each refuelling stop coincided with a wheel change and because of course the Mark 9 was fitted with knock-off hubs, pit stops took the minimum of time. In the early part of the race Chapman/Jopp vied for the class lead with the Porsche of Moss/von Hanstein and shortly after the Porsche made a routine pit stop, the Lotus was able to pull out a lead of three laps in the class while the German car was in the pits. The Porsche was of course fitted with five-stud wheels and pit stops took that much more time. After rising to sixth place overall the Lotus was eliminated by broken timing gear, the Porsche driven by Moss collided with the Cooper-Bristol of Tony Cook that had spun on oil and victory in the 1,500 cc class went to the Connaught driven by Les Leston and Archie Scott-Brown entered by Peter Bell. The Coombs/Young Connaught-powered Lotus retired when a half-shaft broke and the car shed a wheel while John Young was driving. On only the first lap Tony Gaze's Aston Martin DB3S had spun and collided with the front of the Climax-powered Lotus driven by Flockhart. The front suspension of the Lotus was wrecked and after a long rebuild in the pits, the second works car rejoined the race only to retire because of gearbox oil seal failure. Despite a pit stop that lasted 27 minutes, the Page/Emery Lotus finished the race eleventh overall and fourth in the 1,500 cc class.

Of the Lotus entries in this race, the magazine *Motor Racing* made two interesting comments in their 'Pit Patter' in the October 1955 issue. It was commented that after the 9 hour race the brake pads of the Girling disc brakes on the Mark 9 were worn only to the extent of .012 in and that Girling had calculated they should be capable of covering 16,000 racing miles before relining was necessary. 'Pit Patter' also commented that Paul Emery, a very well-known special builder, was the only driver of a Climax-engined car in the race to note that the standard dynamo drive was over-geared. The result was that the Cooper-Climax cars were in trouble with burned-out dynamos due to over revving at full throttle and were forced repeatedly to change batteries. On the Lotus-Climax which Emery drove with Page this was one problem they did not have because of the fitting of a large dynamo pulley.

Two minor international British races followed. On 27 August the *Daily Herald* International Trophy race was held at Oulton Park. Chapman drove the MG-powered car while the Climax-powered works Mark 9 was entered for Cliff Allison. Chapman was delayed by a broken steering arm and eventually forced to retire with oil in the clutch while Allison crashed badly with the 1,100 cc car at Old Hall corner, but suffered only minor cuts and bruises. It did mean, however, that the team had a lot of work to do on this car before the Tourist Trophy on 17 September. The following weekend was the International Aintree meeting where Chapman with the MG-powered car was the winner from a brace of Connaughts, the works car driven by Tony Brooks and Les Leston with the Peter Bell entry.

There was a total of four Lotus entries in the Tourist Trophy, a round in the World Sports Car Championship held on the very difficult and very dangerous Dundrod road circuit in Northern Ireland, a circuit that took a heavy toll in tyre wear and was exceptionally dangerous because of the narrow, tortuous, winding and undulating public roads on which the race was run. Team Lotus entered the MG-powered car to be driven by Mike Anthony and Peter Jopp, while the 1,100 cc car was driven by Chapman and Allison. The Connaught-powered car of Coombs, co-driven by Ian Burgess was also entered in this race under the Team Lotus name. The fourth Mark 9 in the race was Dickie Steed's new Mark 9 co-driven by Peter Scott-Russell. Opposition in the smaller-capacity classes was strong with three works Porsche 550s in the 1,500 cc category and in the 1,100 cc category three Climax-powered Coopers, together with a Kieft and an Elva. The Climax-powered Lotus was the sensation of the race and Chapman and Allison built an ever-increasing lead in their class and led on the complicated handicap Index of Performance until the Lotus broke an oil pipe; as a result of time lost in the pits it fell back to finish eleventh overall and second in the class to the Cooper of Bueb/MacDowel. Steed/Scott-Russell also finished the race in fifteenth place to take third place in the class. The Coombs/Burgess Lotus finished in last place after a succession of pit stops caused by plug trouble.

The race had been dominated by the magnificent duel between the sole works D-type Jaguar of Mike Hawthorn and Desmond Titterington and the works Mercedes-Benz 300SLRs which ended when the Jaguar's engine seized. The race was also marked by a disastrous crash when Jim Mayers (Cooper-Climax) overtook the very slow Mercedes 300SL of the Vicomte de Barry. He hit the left-hand side of the road and struck some concrete pillars at over 100 mph, the Cooper disintegrated and Mayers was killed instantly. Bill Smith with the works Connaught collided with the burning wreckage and also died in the inferno. Wharton crashed his Frazer Nash, unable to see the road, and also involved were Lance Macklin (Austin-Healey), Jim Russell (Cooper-Climax) and Peter Jopp with the Lotus-MG. The principal cause of the accident was the total unsuitability and inadequacy of the Dundrod circuit for motor racing and it was never used again.

Before the end of the season there were a number of minor races. Chapman won the 1,500 cc sports car race at the Members' Meeting at Goodwood on 24 September with the Climax-powered car and the similar entries of Page and Steed took second and third places. At Castle Combe on 1 October Chapman with the Climax-powered car was beaten into second place by Bueb with a Cooper-Climax and later in the day he took another second place to Bueb in the Invitation sports car race. Eight days later Chapman beat Bueb into second place in the 1,200 cc sports car race at Brands Hatch. For the second year in succession the BRSCC held a race meeting at Brands Hatch on Boxing Day. The 1955 meeting was marred by rain, but Chapman drove the Climax-powered Mark 9 to win the fifteen lap Lex Trophy for sports cars up to 1,200 cc from Ivor Bueb's Cooper-Climax.

In the meanwhile Lotus had exhibited at the London Motor Show at Earls Court. Although Lotus was a member of the Society of Motor Manufacturers and Traders as an accessory manufacturer, they were granted a stand in the main hall and not in the Gallery where most of the accessory manufacturers exhibited. Lotus Engineering displayed a Mark 9 chassis with the body panels removed.

With the racing year over, Lotus made available the team cars to the press. John Bolster tested both MG and Climax-powered versions and his report is reproduced in Appendix 1. While Bill Boddy of *Motor Sport* tested only the Climax-powered Mark 9, Peter Garnier of *Autocar* drove the Climax-powered Mark 9 to Cornwall

LOTUS-M.G.

This is the car which has been raced by TEAM
LOTUS this season and driven by Colin Chapman
and Peter Jopp. It has proved to be quite easily
the fastest 1½-litre car in the country. It won
its class at the following International meetings:—
   Johnson Challenge Trophy, Goodwood, 30th May
   British Grand Prix Meeting, 16th July
   Crystal Palace, 30th July
   Aintree International, 3rd September
   Castle Combe International, 1st October
and numerous other smaller events. This is a
genuine two-seater sports car and can be used for
      road or rally work if required.
   It is offered in first-class racing
   condition with various spares: **£1,500**
                  Apply:—
   LOTUS ENGINEERING CO., LTD.,
      7 Tottenham Lane, Hornsey, N.8.
             MOUntview 4044.

Above left *The Mark 9s of Peter Lumsden (nearest the camera) and Dickie Steed fight it out at the BARC Members' meeting at Goodwood in March 1956. (LAT.)*

Above right *An advertisement for the works car in the classified pages of the 21 October 1955 issue of* Autosport.

and back. Chapman's confidence in allowing the press to drive these sophisticated and apparently quite flimsy sports racing cars for extended distances on the road did much to enhance the Company's reputation.

During 1955 only 23 of the Mark 9 were built. Apart from the two cars shipped to the United States for the Sebring race at the beginning of the year, other cars were sold in the United States to Len Bastrup, Duncan Black and G. D. Buchanan. Also finding its way to the Western side of the Atlantic was a Mark 9 for Gerry Polivka of Toronto. Other drivers to handle these cars in the United Kingdom, in addition to those mentioned in this chapter, were Dimitri Kasterine who entered his car under the 'Six Mile Stable' name (this car still survives), Edward Lewis, Mike MacDowel, L. I. Bramley, Peter Ashdown, Tom Barnard and Peter Lumsden. In 1956 Peter Lumsden, as a result of consistent successes in BARC Members' Meetings at Goodwood, won the Brooklands Trophy awarded by *Motor Sport*. With the ex-MacDowel car, John Anstice-Brown won the 1956 Chapman Trophy for cars with Ford 1,172 cc side-valve engines.

It had been a year of hectic activity for Lotus Engineering and Team Lotus, but now Chapman's reputation was firmly established and with new cars in 1956 the company was to grow both in terms of success and reputation. It was the turning point in the building of the company.

Chapter 4

The Mark 10, 1955

During the years 1953-55 the 2 litre class sports-racing cars in Britain grew extremely popular. The leading contenders were the Coopers of Alan Brown and Tony Crook, the Tojeiro of Cliff Davis and, from July 1954, the Lister of Archie Scott-Brown, all of which cars were powered by the Bristol engine. The Bristol, quite simply a British-made version of the pre-war BMW, was a 1,991 cc (66 x 96 mm) six-cylinder unit with inclined overhead valves. The inlet valves were operated by pushrods and rockers from a camshaft in the cylinder block and the exhaust valves were operated by pushrods, transverse pushrods and further rockers. It was normally fitted with three downdraught Solex carburettors. It had powered all post-war Bristol cars, had been developed in higher performance versions to power the Frazer Nash sports cars and had been further developed to power Formula Two cars built by Cooper and ERA. It had also powered the sports-racing 450 coupés built by Bristol themselves from 1953 onwards. It was a readily available, albeit expensive engine, developing around 142 bhp at 5,750 rpm in competition form.

The 2 litre category was not one in which Chapman was particularly interested in competing, but Brighton furrier Mike Anthony, who had raced a Team Lotus Mark 6 in 1954, was keen to have a car to race in this larger capacity class. Chapman considered it practical to adopt the design of the Mark 8 intended for MG power, to take the deeper and heavier Bristol engine. The space-frame chassis was modified by enlarging the engine bay and the problem of installation and removal of the engine was overcome by making two members of the space-frame detachable. In order to install the power train lower in the car, both engine and transmission line were lowered and a Salisbury hypoid bevel final drive was used. The Mark 10 would easily be distinguished by the fitting of a pronouncedly domed and curved engine cover which made the bonnet about 2½ in higher than that of the Mark 8. Chapman was concerned about the braking problems with this faster car and thought that the Girling drum brakes used on the Mark 8 would not be sufficiently powerful. Accordingly Dunlop disc brakes were adopted, mounted at the wheels at the front and inboard at the rear. To compensate for the weight of the Bristol engine and ensure proper weight distribution, the fuel tank was mounted behind the rear axle, together with the fuel pumps, spare wheel and battery. Apart from the domed engine cover, the Mark 10s were distinguishable by the absence of valances over the rear wheels.

Whilst Mike Anthony was the first to take delivery, the word had got round and other cars were supplied to Peter Scott-Russell who previously raced a Frazer Nash, lived at Standlake in Oxfordshire and used to commentate at Silverstone; a third car was supplied to Cliff Davis well known both as a dealer in American cars and for his chequered shirts. The purchasers had to supply their own Bristol engine and gearbox, but in component form the Mark 10 was supplied for £925.

Whilst purchasers of Mark 9 cars, two American owners apart, were forced to wait until later in the season for their new cars, Chapman built the first three Mark 10s very early in the year. There was of course a ready-cash inducement! Mike Anthony's car, a registered PCD 13, was beautifully constructed and immaculately finished in British racing green. For his car Peter Scott-Russell chose a light green finish (his car was registered JBW 648) while Cliff Davis kept his car in unpainted polished aluminium (it was registered NOY 1).

With a weight of only 11 cwt, about 1 cwt lower than Scott-Brown's Lister and, in particular so far as Anthony's car was concerned, in a very high state of tune, the Lotus Mark 10s should have, in theory at least, dominated the 2 litre class in 1955. However the most successful driver of the year in the class was again Archie Scott-Brown, at the wheel of the same Lister-Bristol that he had raced in 1954. It is interesting to look at the reasons why the Mark 10 was far less successful than anticipated (although it did enjoy a reasonable measure of success). Firstly no driver of a Mark 10 matched the sheer bravado, expertise and verve of Scott-Brown. It would also seem that Lister was a much better-balanced car and its handling was vastly superior. In addition the Bristol engines prepared for the Lister by Dan Moore probably gave the Cambridge-built car an extra edge.

Mike Anthony's car was ready first and he drove it in its first few races in unpainted aluminium. On the debut of the Mark 10 at the British Empire Trophy at Oulton Park Anthony crashed and overturned at the Cascades, escaping with cuts and bruises, but with the car too badly damaged to start the race. He took a third place in the 2,000 cc sports car event at Goodwood on Easter Monday, finished second at Ibsley at the end of April and at the International meeting at Silverstone in May both he and Peter Scott-Russell, making his debut with his Mark 10, retired. Incidentally in 1955 Mike Anthony continued to race as a member of Team Lotus. At this time Scott-Russell's car was still unpainted. Anthony won the 2,000 cc class of the Johnson's Trophy race at Goodwood on Whit Monday, but Scott-Brown was otherwise engaged at the Crystal Palace. By the latter part of June Scott-Russell's car had been painted in what one commentator descibed as 'a rather billious green' and he finished third in a race at the BARC Members' meeting at Goodwood. Cliff Davis' Mark 10 did not appear until Brands Hatch on 10 July and initially it ran far from well. Over the August Bank Holiday Mike Anthony finished a poor fourth at the Crystal Palace on the Saturday and at Brands Hatch on the Monday he took second place to Archie Scott-Brown with the Lister in the Kingsland Trophy race for sports cars over 1,900 cc, but he was over 40 seconds behind at the finish of this short event.

In August there were a number of minor international events in Britain and the Lotus-Bristols were well to the fore. On 6 August there was an International meeting on the Charterhall circuit near Greenlaw in Berwickshire. The main event of the day was the *Daily Record* International Trophy, but because of shortage of entries sports

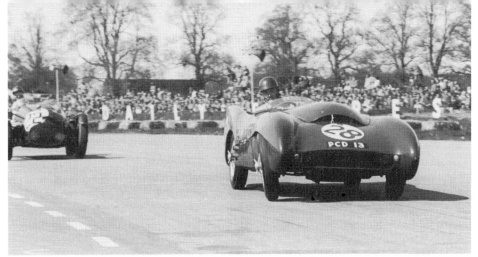

Above *Most successful of the Mark 10 drivers was Mike Anthony, seen here in the sports car race at the International Trophy at Silverstone in May 1955. Just how hard Anthony is trying can be seen from the angle of the front wheels—although, of course, with swing-axle front suspension wheel-angles could be very extreme!* (T. C. March.)

Below *Peter Scott-Russell with his still unpainted Mark 10 leads Tony Brooks with the works lightweight Frazer Nash at the Whitsun Goodwood meeting in 1955.* (LAT.)

Bottom *Another view of Scott-Russell and his Mark 10, now painted British Racing Green, at the British Grand Prix meeting at Aintree in 1955, heading the Gilby Engineering-entered Cooper-Maserati driven by Alan Brown.* (T. C. March.)

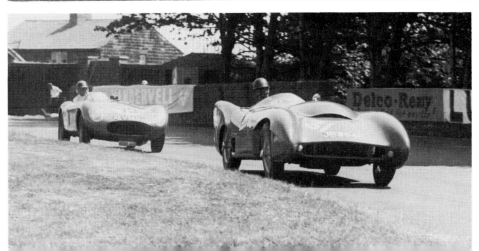

1955 Bristol engine, car completely rebuilt for coming season, exceptionally fast, Goodwood 84 m.p.h., Silverstone 90 m.p.h., max. speed approx. 135 m.p.h. Car has Dunlop disc brakes, engine special Lucas head.
Price £1,650.
Also spare Bristol BS4 engine and gearbox available.
MICHAEL ANTHONY,
15 Selborne Road,
Hove, Sussex.

Left *An advertisement for Mike Anthony's car which appeared in* Autosport *in the same issue as that for the works Mark 9.*

Right *At the 1956 International Trophy meeting at Silverstone in May, Cliff Davis with his Mark 10 leads the Ferrari of Roger Laurent (entered by Equipe Nationale Belge) and the Mark 10 of Peter Scott-Russell. (T. C. March.)*

cars were allowed to run in the first heat. This heat was won by Anthony with PCD 13, (but he did not feature in the final which was dominated by Bob Gerard with Stirling Moss' Maserati). He did however also finish second in the race for sports cars up to 2,700 cc behind Scott-Brown with the Lister. The following weekend it was the turn of the Snetterton circuit in Norfolk to host an international meeting. In the sports car race all three of the Mark 10s were entered. Scott-Brown crashed, Anthony took the lead only to retire with a holed piston, and the Listers of both Cunningham-Reid and Jack Sears retired. The class was won by Roy Salvadori at the wheel of that ill-handling pig of a car, the Cooper-Maserati sports car, concocted by Gilby Engineering because of the shortcomings in British events of their 2 litre Maserati sports car. This was one of the Cooper-Maserati's very few successes and second and third places went to the Mark 10s of Scott-Russell and Davis.

In the Goodwood 9 Hours race Scott-Brown co-drove a Connaught with Les Leston, so only the private Listers of Moore/Holt and Hampshire with Peter Scott-Russell as co-driver were entered. Mike Anthony was co-driving Bob Chase's new Cooper-Bristol driven by Mike Keen but this crashed with fatal results with Keen at the wheel. The more conventional Cooper-Bristol of Tony Crook partnered by Gibson was eliminated when Crook spun in the dark on oil and was rammed by Stirling Moss with a Porsche. The result was that the rather slow, ill-handling Mark 10 of Cliff Davis partnered by Reg Bicknell came through to finish twelfth overall and second in the 2 litre class behind the Lister of Hampshire/Scott-Russell.

The following weekend the *Daily Herald* International Trophy for sports cars was held at Oulton Park. Here the Listers failed and Peter Scott-Russell won the 2 litre class with the only other survivor in the class, Anthony's car, second after a succession of pit stops to top up the radiator and replace water lost through a blown head gasket. A class second followed the next weekend for Scott-Russell at the International Aintree meeting. Here Scott-Brown's Lister retired with a broken crankshaft and victory in the class went to Cunningham-Reid with his private Lister.

At the end of the 1955 season Mike Anthony advertised his Mark 10 in *Autosport*. This very highly tuned car, with the inlet trumpets for the carburettors poking through the bonnet top, a special Laystall-Lucas cylinder head and a claimed top

Two views of Cliff Davis with his Mark 10 in 1956. **Above**, at the International Trophy meeting at Silverstone, Davis leads Austen Nurse with the ex-Hampshire 1955 Lister-Bristol, while, **below**, at the British Grand Prix meeting at the same circuit he is about to be passed by Allan Moore with Ormsby Issard-Davies' 1956 Lister-Bristol. (T. C. March.)

The ex-Cliff Davis Mark 10 Bristol-powered Lotus seen beautifully restored at the Lotus meeting at Donington Park in 1977. (Geoffrey Goddard.)

speed of 135 mph, was offered at a price of £1,650. It was bought by Dimitri Kasterine who painted it black with a prominent white stripe from nose to tail (as on the Mark 9 that he had raced in 1955) and he competed with this in 1956 under the team name 'Six Mile Stable'. Also in the Six Mile Stable was Noel Cunningham-Reid who had of course beaten the Mark 10s on more than one occasion with his Lister-Bristol in 1955. Anthony was to turn his attention to another Bristol-engined Lotus that was to prove even more interesting than the Mark 10, but substantially less successful.

Both Peter Scott-Russell and Cliff Davis continued to race their Mark 10s into 1956. However Scott-Russell went off the road at the May Silverstone meeting, the Lotus caught fire and was burnt out. He spent several years rebuilding it and it was eventually sold. Many years later it appeared in the small ads in *Autosport* for 2 December 1966. It was advertised under a Harlow telephone number and described as 'Taxed for the road, an ugly brute, but potent' at an asking price of £325 ono! Cliff Davis continued to race his car through into 1957 by when it was painted red. It was also used in the film *Checkpoint*.

There were other Mark 10s but none featured so prominently as the three primarily described in this chapter. During 1955 a 'kit of parts' had been sold by Lotus to Dr Vaughan Havard and was built up for him by Bill Short. Apparently Dr Havard was taken seriously ill before the car was completed and it was some while before it was used in competitions; it was driven in a number of sprints and hill climbs by both the owner and Bill Short. Mike Young was supplied with a Mark 10 in component form which he built up with a Connaught 2 litre Formula Two engine. This failed to make its mark on the racing scene, as did the variant raced by George Nixon with a 1,500 cc Turner four-cylinder engine. Perhaps the most renowned of the Mark 10s, despite the fact that it was never raced, was the car without engine that was exported for film star James Dean. This was due to be fitted with an Offenhauser engine before it was delivered to him, but he crashed a Porsche with fatal results before the car arrived.

By the standards of the successes of the MG and Climax-engined cars of the period, the Mark 10 was a failure, especially when compared with the rival Lister-Bristol. It did however achieve a reasonable measure of success in British national club events and certainly gave its owners more than adequate satisfaction.

Chapter 5

The Eleven, 1956

In late 1955 Chapman decided that the company's efforts would be concentrated solely on one model for 1956 and that this would be known simply as the 'Eleven' without any mark number. The result was a Climax-powered sports-racing car of which more than 150 were built. It was a car that came to dominate the 1,100 cc category of racing and it played a major role in the final demise of 500 cc Formula Three racing which was waning in popularity already. For many drivers the Eleven became the gateway to motor racing. Elevens were raced at all levels from ten-lap races in club meetings at Silverstone to major long distance endurance races. Some indication of the degree of domination of the category by Lotus can be gathered that compared with the Eleven production figures, between 1955 and 1957 only around forty of the rear-engined Cooper-Climax cars were built, perhaps the same number from the rival Elva concern and production of the 1,100 cc Tojeiros amounted to a mere four or so cars.

The Eleven represented an evolution of the earlier Mark 9, with a multi-tubular space-frame chassis following the general design principles of the earlier car, and based on tubes of 1 in diameter for the main tubing and with subsidiary tubing of ¾ in in 18 and 20 gauge section, with stressed transmission tunnel. The suspension layout was basically unchanged in design, with swing-axles and coil spring/damper units at the front and at the rear a de Dion tube of 3¼ in diameter located by parallel radius arms and with the ends of the articulated drive-shafts piercing the tube and attached within it to the outboard universal joints. At the front an important change was a lower pivot point for the swing-axles which reduced the understeer that had been so pronounced on the Mark 9. There was now rack and pinion steering. In the tail was a lightweight 12 volt battery and the spare wheel mounted horizontally. The prominent tail fins which had characterized the earlier streamlined Lotus cars were gone and in their place were rear wings with just a very slightly finned effect. There were drop-down doors on both sides. The whole of the front of the body incorporating full ducting and a very small air entry for the radiator, hinged forward to give access to the engine and front suspension. At the rear, again the whole of the body hinged, to reveal the rear axle. Generally the Eleven was much more compact, with the wheelbase reduced from 7 ft 3½ in to 7 ft 1 in, front track from 4 ft ½ in to 3 ft 10½ in, overall length from 11 ft 8 in to 11 ft 2 in. The weight was down from 9 cwt to about 7½ cwt.

In February 1956 Lotus Engineering announced the Eleven in 'Le Mans' and

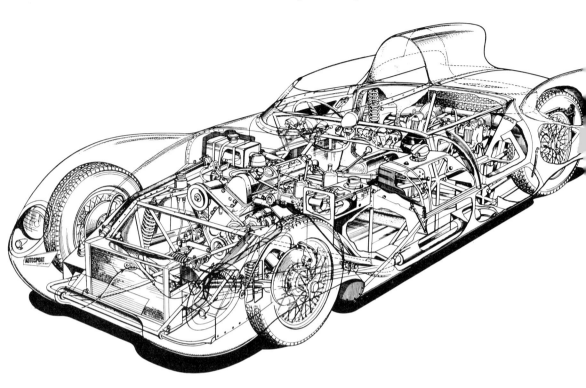

A very detailed cut-away drawing of the Lotus Eleven Le Mans by Theo Page. (Autosport.)

'Club' forms. Both of these cars were powered by the Coventry Climax 1,098 cc FWA engine in unit with a new gearbox, having an Austin 30 casing with Lotus close-ratio gears in the Le Mans specification. The company also stated that the Eleven was available as a sports car for the road with the Ford 100E 1,172 cc side-valve engine, Ford gearbox and full-width curved glass screen with windscreen wipers. There was also talk even of the availability of a hard top for road use. During the year however, the specifications of the different Eleven models were consolidated so that there were in effect three clear versions:

Le Mans

Intended for serious competition work, the Le Mans featured the Coventry Climax FWA engine inclined 10° to the left in the chassis, thereby permitting a carburation arrangement with horizontal induction tracts. It also permitted a lower bonnet line, but modification was required to both the sump and oil intake of the Climax engine. The carburettors and float chamber were flexibly mounted and connected by flexible tubing to prevent fuel frothing caused by vibration. Although, in the ordinary way, the Le Mans was fitted with the FWA engine either in Stage 1 form developing 72 bhp at 6,000 rpm or in Stage 2 form developing 83 bhp at 6,800 rpm, both Team

Lotus cars and private owners who were favoured by Coventry Climax were able to use the new 1,460 cc FWB engine. The Le Mans was initially fitted with the gearbox based on the A30 casing and Lotus close-ratio gears, but later the MGA gearbox was substituted. The Le Mans featured a streamlined head fairing, a perspex wrap-round screen on the driver's side of the cockpit and a metal tonneau cover on the left-hand side. Girling disc brakes, mounted inboard at the rear, were now standard. Whilst the standard 9½ gallon fuel tank mounted in the near side of the body was usually sufficient, an extra 11 gallon tank could be installed in the off side of the body. The headlamps were in the wings under perspex streamlined covers. With the Stage 1 Climax in 'Le Mans 75' form the price was £1,337 and with the Stage 2 Climax engine, the 'Le Mans 85' the price was £1,387. If the 1,460 cc Climax FWB engine was installed, the price was around £250 extra.

Club
In this form the Climax FWA engine and A30/Lotus gearbox were retained, but at the rear there was a live rear axle located by parallel trailing arms. Drum brakes were used, with 9 in drums at the front and 8 in drums at the rear. This version was available with full-width screen, wipers and hood. It was priced at £1,083.

Sports
This version of the Eleven was fitted with the Ford 1,172 cc side-valve engine and a Ford three-speed gearbox. Otherwise the specification was similar to that of the Club. The price of this version was £872.

Whilst of course it was possible to buy a built-up motor car, Chapman was still very anxious to sell the cars in component form, partly because the company had so many orders that it would not have been able to cope with building all these cars up and, partly, because it saved purchase tax. A great deal of the construction of the components for Lotus Elevens was sub-contracted, including the construction of the bodies by William and Pritchard Ltd of Edmonton, chassis construction was sub-contracted and of course many components were simply bought in.

The 1956 Racing Season
At the beginning of the year Chapman concentrated on the preparation of a 1,460 cc Eleven to be sold to Briggs Cunningham to run in the Sebring 12 Hours race to be held on 25 March. Then came the Team Lotus Elevens for Colin Chapman, Reg Bicknell and Cliff Allison. Both Allison and Bicknell were paying their way. Whilst Allison was a young and hungry driver, destined to become a member of the Ferrari team, Reg Bicknell was one of the old school. Born in 1915, he was in the motor trade, running his own business, Revis Car Sales Ltd, in Southampton. He had raced Staride and his own Revis Formula Three cars for some years and in 1955 had built and raced, albeit briefly, his own Borgward-engined Revis sports-racing car. This had not been a success—it showed tremendous speed but horrific handling and had soon been disposed of. He was an enthusiastic but mediocre driver and his successes during 1956 were to be limited. It soon became apparent that the only driver in Team Lotus fully capable of exploiting the potential of the Eleven was Chapman himself.

One other new Eleven was ready at the beginning of the year, an FWB-engined car for Ivor Bueb, the Cheltenham driver, vastly experienced in Formula Three, who had joined Jaguar as a works driver in 1955 and had co-driven the winning D-type at Le Mans. In 1955 Bueb had also driven works Coopers. Now, for the 1956 season, he was setting up his own team with a FWB-engined Cooper-Climax which he normally drove himself and the Lotus Eleven which was to be driven throughout the year by Mike Hawthorn. As the season progressed more and more Elevens were completed and they played an increasingly important role in British sports car events.

In March Chapman flew to Sebring. In practice both he and Len Bastrup were shatteringly fast with Cunningham's new FWB-powered Eleven, but unfortunately Bastrup went off the road, the car caught fire and was very badly damaged. Bastrup suffered minor burns, there was no prospect of having the car ready in time for the race and so Chapman agreed to co-drive the 1,098 cc Lotus entered by Joe Sheppard. So far as can be ascertained this car was a Mark 9. Chapman and Sheppard led their class until the starter motor burned out during a pit stop and the car was disqualified after the back end had been jacked up and the engine fired by spinning the rear wheels.

Chapman was still in the United States when the Eleven, registration number RCR 400, for Bicknell made its debut at the Easter Goodwood meeting. The Eleven was still unpainted and practice revealed it suffering from major handling problems. Bicknell finished fourth in the race for sports cars up to 1,500 cc behind a trio of Cooper entries. The first problem that Chapman faced on his return was to resolve the handling and to make sure that the cars were ready for their next race, the British Empire Trophy at Oulton Park.

Here Chapman was at the wheel of his new FWB-powered Eleven, registration number 9 EHX, the Bicknell car also ran and Mike Hawthorn was driving for Ivor Bueb's Ecurie Demi-Litre team with their new unpainted FWB-engined Eleven. There was strong Cooper opposition with works cars driven by Salvadori, Russell and Stirling Moss who had borrowed a Cooper from the works. The British Empire Trophy was run in three heats according to capacity, with a handicap final. In the heat for cars up to 1,500 cc Bueb crashed his Cooper shortly after the start and Chapman went into the lead pursued by Moss, Russell, Salvadori and with Hawthorn rapidly closing on the leaders. At the finish of the sixteen-lap heat, Chapman led Salvadori by five seconds with Hawthorn third, Moss fourth and Bicknell fifth. The handicapping of the final favoured the smaller capacity cars. Moss led initially, then Chapman went

Top right *A good view of the front of the chassis of the Eleven. This is the Ecurie Demi-Litre car in the paddock at the British Empire Trophy at Oulton Park in 1956. (T. C. March.)*

Above right *Another view in the paddock at Oulton Park in April 1956. Mike Hawthorn chats to Colin Chapman, while Ivor Bueb is on the right of the group. No 11 is the Team Lotus Eleven, No 15 is the Ecurie Demi-Litre car and No 7 is one of the Cooper-Climax entries. (T. C. March.)*

Right *Before the 'off' of the final, Mike Hawthorn at the wheel of the Ecurie Demi-Litre Eleven. No 12 is Reg Bicknell's Team Lotus car and No 61 is Joakim Bonnier's rebuilt Alfa Romeo Disco Volante driven by Ken Wharton. (T. C. March.)*

BENZOLE MIXTURE

9 EHX

At Oulton Park Colin Chapman with the Team Lotus Eleven, appropriately numbered, won his heat and finished second in the final. (T. C. March.)

ahead and began to pull out a lead until he spun at Druids. The Lotur driver rejoined the race to finish second, ten seconds behind Moss, but ahead of Salvadori and Hawthorn.

A week later Team Lotus was in action again at Aintree. In the race for sports cars up to 2,000 cc Hawthorn was the winner from Salvadori and Bicknell with the Team Lotus entry, Chapman had entered his car in FWA 1,098 cc form and won the 1,100 cc class from the Coopers of Gammon and MacDowel. Throughout the year the Coopers and the Elevens fought for success in the 1,100 cc and 1,500 cc classes, but as the year went on the balance of power swung sharply in Lotus favour. At Brands Hatch on 29 April Bicknell won the 1,500 cc sports car race but Graham Hill, at this time a Lotus Engineering employee and without the financial means to race his own car and without the track record to get drives in other people's cars, had been lucky enough to borrow DEC 494, the latest works Eleven, from Chapman. Apart from finishing second to Bicknell in the 1,500 cc race, he won the 1,200 cc race from Gammon's Cooper. He was obviously a driver of considerable potential, but as will be revealed later in this chapter there were occasions when his driving was wild in the extreme.

The main contenders were in action again at the International Trophy at Silverstone on 5 May, but although Hawthorn had been entered with the Ecurie

The fantastic scrap at Goodwood on Whit Monday 1956 between Hawthorn with the Ecurie Demi-Litre Lotus and Chapman with the Team Lotus entry. (LAT.)

Demi-Litre car, he decided he was committed quite enough by driving a works BRM in the main race of the day and so the Ecurie Demi-Litre Lotus was driven by Bueb. The race was won by Salvadori with the works Cooper-Climax and with Chapman in second place. Bueb was fifth and Bicknell sixth. In this race Tony Brooks drove Coombs' Lotus-Connaught, a Mark 9, into eighth place. Allison drove the Team Lotus 1,098 cc car but retired with broken suspension.

By the Whitsun weekend quite a number of Elevens were being raced by private owners. At Snetterton on the Saturday W. S. Frost, Keith Hall (YTN 444) and David Piper all had their new cars. Piper finished second in the twelve-lap final of a race based on two qualifying heats for cars of different capacity, whilst Hall finished second in a five-lap Lotus handicap. The following day at Brands Hatch Cliff Allison won the race for cars under 1,200 cc from Alan Stacey at the wheel of his new car, YKX 55, while Chapman won the race for sports cars under 1,500 cc.

The main event of the weekend was the meeting at Goodwood on the Monday. In the first race, a 26-lap event for sports cars up to 1,500 cc there was the most fantastic dice between Hawthorn and Chapman with Elevens. Team Lotus also entered Bicknell with his 1,500 cc car, still unpainted, together with Allison with the 1,098 cc model. I quote the *Autosport* description of this fantastic race: '. . . both [Hawthorn and Chapman] manifested an urgent desire for the lead. The result was racing at its best. Mike Hawthorn and Reg Bicknell (Lotus) were quickest away at the start, but Mike passed Bicknell on the inside at St Mary's to lead, while Chapman lay third for a lap. Then he got going, caught Bicknell on lap two, then whipped past Hawthorn on lap three. Mike tried one side, he tried the other, and on lap four, in the rush down the Lavant Straight to Woodcote, he took Chapman on the inside, the pair now amongst the tail-enders in the race.

'Lap five, and they whisted past "Pathfinder" Bennett's neat white Fairthorpe-Climax, one to the left, the other to his right, at Fordwater. And at Woodcote Chapman turned the tables on Hawthorn by taking *him* on the inside. Lap six and Mike repassed "outback" but Chapman swiftly retaliated, and this time his opponent tried to pass on the outside at Woodcote. Lap eight and Hawthorn led. Lap nine and it was Chapman. Lap eleven, Hawthorn, and on lap twelve Chapman again. Just then Reg Bicknell, who had been holding third, dropped out, letting Brabham's Cooper come up, followed by Cliff Allison's Lotus, the leading "1,100". And just then, also, Chapman and Hawthorn executed a joint waltz at Madgwick with military precision, contacted briefly, and shot off again.

'Lap fourteen and Chapman led, and Hawthorn slowed, stopped at the pits for a hasty examination of his car, then tore away again. . .

'That Hawthorn/Chapman *pas de deux* at Madgwick broke up the magnificent fight and from then on Chapman was unchallenged, winning at 85.88 mph from Hawthorn, Brabham and Allison, who won the 1,100 cc class. To drive home just how close in performance the duelists were, both shared fastest lap at 88.71 mph—a new class record.'

Hawthorn and Chapman met up again in the *Formule Libre* race, but with only three single-seaters and mainly the contestants from the two earlier sports car races. However Chapman was out of the race with a stripped second gear before the first corner and Hawthorn went on to finish second to the winning D-type Jaguar of Desmond Titterington entered by Ecurie Ecosse.

Another new interesting Lotus to appear at Goodwood was Mike Anthony's special Bristol-powered Eleven. This car, built up by Anthony himself, featured the Bristol engine laid nearly horizontally so as to be accomodated in the Eleven chassis. It was beautifully turned out and taken to races on Anthony's new transporter, a Standard Vanguard with lengthened chassis and Triumph TR3 engine, thereby aping the high-speed 300 SL-engined transporters used by the Mercedes-Benz team in 1955, which were capable of 100 mph and could be used to carry a single car to race meetings. Sadly, Anthony's initiative was wasted and the Bristol-powered Eleven was a complete failure. It was subsequently sold in the United States with the claim that it was the fastest Lotus ever—this may have been true at the time, but it very rarely displayed such performance in British events.

On the Sunday Graham Hill had driven a Cooper-Climax at Brands Hatch and the following day he was entered at the Crystal Palace at the wheel of Tommy Sopwith's new Eleven with 1,098 cc engine. He finished third in the Anerley and Norbury Trophy races, both for sports cars up to 1,500 cc.

At Oulton Park on 2 June yet another variant of the Eleven appeared, a Maserati-powered car driven by J. B. Naylor. Naylor had been racing a Maserati 150S car in

British events. Although Jean Behra had won the 1,500 cc Nüburgring 500 km race in 1955 from strong Porsche and EMW opposition, it was not a suitable car for British short-circuit events and Naylor had been bitterly disappointed with the vast expenditure which had produced such little result. As a result this Stockport-based company director and car dealer acquired an Eleven chassis into which he transferred the Maserati engine and gearbox. At Oulton Park he won a short race for sports cars up to 2,000 cc and this was to be the first of many successes for this new car, registered KJA 90. The Lotus-Maserati was easily recognizable by an aperture cut in the bonnet panel to accomodate the radiator header tank of the Maserati engine.

On 16 June Reg Bicknell drove his FWB-engined car in the City Cup race for sports cars up to 1,500 cc held in Porto over the 4.6 mile Boavista circuit, so called because the main straight was formed by the Avenida da Boavista. Despite handling problems caused by strong cross-winds, the lightweight British cars fared well. The race was won by Salvadori with a works Cooper-Climax from Nogueira with a Porsche and Bicknell crossed the line in third place. The following day the Lotus-Climax with FWA engine competed in a very different sort of event when Charles Bulmer, accompanied by his wife, drove a works-loaned Eleven in the Mobilgas Economy Run over a 640 mile course in South and West England and including an hour spent lapping Goodwood. In the so-called allcomers class the Bulmers brought their Lotus home in second place having averaged 48.49 mpg.

There were four Lotus entries in the Supercortemaggiore Grand Prix held on the combined road circuit and banked track at Monza on 24 June. A Team Lotus entry for Chapman/Sears was withdrawn, as was the Ecurie Demi-Litre FWB-engined car to be driven by Hawthorn/Hamilton because it had developed gearbox trouble on the way to the circuit. Cliff Davis' Mark 10 failed to arrive and Anthony's Bristol-powered Eleven ran in practice driven by himself and Mark Lund. Unfortunately it became a non-starter after several pistons had broken. Originally destined to appear at this race was a Lotus to be entered by Officine Alfieri Maserati. Maserati obviously shared Brian Naylor's view with regard to the 150S and through Piero Taruffi had ordered an Eleven chassis which was to be run in this race with 150S engine and gearbox. Lack of time for development was blamed for its withdrawal. Accordingly the only Lotus starter was a 1,098 cc car driven by David Piper and Mark Lund. Piper was now enjoying a full season's tour of the Continent, competing in minor races and picking up starting and prize money wherever he could, and was shortly to be joined by Bob Hicks. Piper's car, registered RNM 222, appeared only to have qualified because of a confusion by the timekeepers who had credited it with times achieved by Anthony's Bristol-powered car when Lund was at the wheel! The Lotus was delayed by brake problems, cured by fitting a calliper cannibalized from the Ecurie Demi-litre car, and brake problems caused its final retirement from the race when the brakes failed altogether and Piper had great difficulty in stopping the car.

The same weekend Chapman won the 1,500 cc sports car race at Aintree and Archie Scott-Brown, at the wheel of Sopwith's car with FWB engine and registered TMY 400, finished third behind Leston's Cooper. Sopwith's cars, raced under the name Equipe Endeavour, bore the name of the yachts raced by his father in pre-war days and adopted the same handsome dark blue colour finish. They were always immaculately turned out and Sopwith usually secured first class drivers to handle them. He had retired from driving himself at the end of 1955 because of family pressure. It was typical of the trend of the period that Sopwith, a firm supporter of Cooper in 1955 with Climax, Connaught and Jaguar-powered cars, had now switched his allegiance to Lotus, abandoning both the Cooper chassis and also the very expensive 1,484 cc Connaught engine that had now been superseded by the latest Climax.

There followed another important Continental race, the 1,500 cc 12 hour sports car race at the French Grand Prix meeting at Reims. The sole Lotus entry was the Ecurie Demi-Litre car driven by Bueb and Herbert MacKay Fraser (Hawthorn was not available because he was driving a works Jaguar in the sports car race for cars of unlimited capacity that followed). The Lotus was second fastest in practice to the Cooper-Climax of Stirling Moss/Phil Hill. In the race the Cooper was soon out of contention with carburation and gasket problems, the race was initially led by the Osca of Maglioli, but the Lotus came through to hold second place and for a short while took the lead. Over the next couple of hours the Lotus and the Porsche driven by von Frankenberg/Storez swapped places, but after seven hours forty minutes of racing the Lotus was in the pits with gearbox trouble. MacKay Fraser rejoined the race with the use of top gear only, still holding second place, but falling further and further back until during the eleventh hour the Lotus stopped in the pits with a holed sump. Mike Anthony's Bristol-powered Lotus had been entered in 12 hour race for unlimited capacity cars, but once again non-started.

On 7 June Bicknell won the 1,500 cc sports car race at Mallory Park from Leston's Cooper and Hall's Lotus. However the most interesting Lotus in this race was the unpainted aluminium finished car of Graham Hill, registered XJH 902, a Team Lotus car running in sports trim in the *Autosport* Series Production Sports Car Championship. Hill won his class and finished third overall behind the Austin-Healey 100S cars of John Dalton and David Shale.

The following day the Team Lotus and Équipe Endeavour cars ran at Rouen, a meeting with important international 1,500 cc and unlimited capacity sports car races. The Rouen Grand Prix for unlimited cars produced an exciting battle won by Castellotti (Ferrari) from Moss (Aston Martin), but in the earlier Coupe Delamare Debouteville the Lotus Elevens had displayed complete domination. Harry Schell led initially from Chapman, Phil Hill (with the Ecurie Demi-Litre Cooper), MacDowel (Cooper) and Allison (1,098 cc Lotus). Schell spun on the fourth lap, Chapman went into the lead, Hill retired and so the order was Chapman - MacDowel - Schell - Allison - Hawthorn (Ecurie Demi-Litre Lotus). Hawthorn soon retired with a broken gearbox, MacDowel visited the pits and dropped right to the tail of the field and at the finish of this race lasting 75 minutes Chapman crossed the line the winner, having averaged 87.93 mph, ahead of Allison and Schell. It was a magnificent triumph for Lotus. Continental critics had been forming the conclusion that the Lotus Eleven was little more than a British lightweight, excessively fragile ten-lap sprint car. Now they were beginning to change their minds.

On 14 July a significant race was held at the British Grand Prix meeting at Silverstone. This was the first ever 1,500 cc Formula Two race, held in anticipation of

Above *In the first 1,500 cc Formula Two race which was held at the British Grand Prix meeting at Silverstone in July 1956 Chapman finished second with this Team Lotus Eleven.* (T. C. March.)

Below *Another shot from the Silverstone Formula Two race with Reg Parnell at the wheel of the Équipe Endeavour Eleven leading the old Gordini of André Pilette.* (T. C. March.)

Above In the pits at Le Mans in 1956 are the 1,460 cc Eleven of Chapman/MacKay Fraser and the 1,098 cc car of Cliff Allison/Keith Hall. (Geoffrey Goddard.)

Below The line-up of Team Lotus entries at Le Mans in 1956. From left to right, the 1,100 cc Elevens of Bicknell/Jopp and Allison/Hall and the 1,460 cc car of Chapman/MacKay Fraser. (Geoffrey Goddard.)

the new Formula Two which was to come into effect in 1957. In fact it was not to be the only race to be held to the new Formula during 1956, but the only constructors to have single-seater cars ready during that year were Cooper, who were well advanced with their plans for what amounted to a single seater version of the 'Manx-tail' sports car (and as a result concentrated on this more and more at the expense of the sports cars which they finally abandoned in mid-1957) and Francis Beart's Beart-Rodger-Osca. Lotus were not able to show their Formula Two cars to the public until the end of 1956, but that Formula Two car was both important in itself, and also as an influencing factor, on the design of future Lotus sports-racing cars.

At Silverstone Team Lotus entered cars for Chapman, Allison and Bicknell, while Reg Parnell was at the wheel of the Équipe Endeavour Lotus. It does seem however, that Équipe Endeavour had optimistically expected a Climax single seater to be delivered to them in time for this race, because that was what they had entered and that is what appeared both in the race programme and in several race reports. Other Lotus drivers included Graham Hill, at the wheel of J. J. Richards' 1,098 cc car (at this time in his career Graham would drive owt for nowt!). Salvadori with the single-seater Cooper was fastest in practice, but Chapman with a sports Lotus was only a second slower and Cliff Allison two seconds slower than his Team Lotus team-mate. Chapman led the race initially, but Salvadori rook the lead on lap ten and the final results were Salvadori - Chapman - Bueb (Ecurie Demi-Litre Cooper) - Allison.

Later in the day, after the Grand Prix, there was an unlimited capacity sports car race for cars over 1,500 cc and Mike Anthony had entered his Lotus Eleven-Bristol with Mark Lund at the wheel. He had been slower than the entire field in practice, 10 seconds slower than Allan Moore at the wheel of one of the latest Lister-Bristols and 9 seconds slower than Austen Nurse at the wheel of a similar car. In the race however, Lund soon moved into the lead in the 2 litre class with the radical Eleven-Bristol, finished seventh overall ahead of some much heavier opposition, winning the 2,000 cc class from Moore (Lister-Bristol) and Davis (Lotus Mark 10-Bristol).

Following the 1955 disaster at Le Mans, a number of modifications were made to the circuit in the interests of safety, including the shortening of the circuit by some 140 yd and as a result of these modifications the race was postponed until 28-29 July. As another result of the accident, there were special rules governing the race, with the result that it did not count as a round in the Sports Car World Championship. There was a ban on prototypes of over 2,500 cc, but both the Aston Martin DB3S and the Jaguar D-type were accepted as production cars, not withstanding the fact that the cars raced by the works teams were very different mechanically from those being offered to private purchasers. Ferrari was obliged to run 2.5 litre cars with engines derived from their old 1955 Tipo 625 Grand Prix cars. Other regulations were that a full-width windscreen had to be fitted, there must be a tonneau cover of flexible material and there was a miniumum width prescribed for the two seats. Refuelling could not take place before 34 laps had been covered and thereafter at intervals of not less than 34 laps. There was a maximum fuel tank capacity limit of 29 gallons (130 litres and at fuel stops a maximum of 26½ gallons (120 litres) could be taken on board. In other words everyone had to average not worse than 11 mpg. The fuel consumption regulations of course did not affect Lotus at all, but the three Team

Lotus entries that were accepted for the race had to be substantially modified, so far as bodywork was concerned, to comply with the regulations.

Because of the minimum width regulation, what were described as special cars were built for the race, with the chassis frames wider at the centre and sweeping in just ahead of the rear wheels. All three cars, however, bore registration numbers already seen during the year's racing, but it is true to say that with works team cars, they are so frequently rebuilt during the year that it is impossible to ascertain what is new and what is not. Other changes included the mounting of additional headlamps behind plastic covers in the nose of the car, a full-width perspex windcreen, and perspex side portions attached to the drop down doors. Like several other entrants, Chapman was optimistic enough to expect the windscreen wiper to work on fly-spattered perspex, but at least trying to look over the top of the Lotus windscreen was not quite as bad as it was with some cars.

Once again Team Lotus was managed by John Eason Gibson and to comply with the requirement that signalling had to be carried out from special pits just round the Mulsanne corner, amateur Lotus driver John Lawry maintained contact with the main pits and operated the necessary signals for the drivers.

The performance of the team Lotus entries and their details can be summarized as follows:-

No 32, registered 9 EHX (the same registration as the 1955 MG-powered Mark 9) 1,460 cc FWB engine, driven by Colin Chapman/Herbert MacKay Fraser
This Lotus ran extremely well for much of the race, progressing steadily through torrential rain that inundated the circuit after midnight. By dawn on Sunday this Lotus was in second place in its class, but a long way behind the Porsche 550 of von Frankenberg/von Trips which eventually won the class. With slightly under 4 hours to go to the 4 pm finish this Lotus was eliminated by a broken big end bolt. On the Mulsanne Straight the FWB-powered car had been timed over the kilometre at 128.2 mph, admittedly substantially slower than the 138.09 mph of the class-winning Porsche.

No 35, registered DEC 494, 1,098 cc FWA engine, driven by Cliff Allison/ Keith Hall
The car ran exceedingly well until the early hours of Sunday morning when, in the period before dawn when the circuit was enveloped with mist, Allison collided on the Mulsanne Straight with a large dog. The dog was of course killed and the front of the Lotus so badly damaged that there was no alternative but to withdraw the car.

No 36, registered XJH 902, 1,098 cc FWA engine, driven by Reg Bicknell/ Peter Jopp
Throughout the race the Lotus 1,100 cc cars battled with the Cooper-Climax driven by Hugus/Bentley. In the closing hours of the race this Lotus moved ahead of the Cooper into eighth place and at the end of the race it was a clear lap ahead. Apart from winning the 1,100 cc class, the Lotus finished seventh overall and fourth in the Index of Performance.

The race was a great British success with the Ecurie Ecosse-entered Jaguar D-type of Ron Flockhart/Ninian Sanderson winning from the Aston Martin DB3S of Stirling

Above *During 1956 Mike Anthony raced a Bristol-powered car. Apparently Anthony had asked Chapman to build him a special car, but the reply was that it would have to be a 'Mark Anthony', in other words a 'Special' built by Anthony himself. This photograph taken at the International Trophy meeting at Silverstone shows the canted engine (which was converted to dry sump) with three semi-downdraught SU carburettors. Anthony was obsessed by the number 13, he raced with that number whenever possible and here it can be seen on the boss of the steering wheel. (T. C. March.)*

Below *A view of the rear end of the Eleven-Bristol showing the standard Lotus layout. Note the coil spring/damper mounting, the inboard brakes and the mounting of the spare wheel. (T. C. March.)*

Moss/Peter Collins. It was of course Jaguar's fourth victory in the race.

On August Bank Holiday Monday there were race meetings at both Brands Hatch and the Crystal Palace. Mike Hawthorn drove the Ecurie Demi-Litre Eleven at Brands Hatch with a 1,290 cc engine. He won his heat of the 1,500 sports car race, but this was in wet conditions, and in the dry final he was out-paced. The race winner was Reg Bicknell with his Team Lotus car. Bicknell also finished second in the Formula Two race behind Salvadori's single-seater Cooper. Graham Hill was the highlight of the *Autosport* series Production Sports Car Championship race with the Ford-powered Lotus, now painted yellow, but his prominence was for all the wrong reasons. Having come through the field to challenge the leaders, he repeatedly spun off and was eventually black-flagged and disqualified. The same day at the Crystal Palace Keith Hall, whose private car was now fitted with Weber carburettors, succeeded in beating Team Lotus driver Cliff Allison in the August Trophy race, held as two qualifying heats and a final.

The *Daily Herald* International Trophy meeting was held at Oulton Park on 18 August. Because of torrential rain that had flooded the circuit and time spent trying to pump it clear of water, both the main race for unlimited capacity cars (in which the only Lotus was Anthony's car driven by Lund who retired), and the 1,500 cc *Sporting Life* Trophy were shortened. Mike Hawthorn was again at the wheel of the Ecurie Demi-Litre 1,500 cc Eleven; the only Team Lotus entry was the 1,098 cc car of Cliff Allison. For an account of what happened in this race, I quote from *Roy Salvadori: Racing Driver* (Patrick Stephens Ltd, 1985): 'In the 1,500 cc race Moss took an early lead with his Cooper, but I was well in the hunt in second place and narrowly leading Mike Hawthorn at the wheel of Bueb's Lotus. As we approached Nicker Brook Mike went ahead; I thought that he was motoring too fast on the approach to the corner, but he seemed to be holding a good line and it looked as though he was going to get away with it. Suddenly the back of the Lotus broke away, the car mounted the bank and turned a complete somersault. I tried to avoid the Lotus and instinctively ducked as parts of Mike's disintegrating car landed on top of my Cooper, hitting me on the head and breaking the windscreen. Completely dazed, I went off the road, just missing a small concrete building; the car spun and carried on backwards until I managed to get it pointing in the right direction and I cruised round to the pits. "Lofty" England of Jaguar, a great friend of Mike's, was in the pits and asked what happened to Mike. Still badly dazed, I said "he's dead". This caused considerable, but rather needless panic, for, although he had been thrown out of the car, he had only suffered bad bruising and a sprained wrist. For the first time in my career I opted out of a race for other than mechanical reasons and this indicates clearly just how stunned I was.' Moss duly won the race and Keith Hall and Cliff Allison with their 1,098 cc cars took second and third places.

Another, albeit minor success was achieved in the Brighton Speed Trials where Mike Anthony won the 1,501-2,000 cc sports car class with his Lotus-Bristol at a new class record time of 28,73 seconds. At the September Goodwood meeting Keith Hall won the Madgwick Cup race for sports cars up to 1,100 cc with Cliff Allison third (behind MacDowel's Cooper) and with Alan Stacey in fourth place. The Woodcote Cup race for cars up to 2,000 cc was won by Salvadori with the Formula Two Cooper,

C. M. Lund with Mike Anthony's Lotus-Bristol leads a Cooper-Climax and a Formula 2 Connaught at Goodwood in September 1956. (Geoffrey Goddard.)

but Chapman finished second and Bicknell was fourth. The following day at Brands Hatch Bicknell won the race for sports cars under 1,500 cc with Allison second and Chapman won the Formula Two race. Also in September the Gold Cup race at Oulton Park was held for Formula Two cars. Lotus still forced to race sports cars, whilst by now there was a total of four Cooper-Climax single-seaters running. The Coopers of Salvadori (works car) and Tony Brooks entered by Rob Walker took the first two places, but Ron Flockhart at the wheel of John Coombs' Eleven finished third and Chapman, his Lotus almost brakeless, finished fourth. During this race Bicknell, travelling through the Cascades at speed, suffered a locked brake and slid straight over the bank and into the lake. He made his escape without injury. At the same meeting Graham Hill drove the Ford-powered car in the final of the *Autosport* Production Series Sports Car race. Graham was second quickest in practice to Ken Rudd's AC Ace-Bristol, but in the race, which lasted three hours, having held third place overall, he collided with an Austin-Healey. The Lotus subsequently lost all its water as the result of a broken fan pulley and with the oil pressure sagging the Lotus put a connecting rod through the block, Graham pulled out of the race leaving behind him a trail of oil down the road.

At the beginning of September Lotus had taken to Italy a modified Le Mans car with streamlined bubble canopy which was intended for record-breaking attempts in International Class G at Monza. The driver was to be Stirling Moss and the attempt was to take place the day after the Italian Grand Prix. Moss established a 50 km record at 135.54 mph and 50 mile record at 132.77 mph when the attempt had to be abandoned because the exceptional bumpiness of the banked circuit had caused the rear sub-frame to fracture and the tail of the Eleven to become detached. Team Lotus returned to Italy after the Gold Cup race at Oulton Park and Team Lotus Elevens were driven by Herbert MacKay Fraser and Cliff Allison in the Shell Grand Prix at Imola. Allison led initially, but went off the course, and the winner was Castellotti with an Osca. MacKay Fraser finished fifth. After Imola the Lotus team went back to Monza to continue their record-breaking attempt with MacKay Fraser at the wheel. The team broke the following International Class G record for cars up to 1,100 cc:

50 km:	135.15 mph	50 miles:	135.24 mph
100 km:	135.45 mph	100 miles:	137.5 mph
200 km:	137.5 mph	1 hour:	137.5 mph

In addition the bubble-top Lotus achieved a fastest lap round Monza of 143 mph. On the Castfelusano circuit, a fast 4-mile course near Ostia, Team Lotus competed in the Rome Grand Prix held on 20 and 21 October. Cliff Allison and Ron Flockhart retired their 1,500 cc cars, but whilst Luigi Musso won the 1,500 cc event with an Osca, Brian Naylor finished second with his Maserati-powered Eleven and MacKay Fraser and David Piper took first and second places in the 1,100 cc class.

As has been mentioned earlier in this chapter, throughout 1956 David Piper and Bob Hicks had been competing all across Europe with their 1,098 cc Elevens. Apart from Piper's performance at Ostia, Piper and Hicks had taken first and second places at Les Sables d'Olonne in July, finished first and second in the Sila Cup race at Cosenza in Italy (a typical Italian street race) and Piper had won the 1,100 cc class in the Coupe du Salon at Montlhéry in October. It had been a surprisingly successful year for these two under-financed and very optimistic campaigners.

At the London Motor Show Lotus Engineering had exhibited their long-awaited Formula Two car. Although the history, and comparative failure, of the Formula Two Lotus does not fall within the scope of this book, the car nevertheless played a significant part in the development of Lotus sports-racing cars, as from now onwards design features tried on the single-seaters were adapted on the sports-racing cars. Also exhibited at Earls Court were two cars to the specification raced at Le Mans and complying with the new International Sports Car regulations to be adopted for 1958, that is with fully-open cockpit and full-width screen. One car was complete, but the other was displayed without the body panels in place.

Reference must be made to one other Lotus Eleven that appeared in 1957. At Geneva Motor Show there had been exhibited an Eleven with Ghia drophead coupé bodywork. It was an exceptionally elegant car and it ran in a few continental hill climbs in 1957.

In November Lotus loaned one of the Le Mans cars, DEC 494 to Ian Smith, the

The Hon Edward Greenall at the wheel of his Series 1 Eleven in the 1957 British Empire Trophy at Oulton Park. (T. C. March.)

Secretary of Club Lotus who drove it over a distance of 892 miles from Lands End to John O'Groats via Appleby in what is now Cumbria. The Lotus averaged 51.06 mph and 35.525 mpg. Overall during a four day period Smith covered 2,000 miles. The only problem suffered was breakage of the chassis sub-frame above the battery on the near side of the car. This was repaired overnight and did not in any way delay the drive.

During the year Lotus had built and sold around 150 Elevens, of which over sixty were sold in the United States. Whilst Chapman was to become more and more involved with design and construction of single-seater cars, Lotus sports car production continued throughout the winter and the Eleven still had a very long racing career ahead of it.

Chapter 6

The Eleven, 1957-58

For 1957 Lotus Engineering introduced the Eleven Series Two. The principal change was the adoption of the Formula Two front suspension by double wishbones with the leading member of the upper wishbone also acting as an anti-roll bar and, of course, with combined coil-spring damper/units. At the rear the de Dion tube was increased in diameter to 3⅝ in and Hardy Spicer drive-shaft joints passing through the tube were adopted. To comply with the new International Appendix C regulations, the cars were now usually built with the wider chassis, two bucket seats, full-width perspex windscreen and with a wiper blade. In fact this layout was not required for British National events and many cars still raced with the metal tonneau over the passenger side and a wrap-round perspex screen on the driver's side. The different models offered by Lotus Engineering in 1957 may be summarized as follows:

Le Mans 150
This car was fitted with the new Coventry Climax FPF 1,475 cc twin overhead camshaft engine. Obviously this engine was available only in very limited numbers, but when it was supplied in a completed car, the basic price was £2,885.

Le Mans 85
This was similar to the 150, apart from the fact that the rear body contours were slightly narrower as the 1,098 cc cars had smaller tyres. The Climax FWA engine was fitted in Stage 2 form and the price was £2,501 basic.

Le Mans 75
Absolutely identical to the 85, except that the Stage 1 FWA engine was fitted. The basic price was £2,405.

Club 75
This model was fitted with the Climax FWA 1,098 cc engine in Stage 1 tune, but the original swing-axle front suspension layout was fitted and there was a rigid rear axle of the type made by BMC for the Nash Metropolitan.

Sports 45
This was powered by the Ford 1,172 side-valve engine, Ford three-speed gearbox, Nash Metropolitan rear axle, and, like the Club 75, drum brakes.

Team Lotus was organized into two divisions, the first team consisting of Herbert MacKay Fraser, Cliff Allison and Colin Chapman, while there was to be a second division team of private owners, Peter Ashdown, Keith Hall and Alan Stacey who would be racing their own Series Two 1,098 cc cars with works support.

Although many owners continued to race their 1956 cars and other 1956 cars passed into new ownership, there was a long queue of people awaiting delivery of Elevens in complete or component form. Foremost amongst the private owners were Brian Naylor who bought an Eleven Series Two chassis to be powered by a 2 litre Maserati engine and that invariably successful entrant John Coombs, whose standard Eleven was to be fitted with the Climax FPF twin-cam engine.

The 1957 Racing Season

Early in 1957 four Elevens, all complying with Appendix C regulations including the fitting of a hood, were shipped from Liverpool to the United States for the Sebring 12 Hours race. Later Colin Chapman flew out to combine driving in the race with a trip to meet American Lotus distributors. Chapman co-drove a 1,098 cc car with Joe Sheppard and Dick Dungan. Despite problems with the officials during scrutineering as to the eligibility of the Lotus bodywork, which was resolved before the race, this car went magnificently and finished eleventh overall, first in the 1,100 cc class and third in the Index of Performance.

The other Lotus entries were less fortunate. Another 1,098 cc car driven by Merina/Pedreira and entered by the Puerto Rico Club finished 32nd, but the 1,100 cc car driven by Jay Chamberlain (the American Lotus distributor) and Ignacio Luzano ran out of fuel and Chamberlain pushed it halfway round the circuit before finally throwing in the towel. The fourth entry had a Climax FWB 1,460 cc engine and was driven by Moran and another, but was eliminated by failure of the timing gears.

Britain faced petrol rationing, the result of the Suez crisis, and this had its effect on motor racing. Because of the rationing, there was likely to be a problem with attendances at races and for this reason the International Trophy Race, usually held at Silverstone in May, was postponed until September. The first important race of the year, the British Empire Trophy at Oulton Park, was held simply as three class races, without the usual handicap final. The first of the races at Oulton Park was for cars of up to 1,200 cc and Graham Hill won at the wheel of Dr Edward Manton's Series Two Eleven, unpainted and registered 4 HMC, from Tom Dickson with a similar car and with other Elevens driven by Ashdown, Piper, Ireland and McMillan finishing in the next four places.

McMillan's car was of special interest, as it was powered by a Stanguellini engine. The Modena-built engine featured a large number of aluminium castings, it was fitted with twin Weber twin-choke Tipo 35 DCO3 carburettors, was said to develop 95 bhp at 7,300 rpm and was used with a modified Fiat gearbox. McMillan who raced the car as a member of the Northern Racing Team together with John Higham and Neil Campbell Blair (who raced the Bristol 'Barb') abandoned the Stanguellini engine later in the year. The car was plagued by a weak clutch and eventually the engine blew up at Roskilde in Denmark after which the usual Climax engine was

The four Sebring cars awaiting despatch from the works.

*LOTUS ENGINEERING COMPANY congratulates
LOTUS owners and drivers on winning their classes
in every important sports car race entered so far
this year.*

SEBRING 12-HOUR RACE   **BRITISH EMPIRE TROPHY RACE**
1100 cc Class - 1st & 3rd   2 Litre Class - 1st, 2nd, 3rd, 4th
(3rd on Index of Performance)   1100 cc Class - 1st, 2nd, 3rd, 4th, 5th, 6th, 7th

GOODWOOD INTERNATIONAL MEETING — EASTER MONDAY
2 Litre Class - 1st & 3rd   1100 cc Class - 1st, 2nd, 3rd, 4th, 5th, 6th
1500 cc Class - 1st, 2nd   1100 cc Series Prod. Class - 1st, 2nd, 3rd

MEXICAN G.P. of AVANDORA   **COUPE DE VITESSE-MONTLHERY**
1100 cc Class - 1st   1100 cc Class - 1st
General Classification - 4th   General Classification - 3rd

S.C.C.A. PALM SPRINGS MEETING   1100 cc Class - 1st & 2nd

All enquiries to :—

LOTUS ENGINEERING CO., LTD.
7 TOTTENHAM LANE, HORNSEY,
LONDON, N.8   *Tel: MOUntview 8353*

Above *One of the Team Lotus
Elevens prepared for the 1957
Sebring 12 Hours race seen, complete with hood and full-width
windscreen, at Hornsey before it
was shipped to Florida.*

Left and right *Two advertisements for Lotus which appeared
on the back cover of* Sports Car
and Lotus Owner *during 1957
and 58.*

– *FOR THE SECOND YEAR RUNNING* –
LOTUS CAPTURE WORLD'S RECORDS

50 Kms.	141·9 m.p.h.
50 Miles	140·8 m.p.h.
100 Kms.	141·0 m.p.h.
100 Miles	140·0 m.p.h.
200 Kms.	139·9 m.p.h.

Subject to official confirmation

AT MONZA AUTODROME ON TUESDAY, 3rd DECEMBER, CLIFF ALLISON, DRIVING A MODIFIED PRODUCTION MODEL LOTUS ELEVEN LE MANS ACHIEVED THESE TIMES.

The car was powered by a COVENTRY CLIMAX 1100 c.c. F.W.A engine and a LOTUS five speed gearbox was used. The records were taken under considerable difficulty, due to frost on the bankings. In spite of this a fastest lap of 145·5 m.p.h. was recorded.

LOTUS Engineering Co. Ltd. 7 TOTTENHAM LANE · HORNSEY LONDON N.8 · TEL. FITzroy 1777

Left *During 1957 Alex McMillan raced a Stanguellini-engined Eleven, NBU 777, distinguished by a prominent bulge in the bonnet. Here at Mallery Park in April, McMillan chases Len Gibb's Climax-powered car through Shaw's Corner.*

substituted. So long as it was raced however, the Stanguellini engine car made an interesting difference in what was usually a field of otherwise entirely Climax-powered cars and its appearance was distinguished by a very non-Lotus bulge in the bonnet.

In the race for cars up to 2,000 cc the strongest contenders were Colin Chapman with a new works Eleven and Ron Flockhart at the wheel of Coombs' 1956 car, registered 5 BPB, both of which were powered by the 1,460 cc Climax single-cam engine. Chapman's car was also fitted with the latest 'wobbly web' magnesium alloy wheels, as used on the team's Formula Two cars. Flockhart led the race initially, but then Chapman took the lead only to spin and rejoin to finish second behind the Coombs-entered car.

David Piper, who had finished fourth in his class at Oulton Park, was still racing all over Europe with his Eleven, together with Bob Hicks. There were now another pair following the same trail, Dan Margulies and Tony Hogg (the latter, later Editor of *Road & Track*). On the day after the Oulton Park race, David Piper was in action again at Montlhéry where he won his class and finished third overall in the Coupe de Vitesse, held on the banked French circuit.

The Elevens were well to the fore at Goodwood on Easter Monday. The Goodwood race meetings always had a delightful country garden party atmosphere and attracted good British entries, but there were usually few foreign runners, even in the Formula One events. The first race of the day was the *Autosport* Series Production Sports Car race, and one of the contenders was Ian Walker at the wheel of the Lotus Eleven that Graham Hill had driven in some 1956 events. It was powered by a Ford engine of course, but it was now fitted with a special Willment cylinder head with overhead inlet valve conversion. Although Walker was only second in his class at Goodwood, he was destined to win the Championship overall that year.

In the Formula Two Lavant Cup both Flockhart (with a Coombs-entered car) and MacKay Fraser were at the wheel of sports Lotus Elevens, in the latter case simply because Lotus Engineering had not succeeded in completing more than the one car. Single-seater Coopers took first two places and Flockhart finished third with

Above *The 1,100 cc category at the British Empire Trophy, Oulton Park in 1957 was won by Graham Hill with Dr Edward Manton's Series 2 Eleven, followed here by Alan Stacey's 1956 car. (T. C. March.)*

Below *At Oulton Park Chapman drove this new Series 2 Eleven into second place in the 2,000 cc race behind Ron Flockhart with a Lotus entered by John Coombs. (T. C. March.)*

The installation of the Maserati 2 litre engine in the chassis of Brian Naylor's Eleven, seen in the paddock at the British Empire Trophy in 1957. (T. C. March.)

Coombs' car. MacKay Fraser went straight through the chicane just before the start at the pits straight and wrecked the front section of the bodywork. The cause of the trouble had been locking brakes. However this did not stop Chapman driving the car in the 1,500 cc sports car race. The Eleven was hastily fitted with the nose section from Coombs' new twin-cam Eleven which had been present at the circuit, but not run because of mechanical problems. Despite potential brake problems and despite misaligned front wheels, Chapman won this race, the Chichester Cup, by the margin of less than a second from Flockhart and with other Lotus entries in the next four places. The Elevens of Hill and Ireland took the first two places in the 1,100 cc class. The final race of the day was the Sussex Trophy for sports cars over 1,500 cc and in this race Brian Naylor won the 2,000 cc Class with his Maserati-powered Lotus.

In 1957 Gregor Grant, Editor of *Autosport* arranged with Colin Chapman to borrow one of the 1956 team cars, 9 EHX, to drive in the 1,100 cc sports car class of the Mille Miglia race in Italy. This was to be the last year in which the 1,000 mile race over closed public roads in Italy was to be held as the race was banned following the fatal crash of the Marquis de Portago with a works Ferrari. Grant took the car to Italy on a trailer borrowed from Cliff Davis, towed behind the MG Magnette Saloon which he had driven in the 1956 race. He had made arrangements with the Ecurie Ecosse team, which had entered a D-type Jaguar for Ron Flockhart, to use their refuelling and other services during the race providing that it did not interfere with their work on the D-type. A second Eleven was driven by private owner Bruno

Ferrari (no relation to Enzo!), but this retired early in the race because of gearbox trouble.

Throughout the race Grant was plagued by leaking fuel, but he rose through the field to hold fourth place in the 1,100 cc sports car class, and then, by the time he had reached Siena, he had moved up into second place in the class. Blinded by petrol vapour, he spun on the Futa Pass, clouting a wall with the offside rear wheel, but managing to carry on, despite the wheel wobbling badly, until he reached Bologna. It was only at Bologna that the Ecurie Ecosse team noticed that the fuel tank was leaking, and petrol was running out almost as fast as it was hosed in. An emergency repair was effected and Grant went on, passing the Osca which was holding second place in the class. More problems with the fuel pump followed, the steering deteriorated, and then, finally, on a very fast stretch of road between Cremona and Mantova the tank burst flooding the cockpit with fuel. To quote from Grant's report of the race in *Autosport,* 'when my fuel tank burst, I was drenched with about 80 litres of high octane fuel, and had to bale out rapidly with only 70 miles left to go. By a miracle the Lotus did not catch fire, nor did it hit anything when it came to rest gently by the roadside. Main danger was when cigarette-smoking Italians came running to help me to my feet. When I saw them coming I took to my heels yelling "benzina-benzina, pericolo!" It had the desired effect.'

With a jury-rigged jerrican as a fuel tank, Grant managed to drive the Lotus to the finish, too far behind to qualify, in considerable pain from petrol burns, but at least he had the satisfaction of completing the last ever of these great road races.

The same weekend the Spa Grand Prix was held over 132 miles on the exciting and difficult Spa-Francorchamps circuit. The race was dominated by the Aston Martin DBR1s of Tony Brooks and Roy Salvadori, but Brian Naylor won the 2,000 cc class with his Lotus-Maserati and Herbert McKay Fraser won the 1,500 cc category with a Team Lotus entry. At Brands Hatch on 19 May Graham Hill won the 1,100 cc sports car race with Manton's Eleven and with Hall in third place. At the same meeting Cliff Allison with a Team Lotus car won the event for sports cars up to 2,000 cc and Mike Anthony, still at the wheel of his very special Eleven-Bristol, finished fourth despite the fact that there was an air-lock in the cooling system that had caused the engine to completely overheat. On the same day Tom Dickson and Bill Frost finished first and second with their sports Elevens in the Formula Two race at Snetterton.

Sebring and Le Mans apart, Lotus entries in World Sports Car Championship races were unusual. However at the Nürburgring 1,000 km sports car race held on the tortuous 14.12 mile circuit through the Eifel mountains on 26 May three Elevens were entered. David Piper had entered two cars to be driven by permutations of himself, Bob Hicks and Tony Hogg, while Dan Margulies' car was driven by MacKay Fraser. The Nürburgring was a pounding, hard race that sought out and destroyed weaknesses in chassis design. Retirements because of structural failure were frequent and it was common enough for cars to finish the race with broken chassis. The Elevens, of course, had a reputation, more accurately a notoriety, for fragility and if there was to be one race the standard Elevens would not finish, it would be the Nürburgring. Nevertheless, albeit at the tail of the field, one of the Piper cars did

Above *The Team Lotus entries of Colin Chapman (left) and Keith Hall (right) battle for the lead in the Anerley Trophy at the Crystal Palace in June 1957. (LAT.)*

Below *Another shot from the Crystal Palace in June 1957 with Chapman hot on the exhausts of Salvadori's Cooper which he passed shortly before the finish. (LAT).*

finish the race despite running out of fuel, brake problems, leaking fuel and fuel blockage troubles—but no broken chassis!

Over the Whitsun weekend there was the usual spate of races in the United Kingdom. At Brands Hatch on the Sunday Chapman won the sports car race for cars up to 2,000 cc from Salvadori's works Cooper. Chapman's car was fitted with a single-cam engine, whereas Salvadori had the new FPF twin-cam engine in his car. In the 1,100 cc race Lotus entries took the first five places with Hall leading across the line Ashdown, Stacey, Hill (with Manton's car) and Bueb in fifth place. The results were much the same on the Monday at the Crystal Palace where Chapman won the Norbury Trophy race for sports cars up to 2,000cc from Salvadori and this was in fact the last occasion on which a works sports-racing Cooper was entered. Keith Hall again won the 1,100 cc race, the Anerley Trophy, from Chapman and with Hill in fourth place. On the Monday there was also a race meeting at Goodwood. The race for sports cars up to 1,100 cc was held over 100 km (26 laps) and although Innes Ireland, very much an up-and-coming driver, led until a timing wheel stripped, the eventual winner was Alan Stacey with his Lotus.

Colin Chapman was persistently over-ambitious in his plans for Lotus, over-stretching the Company financially, and trying to do far more than its technical resources and manpower would permit. Apart from the ambitious Formula Two programme in which Lotus, depite the technical ingenuity of the front-engined cars, ran a constant poor second to Cooper, Team Lotus was running a very extensive sports car programme that included an all-out onslaught at Le Mans.

If the single-seaters failed, then the sports-racing cars were overwhelmingly successful at Le Mans and Chapman's financial 'tightrope-walking act' managed to pay off. A grand total of five Lotus Elevens were entered at Le Mans, three of them Team Lotus entries, and two from private owners who were running in conjunction with the works. Although there was the usual frantic rush to get the cars ready for the race, what was lacking in time for the mechanical preparation had not interfered with Chapman's thinking and for some while he had been considering the best way to circumvent the difficult regulations that demanded a full-width cockpit with two proper bucket seats and exploit the aerodynamic potential of the Elevens on the high-speed Le Mans circuit to the maximum. He decided that the best way to deal with the situation would be to raise the rear tail section of the car at the rear of the cockpit to the same height as the windscreen, from which point it fell backwards in a gentle curve to the tail itself. At the sides of the very curved windscreen, perspex side-pieces swept back to meet the rear decking. Over the passenger side of the cockpit there was a plastic tonneau. Chapman had originally conceived the idea of fitting a pnuematic cover on the passenger side. This bag-shaped cover would have been capable of being inflated so as to give a firm upper surface and the necessary uninterrupted air flow over the top of the cockpit. There was no time to deal with the question of air bags, however, and this idea was reluctantly abandoned.

Chapman decided not to drive in the race himself, but to concentrate on team management. The performance of the different cars entered in this race was as follows:

At Le Mans the Class and Index of Performance-winning 750cc Eleven of Allison and Hall is lapped by Duncan Hamilton's D-type Jaguar. (LAT.)

No 37, 1,475 cc, driven by Herbert MacKay Fraser/Jay Chamberlain
When the car arrived at the circuit, it was barely finished and lacked even an exhaust system. During practice the engine broke a valve, not unusual with early Climax FPF engines, and this car did not start the race.

No 41, registered YAR 527, 1,098 cc, entered by André Héchard, driven by Héchard/Roger Masson
This was the first of the Le Mans entries to be completed, it enjoyed a complete trouble-free race apart from running out of fuel on the circuit when Masson pushed it four miles back to the pits. It finished sixteenth overall and fourth in the 1,100 cc class.

No 42, registered UDV 609, 1,098 cc, entered by Bob Walshaw, driven by Walshaw/John Dalton
Apart from a minor problem during the race, when the dipstick became dislodged and some oil was lost through the dipstick hole, this car too completed a trouble-free race to finish thirteenth overall and second in the 1,100 cc class.

No 62, registered DEC 494, 1,098 cc, entered for Peter Ashdown/Alan Stacey, but taken over for the race by Herbert MacKay Fraser/Jay Chamberlain
After the failure of the twin-cam car, it was decided to switch the leading pair of drivers to the 1,098 cc car. Like the other entries in the race, it ran like clockwork, finishing ninth overall, winning the 1,100 cc class and was classified second in the Index of Performance.

No 55, registered XAR 11, 744 cc, driven by Cliff Allison/Keith Hall
This car, powered by a one-off Climax engine, was aimed at a victory in the Index of Performance, a category previously dominated by the French DBs and Panhards. Its

entry had been accepted with reluctance by the Automobile Club de l'Ouest because it represented a serious threat to French domination. It was finally accepted for the list when Héchard/Masson switched from their original entry of a DB-Panhard to the Lotus and accordingly there was little the organizers could do but to accept the entry gracefully. Throughout the race this car steadily pulled away from the French opposition and it finished fourteenth overall, and winner of the 750 cc class and the Index of Performance.

For Lotus the race was, of course, a magnificent triumph with much-needed financial rewards to match, but it also proved a remarkable British triumph. The race was dominated by Ecurie Ecosse whose D-type Jaguars driven by Ron Flockhart/Ivor Bueb and Ninian Sanderson/John Lawrence took the first two places, with other Jaguars third, fourth and sixth. In addition the winner in the 3,000 cc class was the private Aston Martin DB3S of Colas/Kerguen; second place in the 2,000 cc class went to the AC-Bristol of Ken Rudd/Peter Bolton and in third place in the 1,100 cc class, splitting the Lotus Elevens, was the hastily prepared Cooper-Climax of Jack Brabham/Ian Raby.

In his technical review of the race in *Autosport*, John Bolster had some interesting comments to make on the Lotus performance. 'The French-entered Lotus showed a much heavier fuel consumption than its British brothers, and ran out of petrol in consequence. This was due to the considerable use of the gearbox and very high engine revolutions in which its drivers indulged. Without wishing to belittle the heroic pushing feat of Masson, I do feel that this marathon business is not what motor racing spectators pay to see. Surely it is time that a really accurate gauge was fitted.'

Further Lotus successes followed at the French Grand Prix meeting at Rouen on 7 July. On the morning of the Grand Prix there were two sports car races. The Team Lotus cars had been transported directly from Le Mans to the circuit after a check-over at Le Mans and ran in very much the same trim as at Le Mans. In the first race for cars of up to 1,100 cc Alessandro de Tomaso took the lead at the start, with Chapman at the wheel of DEC 494 in hot pursuit followed by other Elevens driven by Hicks, Margulies, Ross and Allison with the Le Mans 750 cc car. After a tight battle, with the two leading drivers constantly swapping places, Chapman went ahead, only to slow unexpectedly because of overheating. After pit stop for the radiator to be topped up, Chapman rejoined the race to finish second to de Tomaso with Hicks and Margulies in third and fourth places and Allison clear winner of the 750 cc class. Argentinian de Tomaso, at that time a leading private driver of Osca sports-racing cars, is now a leading industrialist in Italy and controls the Innocenti and Maserati factories, as well as the Moto-Guzzi and Benelli Motor Cycle concerns.

The second race was for cars up to 1,500 cc and the race was dominated by Ron Flockhart, at the wheel of Coombs' twin-cam Eleven painted blue, apparently as a tribute to Ecurie Ecosse's victory at Le Mans, and at the finish Flockhart was well ahead of Jay Chamberlain with his Team Lotus entry. Herbert MacKay Fraser retired from the race when a hub fractured.

The team moved straight on to Reims for the Formula Two race. Cliff Allison was entered with a Formula Two single-seater, but was plagued by the habitual Lotus gear-selection problems, and the front runner for the team was MacKay Fraser with an Eleven sports car fitted with the twin-cam engine. Out in front Trintignant (Ferrari) and Salvadori and Brabham (Coopers) battled for the lead, but MacKay Fraser was going exceedingly well with the Eleven and holding sixth place until he crashed badly at the very fast Garenne curve and suffered injuries which proved fatal. It was a terrible blow for the Lotus team because MacKay Fraser had been one of their swiftest and most reliable drivers. Only a week previously in *Autosport* Gregor Grant had written 'Fraser is one of the fastest of present-day small-capacity sports car drivers, and is entirely amenable to pit discipline.'

In minor events Lotus continued to achieve tremendous success, taking first three places in the order Hall, Stacey, and Bueb in the 1,100 cc sports car race held on a streaming wet track at the British Grand Prix meeting at Aintree. At Snetterton on 28 July, Ashdown and Stacey took the first two places in the 1,100 cc sports car race and in the combined event for cars up to 1,500 cc and 2,000 cc Naylor with the Lotus-Maserati was the winner, whilst Gawaine Baillie won the 1,500 cc class with the Équipe Endeavour car. There were race meetings on August Bank Holiday Monday at both Brands Hatch and the Crystal Palace. At Brands Hatch Allison, Ashdown, Bueb and Ireland took the first four places in the 1,100 cc race, whilst Chapman, Hill and Frost took the first three places in the 1,500 cc event. Mike Anthony was still persevering with his Bristol-powered car, but at the Kent circuit retired in a cloud of blue smoke from a broken oil pipe in the race for sports cars over 1,900 cc. The same day at the Crystal Palace Keith Hall won the August trophy race for sports cars up to 1,100 cc, setting a new lap record of 77.70 mph. The following weekend, on 11 August, several Lotus drivers competed in the Swedish Grand Prix, but no success was gained.

Team Lotus was out again at the RACB Grand Prix for sports cars on the Spa-Francorchamps circuit on 25 August. The race proved another Aston Martin benefit, with Tony Brooks winning from a brace of Ferraris and with Salvadori fourth. In the 1,500 cc class, throughout the race, there was a battle between the red Osca of de Tomaso and Cliff Allison with the twin-cam-engined Lotus Eleven. Two laps from the finsih de Tomaso retired with engine trouble and Allison went on to finish first in the 1,500 cc class. David Piper was fifth in the class with his 1,098 cc Lotus and Hicks was two places behind.

Another victory for Lotus followed at the International Trophy meeting at Silverstone, postponed from its usual date in May until September because of petrol rationing, and here Ron Flockhart with John Coombs' twin-cam Lotus, registered 5 BPB, won the 1,500 cc sports car race from Keith Hall's 1,098 cc Lotus. Cliff Allison had led with his Team Lotus entry until forced to stop at the pits with fuel-feed problems. In the over 1,500 cc sports car race Brian Naylor finished second overall with the Lotus-Maserati and won the 2,700 cc class. A fortnight later Roy Salvadori with the Coombs car turned in a magnificent drive at Goodwood, finishing fourth overall and winning the 2,000 cc class of the Goodwood Trophy. Naylor crashed heavily with the Lotus-Maserati and thereafter raced his own JBW cars. On 12 October the 3 hour final of the *Autosport* Series Production Car Championship was held at Snetterton. Although the race overall was won by Ken Rudd with his AC

Above With this 1956 yellow-painted Lotus Eleven fitted with Willment IOE cylinder head Ian Walker won the Autosport Series Production Sports Car Championship in 1957. He is seen at Mallory Park in July. (T. C. March.)

Right In 1957 Innes Ireland with his 1956 car, 5 BPH, won the Brooklands Memorial Trophy awarded for performances at BARC Members' meetings at Goodwood. He is seen at Goodwood in September after clinching the Trophy win. (LAT.)

Below Brian Naylor with the 2 litre Lotus-Maserati at the International Trophy meeting at Silverstone, held in 1957 in September. (T. C. March.)

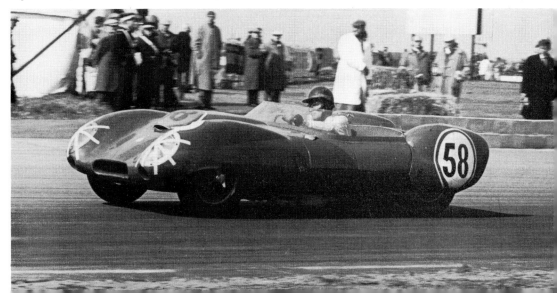

At Goodwood at the end of September 1957 Roy Salvadori turned in a fantastic drive with Coombs' twin-cam Series 2 Eleven to win the 2 litre class of the Goodwood Trophy. (LAT.)

Ace-Bristol, Ian Walker, fourth on the road with his Lotus-Ford, won his class and on the basis of his successes earlier in the year clinched victory in the Championship with a total of 73 points to the 70 of Rudd/Jennings with the AC. Other Lotus drivers, Barnard, Lawry and Williamson finished third, sixth and seventh in the Championship.

In the issue of *Autosport* for 29 November, John Bolster reported on his drive with the Lotus that Williamson had driven in the *Autosport* Championship. Apart from the fact that this had the Willment light alloy IOE cylinder head, it was fitted with a Laycock de Nomanville overdrive to the Ford three-speed gearbox. This in effect gave six speeds. Bolster found that the modified Ford engine would rev up to 7,000 rpm and reported that this Lotus had achieved 126 mph with a wrap round screen and head fairing.

At the beginning of December Lotus again went record breaking at Monza. The car used was a Series Two Eleven, with perspex 'bubble' canopy over the cockpit, the front brake assemblies removed to reduce weight, and a five-speed gearbox of the type used on the Formula Two cars. The aim was to run the car with both 750 cc and 1,100 cc engines fitted with Roots-type superchargers. The driver was Cliff Allison and he broke the following 1,100 cc (Class G) records:

50	km	141.9 mph	100	miles	140.0 mph
50	miles	140.8 mph	200	km	139.9 mph
100	km	141.0 mph			

In addition Allison completed a fastest lap of the Monza circuit at 145.5 mph. The record attempt was abandoned when the engine started to run on three cylinders. An attempt was made to break records with the 750 cc engine, but it was abandoned when the supercharger began to seize up.

Mike Costin wrote the following about the record attempts in *Sports Car*. 'Now the Monza track may be the only place in Europe for really high speed record runs, but it is by no means perfect for the job. Firstly the track is extremely bumpy, being made up of concrete sections mounted on pillars. Bumps between section and section tend to increase as parts of the structure are always on the move. During the winter months parts of the banking become almost permanently frozen—as during the 1,100 cc runs—because the sun never reached them. And for most of our stay matters were complicated by the fog hazard.'

All in all it had been yet another magnificent Lotus effort.

Team Lotus made one further racing appearance in 1957, at the Boxing Day Brands Hatch meeting. Mike Costin himself drove and won the race for 1,100 cc sports cars from the private Lotus of Prior. There was a second race during the day for 1,100 cc sports cars, the Christmas Trophy, won by Graham Hill. In this race Innes Ireland was entered with the Team Lotus car, but on the second lap he collided with his own car being driven by Clarke! On the same day there was a race meeting at the Mallory Park circuit and here R. B. Schofield at the wheel of the ex-Mike Anthony, ex-Kasterine Lotus Mark 10, now registered RN6, won two races.

By the end of the 1957 season Lotus was established as a successful international competitor in sports car racing but still struggling to find its feet in single-seater

The Lotus Eleven with Ghia bodywork competing in a continental hill climb.

Three views of the newly opened Showroom and drawing office of Lotus early in 1958. Inside the showroom is the prototype Elite. Parked by the side door is one of the very early Sevens and to the left of this photograph can be seen the tail of the Porsche driven by Colin Chapman for 'quality appreciation' reasons in the development of the Elite. At the rear of the premises there are stacked Eleven chassis and bodies.

racing. Production still continued on a large scale with the Eleven, and the cars were being raced at all levels from club meetings to international events by a vast number of private owners. Weekend after weekend during the racing season, both in the United Kingdom and in the United States, Lotus Elevens were winning races, so many and so frequently that it would be a tedious catalogue to repeat all the performances here. For the time being at least Lotus was the dominant force in amateur sports car racing and the 500 cc Formula Three races, which for so many years had been the proving ground for young aspirants, were now rapidly being pushed into obscurity by the popularity of the Lotus sports cars and the many races held for cars of 1,100 cc capacity. The Cooper was now quite eclipsed and the Elva a poor second runner, way, way behind Lotus in numbers and in success. In addition

Lotus had exhibited the new GT Elite at the 1957 London show and the new Seven, a very basic sports car, had also appeared.

The 1958 Racing Season

In 1958 Lotus introduced the 15 and this was to be the car campaigned by Team Lotus throughout the year. However the successes of the Eleven continued. In the RAC International Rally in March, Edward Lewis partnered by Denis Pratt drove an Eleven, XAR 11, borrowed from the works. He had used this for hill-climbing in 1957, while waiting delivery of the first of the Sevens and retained it to drive in the rally. The rally was run in appallingly cold icy conditions and the driver had a thoroughly miserable time. In Wales the Lotus holed its sump, the repair was bodged and the car carried on only to collide with a lorry. The Lotus eventually finished fourth in the class for special production touring cars and normal and modified GT cars up to 1,300 cc behind two Standard Pennants and a Standard 10.

At the Sebring 12 Hours race three 1,098 cc cars were entered by Team Lotus. These were driven by Colin Chapman/Cliff Allison, Jay Chamberlain/Bill Frost and Weiss/Tellakson. In a race in which the Aston Martins and Jaguars failed, and the results were dominated by Ferrari which took the first two places ahead of the Porsche of Schell/Seidel, the Elevens ran faultlessly. Weiss/Tallakson finished fourth overall, winning the 1,100 cc class with Chapman/Allison sixth and Chamberlain/Frost ninth. It was in fact, although not greatly remarked upon at the time, one of the best performances achieved by Team Lotus during this period.

In the United Kingdom, Lotus successes continued unabaited. At Snetterton on 30 March the 1,100 cc sports car race was won by John Campbell Jones from Innes Ireland with his new car, 100 RMI, with Keith Greene, who had swapped from Cooper to Lotus, third at the wheel of his new car 20 KVX. In addition Tony Marsh won the race for cars up to 1,500 cc. Alan Stacey won the 1,100 cc sports car race at Brands Hatch on Easter Monday and on the same day at Goodwood John Campbell Jones won the race for 1,100 cc cars from other Lotus Eleven entries driven by Tom Dickson, Roy Salvadori, Keith Hall and Innes Ireland. Keith Hall won the 1,100 cc heat of the British Empire Trophy from Stacey and Ashdown. Yet another Lotus win followed at Aintree later in April when Keith Hall won the 1,100 cc sports car race. Stacey was second overall and won the 1,100 cc class in the 1,500 cc sports car race at the International meeting at Silverstone in May, with Hall third and Campbell Jones fourth. A win for Alan Stacey with his Team Lotus Eleven, 1077 BP, followed in the 1,100 cc sports car race at the Crystal Palace, with Innes Ireland second. A total of four Elevens were entered in the Nürburgring 1,000 km race, but again the Lotus entries were out of luck and the best finish was fifth in the 1,500 cc class by David Piper/Keith Greene.

Following their successes in 1956 and 1957, Lotus were out in force at Le Mans in 1958. There was a total of six entries. Two of these cars were 15s and their performance will be described elsewhere. The 1958 race was run in the most appalling wet weather and the Lotus team was plagued by mechanical failures that resulted in disaster, in stark contrast to the success of the two previous years. The performance of the various Elevens is discussed below:

Above *Alan Stacey entered by Team Lotus leads the 1,100 cc heat of the 1958 British Empire Trophy at Oulton Park. (T. C. March.)*

Below *Victory in the heat went to another Team Lotus entry driven by Keith Hall. (T. C. March.)*

Bottom *Keith Greene at the wheel of his Gilby Engineering-entered Eleven at the International Trophy meeting at Silverstone in May 1958. (T. C. March.)*

No 38, 1,098 cc, entered by Team Lotus, driven by Innes Ireland/Michael Taylor

Like all the Lotus entries, this Eleven was fitted with an inflatable tonneau cover over the passenger seat (an experiment which proved very successful), higher, more aerodynamic tail, and a lip running around the top of the windscreen which reduced buffeting at speed. On the Saturday evening Taylor went off course, slightly damaging the bodywork and putting one headlamp out of action; with Innes Ireland driving for most of the night, this Lotus survived until the Sunday morning when the distributor drive failed.

No 39, 1,098 cc, entered by Car Exchange (Brighton) Ltd, driven by Bill Frost/Bob Hicks

The car was leading the 1,100 cc class but spun off at the kink on the Mulsanne Straight and the gendarmes refused to permit Hicks to remove the car. Later in the race an Alfa Romeo collided with the Lotus and almost completely destroyed it. Bill Frost did not even get a drive.

No 55, 744 cc, entered by Team Lotus, driven by Alan Stacey/Tom Dickson

The two 750 cc cars entered both had live rear axles to reduce transmission power losses, drum rear brakes with disc brakes at the front and magnesium-alloy bolt-on wheels because tyre changes were not anticipated during the race. This car was intended to run in the race with the new Coventry-Climax FWMA 745 cc (64.3 x 57.2 mm) engine. However this engine suffered bearing failure and ignition trouble in practice and for the race was replaced by the 744 cc FWC engine used in 1957. Dickson spun this car into the sand at Tertre Rouge early on the Sunday morning. By the time he had managed to dig the car out and time had been wasted in the pits beating the bodywork back into reasonable shape and repairing the brake lights, it was running at the tail of the field. It eventually finished twentieth and last.

No 56, 745 cc entered by Équipe Lotus France, driven by André Héchard and Roger Masson

This car ran in the race to the same specification as the Team Lotus 750, but it retained the FWMA engine. Early in the race it overheated and lost water because of a faulty hose clip; subsequently it was involved in a three-car accident at White House corner, and was eliminated from the race.

All in all it was a thoroughly disastrous outing for Lotus, and indeed the team was never to display again the fine form seen in the two previous years.

In July Innes Ireland drove his car powered by enlarged 1,290 cc engine, 100 RMI, with Pete Lovely as co-driver in the 12 hour race for GT cars at the French Grand Prix meeting at Reims. Qualification for running in the race was that a hundred of the cars had been built during the last twelve months. Ferraris dominated the outright results taking first-fifth positions together with seventh, but the Innes Ireland-entered car won its class. On 27 July Innes Ireland drove his Lotus in 1,098 cc form in the Circuit d'Auvergne on the new Clermont-Ferrand circuit. On this difficult, winding,

Mike Pressly's beautifully restored Eleven at Wiscombe Park hill climb in May 1965. Note the temporary windscreen!

circuit Ireland came through to take the lead in the 3 hour GT race and won outright from the Ferraris of Trintignant, Mairesse and Gendebien. It was a magnificent triumph, but one not very widely recognized in the United Kingdom.

Throughout 1958 there was a gradual move away from races for 1,100 and 1,500 cc sports cars in favour of larger capacity events. However there was a 1,500 cc sports car race at Brands Hatch on August Bank Holiday Monday and it was won by Alan Stacey with his Team Lotus 1,098 cc car. In the Tourist Trophy, a round in the Sports Car World Championship, and revived after an interval of three years at the Goodwood circuit in September, Aston Martins took the first three places overall. However victory in the 1,100 cc class went to the Eleven entered by Team Lotus and driven by Peter Ashdown and Gordon Jones who finished seventh overall. Second place in the class went to Keith Greene and Michael Taylor who were tenth overall. There was a very strong Lotus entry in this race, but many of the cars were plagued by starter motor overheating problems.

Team Lotus entries apart, the most successful Elevens in 1958 were prepared by Innes Ireland who ran his own company, Innes Ireland Ltd in the grounds of the Golden Acres Country Club at Elstead in Surrey. In all Innes Ireland Ltd looked after six cars during the year, his own, and those of Michael Taylor, Doug Graham, Peter Heath,

An interesting private development of the Eleven was this fixed head coupe seen at the Lotus meeting at Donington Park in 1977. (Geoffrey Goddard.)

Chris Martyn and Jack Westcott. The whole basis of the system on which Innes Ireland operated was that he accepted entire responsibility for the entries, race preparation and transportation of both the cars and spares to the circuit. All the drivers had to do was to turn up at the circuit for practice and take the wheel. A vast number of successes were gained in minor events during the year, apart from Ireland's own two International victories, and undoubtedly the most successful of the drivers was Michael Taylor. In all Taylor, in his first year of racing, competed in 27 events. He was placed in 26 of these races, taking ten outright wins and won the Brooklands Memorial Trophy for his consistent performances at BARC Members' meetings. His only non-finish came in a multiple shunt.

Although Lotus Elevens were to be raced for many years to come, the 1958 season was their last year at the forefront of racing. After this, they were in the main seen only in minor events and the emphasis so far as Lotus were concerned had switched more and more to the 15, raced with engines from 1,500 cc upwards. As far as Chapman was concerned, the Eleven was now becoming outdated and was replaced the following year by the 17. Sadly, as will be recounted, the 17 was no match for the new Lola-Climax and 1958 proved the last season of domination by Lotus in the 1,100 cc class.

Chapter 7

The 15, 1958-59

Historical perspective has tended to condemn the 15 as an exceptionally ingenious sports-racing car that failed to fulfil its design objectives as a result of its excessive complications and was notoriously unreliable. Certainly the 15 incorporated many design features of Chapman's largely unsuccessful front-engined single-seaters, and certainly it had more than its fair share of mechanical failures during its racing career. It did, however, achieve a substantial measure of success and its career was cut short more by the switch in design philosophy to rear-engined competition cars rather than to its own inherent design faults.

The multi-tubular space-frame was a direct evolution of that of the Eleven and was built from 1 in and ¾ in square and round tubing of 18 and 20 gauge steel. The propellor shaft tunnel and floot were stressed members, forming an integral part of the frame. At the front the engine was carried on two rubber mountings, while there was a single rubber mounting at the rear attached to the bell housing.

Although the suspension at the front had been designed to suit this particular car, its basic layout was similar to that both of the Formula Two car and Eleven Series 2. It consisted of double wishbones, with the front member of the top wishbone also acting as an anti-roll bar, and coil spring/damper units. At the rear there was the famous Chapman 'strut' system consisting of a coil spring/damper unit (the strut) rigidly aligned with a substantial hub casting controlling vertical motion, a fabricated forward radius arm locating the hub fore and aft and a fixed length half-shaft providing lateral location. Although when first used on the Formula Two cars there had been problems with failure and twisting of the half-shafts, these problems had been resolved by the time the suspension layout was adopted on the 15. The steering was rack-and-pinion and there were disc brakes, with 9½ in discs, mounted outboard at the front and inboard at the rear. The standard wheels offered to customers were 15 in centre-lock, but the Team Lotus cars were fitted with magnesium-alloy 'wobbly-web' wheels which were also available as an optional extra on cars sold. Obviously these alloy wheels were unsuitable for long-distance racing in which speedy wheel changes would be required . These wheels had first been seen on the 12 Formula Two cars and of course they were also used on Formula One Vanwalls in 1958.

The standard power unit was the Coventry Climax FPF twin overhead camshaft 1,475 cc unit, but in fact this engine was available in a range of capacities up to 2.2 litres. The Climax engine was centred 60° to the right to reduce frontal area, offset

7½° from the chassis centre-line and fitted with special curved inlet manifolds and twin horizontal Weber carburettors. It was used with a twin dry-plate clutch of 7.25 in diameter, hydraulically operated, and used with the Chapman-conceived gearbox designed by Richard Ansdale and manufactured for Lotus by the German ZF company. This gearbox was in unit with the final drive which incorporated a limited slip differential. The gear-change mechanism was of the positive-stop type with the gears in a straight line, and with neutral situated between first and second, and reverse obtained with the lever in neutral by means of a separate linkage and a selector knob on the driver's left at the rear of the passenger seat. The reason for this choice of change was that racing drivers would normally change gear through the box, without missing any gears, and accordingly this simple arrangement would be sufficient for racing purposes. However a number of drivers considered the arrangement to be lethal as it was very easy to select the wrong gear by going straight through the box and in a downward change this could result in the locking of the rear wheels and catastrophe. On John Coombs' cars, Coombs reduced the risk of this by fitting a safety catch that prevented the selection of first and second gears once the car was off the line. A whole range of different final drive ratios was available to suit different circuits.

The fuel tank, together with engine oil and gearbox oil tanks were mounted in the tail of the car, with the spare wheel mounted vertically to the right so that the upper part of the spare wheel was housed within the streamlined headrest. Fuel capacity was 19 gallons. The shape of the body was basically an evolution from that of the Eleven, and although very much in the Frank Costin-style, was in fact the work of Williams and Pritchard Ltd. As on the 1957 Le Mans cars, the decking of the rear tail section was aligned with the top of the curved perspex windscreen and the driver sat so that he looked over the top of rather than through the windscreen. Front and rear, the body panels were hinged and quickly removable.

The 15 had a wheelbase of 7 ft 4 in, front track of 3 ft 11 in and rear track of 4 ft. The overall length was 11 ft 5 in, overall width 5 ft and the height to the top of the scuttle a mere 2 ft. Ground clearance was 5½ in in standard form without fuel and the weight was a mere 980 lb.

The first 15 was driven by Graham Hill at Goodwood on Easter Monday, 1958. It was powered by the Coventry-climax FPF twin-cam engine in 1,960 cc form. Hill set a new 2 litre sports car lap record before retiring with gearbox trouble. He was quoted at the time as saying 'It was like stirring a box full of nothing'. This prototype car was subsequently sold to Pierre Berchem, a Belgian driver, and it seems that the sale was negotiated through John Coombs. As sold, the car was fitted with a 1,475 cc FPF engine and Coombs arranged for Roy Salvadori to drive it in the British Empire Trophy at Oulton Park the following weekend. In the same race there were two 15s entered for Graham Hill and Cliff Allison by Team Lotus, but these arrived only at the circuit after a frantic panic to get them ready in time. All three cars had painted on them the trade plate number 007 MH!

The British Empire Trophy was again run as three qualifying heats and a final. In the heat for cars up to 2,000 cc the winner was Cliff Allison with Salvadori in second place. Hill's car, which had been the last to be prepared, set the fastest lap in the heat

Graham Hill at the wheel of his 2 litre 15 in his heat of the British Empire Trophy at Oulton Park, 1958. All three 15s in this race had the painted trade plate 007 MH. (T. C. March.)

at 89.70 mph, but Hill was delayed by a pit stop when a plug fell out and it took a long time to get the new plug on to the damaged thread. Unfortunately, Hill was too far behind at the finish to qualify for the final. In the final both 15s fell by the wayside. Salvadori was eliminated by a broken rear hub race amd Allison was eliminated by loss of oil pressure. The final was won by the Aston Martins of Stirling Moss and Tony Brooks. Since the 15 had first been revealed to the press, additional openings had been made in the front of the bodywork to cool the front brakes and at Oulton Park centre-lock wheels were fitted.

The sheer speed and excellent handling of the 15s had impressed and in the May 1958 issue of *Sports Car*, Graham Hill gave his impressions of the 15: 'What do I think about the Lotus Fifteen? Well, I suppose it can be summed up in two, or rather three, words—It's b—— fast." That is how Graham Hill, Team Lotus driver and Oulton Park lap record holder, jointly with Stirling Moss (Aston Martin) summed up his impressions of the new car after the British Empire Trophy meeting.

'He subsequently pointed out not only was the car (which he called a projectile - a "thing") different, by comparison with the Eleven, but so was the circuit. Most of the Oulton Park corners seemed to have become much sharper than last year, and the straight was much shorter.

'What about the two litre Coventry Climax engine? "Fantastic. Never known any engine like it."

'Even on the twisty Oulton Park circuit, with a final drive ratio of four to one, the torque of the 1,960 cc engine is such that Hill and Allison were able to use third and fourth gears practically all the way round, selecting fifth at the straight between Esso Bend and Knicker Brook. The gear ratios in the box are extremely close, but (by contrast with the standard 1,500 cc FPF engine) it is not necessary to make constant use of the gears in order to maintain high rpm—the engine pulled magnificently from well under 4,000 rpm to a limit of 6,800 rpm.

'Graham and Cliff Allison went to Oulton Park on the Thursday prior to the Empire Trophy meeting in order to try out the new cars for the first time.

'Eventually Graham and Cliff got out on to the circuit at about 6.30 pm. They were asked to avoid making too much noise, but as Graham said, "that was rather silly really, because once the engine was started you just couldn't hear yourself speak."

'Graham soon found a few modifications would be necessary—for instance he had to "bend the steering wheel" in order to get his left foot on the clutch pedal. This achieved, the gear-selector now worked very well, but further attempts at practice were cut short by the onset of darkness.

'On Friday, the official practice day, Graham and Cliff had the opportunity to sample the 2 litre Fifteen in more suitable conditions. A number of modifications had been made during the night and most of the snags which had suggested themselves during the dusk trials were thus ironed-out.'

The 15s next race was at Aintree in the International meeting on 19 April. For Lotus the race proved something of a shambles. On the warming up lap the distributor cap on Hill's car broke. Allison stalled the engine of his car and when the flag came down, Hamilton's Jaguar accelerated into the back of the stationary 15. Hill succeeded in damaging the gear selectors when moving off the grid. After repairs in the pits, Allison's car rejoined the race but he was too far behind to feature in the results, although he set a new 2 litre class record. At the International meeting at Silverstone in May Graham Hill was entered with a 1,500 cc 15 and John Coombs had now taken delivery of one of these cars which was driven by Roy Salvadori. Hill won the race at 93.07 mph, but Salvadori retired when the engine cut out. In the race for unlimited capacity sports cars Allison was at the wheel of a 2 litre 15, but retired.

At Le Mans, Team Lotus entered two 15s. No 26 was a 1,960 cc-powered car, driven by Cliff Allison/Graham Hill, but after only three laps Allison brought this car into the pits with a blown head gasket. There was little alternative but to retire the car immediately. The second 15 was a 1,475 cc car driven by American Jay Chamberlain/Pete Lovely and distinguished by blue and white stripes. Mechanical trouble meant a lot of time wasted in the pits and although the car ran strongly, it was always well down the field and was eliminated in heavy rain during the first quarter of the race when Chamberlain hit the bank near the Dunlop Bridge in avoiding a French car, and was himself hit by Picard's Ferrari. The Lotus was very badly damaged and Chamberlain suffered minor injuries. The 15s at Le Mans ran with the engines mounted in the vertical position and this feature was to become standard on the production version in due course.

On the weekend prior to the British Grand Prix meeting at Silverstone, the following advertisement appeared in *Autosport*:

TEAM LOTUS

In view of their increased activity in Formula One events, Team Lotus are reluctantly compelled to reduce their racing stable by two 1958 1,500 cc Lotus 15s.

These are the actual "British Empire Trophy" cars (current Oulton Park lap record) and carry all the latest works modifications. Raced four times only, offered immediately, ready for racing, at

£2,500 each

Apply Team Manager, Team Lotus, 7 Tottenham Lane, London, N.8. Fitzroy 1777.

Despite this advertisement there were three 1,500 cc Lotus 15s entered in the sports car race at Silverstone meeting, driven by Cliff Allison, Graham Hill and Pete Lovely. In addition Roy Salvadori was at the wheel of Coombs' 15, now fitted with 1,960 cc engine and painted white. The race was won by Moss with a works Lister-Jaguar, Salvadori took second place overall (winning the 2,000 cc class) and Allison was third, taking first place in the 1,500 cc category. Hill spun his car, fought his way through the field to make up ground, stopped at the pits and then retired with a con-rod through the block. Lovely also failed to feature in the results.

Allison also drove a Team Lotus 15 in the 1,500 cc sports car race held before the German Grand Prix on the Nürburgring. He came through to hold third place in this six-lap race, but was eliminated when a rear radius arm mounting broke. There were two other Lotus entries in this race, Piper with his Eleven who finished ninth and Berchem with his prototype 15 who took twelfth place.

In August 1958 Lotus had announced the Series 2 Lotus 15, an attempt by Chapman to get away from all the problems of complexity faced by the design of both the 15 and his troublesome single-seater car. One of the most important changes was that the FPF Coventry Climax engine was installed at an angle of 17° to the left (ie to the near-side of the car). Straight induction tracts could be used and the carburation problems suffered by the earlier cars were eliminated. The composite five-speed gearbox/final drive unit had been replaced by a BMC B-Series four-speed gearbox mounted in unit with the engine and there was a new final drive consisting of a Lotus casing with BMC gears. Whilst it was said that the existing model would continue in production, and that the new car was mainly intended for export, it clearly represented an acknowledgement by Chapman of the shortcomings of the original 15.

In the Tourist Trophy, now held on the Goodwood circuit, Team Lotus entered a 2 litre 15 for Allison/Hill. Although this car ran well during the early laps of the race, and at the end of the first hour was in seventh place, it retired with valve problems not long after Graham Hill had taken the wheel. A week later Roy Salvadori with Coombs' 2 litre Lotus won the 125 mile sports car race at the Oulton Park International meeting, completely unopposed, and by a margin of 30 seconds from Ivor Bueb's works Lister-Jaguar. At Snetterton on 11 October Graham Hill drove a 2 litre 15 and won a ten-lap race for sports cars from Halford's Lister-Jaguar. In short British events the faster Elevens and the 15s were now a match for most of the larger-capacity Jaguar-engined sports-racing cars, although of course it was very much a different story in endurance racing.

Overseas Derek Jolly had been racing a 15 with success in Australia, Pete Lovely

With John Coombs' 15, Roy Salvadori finished second overall and won the 2,000 cc class in the sports car race at the British Grand Prix meeting at Silverstone in July 1956. Note that this car is fitted with centre-lock wire wheels. Lotus Engineering used this actual photograph in their advertisements soliciting orders for the 15 for 1959, but, ironically, Coombs switched to Cooper Monacos for 1959. (T. C. March.)

had taken delivery of a Series 2 car to race in the United States and Pierre Berchem had enjoyed a good run of success in continental events with his prototype 15. Perhaps his outstanding success of the year was an outright win, by a margin of three laps, in the face of negligible opposition in the Belgian Congo Grand Prix held over three hours at Leopoldsville.

Although the Team Lotus 15s had achieved a reasonable measure of success in 1958, both their development and their racing programme had been overshadowed by the concentration of the team's efforts on Formula One racing. The sports-racing cars now took very much of a subsidary role in Team Lotus activities. And inevitably with a Formula One programme that was really beyond the resources of Lotus, it was hardly surprising that the preparations of the 15s suffered.

The 1959 Racing Season

Two basic modifications were made to the 15 for the 1959 season, affecting the front suspension and also the cooling system. So far as the suspension was concerned the change was that the anti-roll bar, forming part of the upper wishbone, was now behind the wheel-centre, which enabled a larger radiator and oil cooler to be fitted. The front of the chassis was stiffened and front track was reduced to 3 ft 10 in. The 15 was offered in both the Series 2 form with the BMC B-Series gearbox in unit with the engine and also with the five-speed positive stop change and Lotus gearbox in unit with the final drive. In this form the 15 was known as Series 3. As Team Lotus plans were originally announced, there was no provision for works cars to be raced, but in fact they made quite a number of appearances through the year. The driver was usually Graham Hill and he appeared with a works 15 at Goodwood on Easter Monday, at the British Empire Trophy at Oulton Park and subsequently at Aintree.

In *Sports Car & Lotus Owner* for May 1959 Graham Hill reflected on the latest version of the 2 litre 15: 'The Series Three Fifteen shows quite a number of changes from the car we raced last year, the most obvious being the use of a stiffer chassis frame, "reversed" front suspension and a conventionally-mounted four-speed gearbox.

'My first outing in the new car, at Goodwood, was extremely disappointing, for in practice the handling was not right and on race day the distributor drive sheared on the warming-up lap, which explains why the engine would not fire following the Le Mans-type start.

'As the engine was taken out for repairs the following week there was no time to test the car before the British Empire Trophy meeting at Oulton Park. It went very well in practice, however, and I managed to do the fastest lap with a time of 1 min 52.2 sec—quicker than all of the Formula Two cars but 1.4 sec slower than my record last year, which was set up in a similar car with a five-speed rear-mounted gearbox and with the engine inclined at 60°. Despite this I regard the current car as potentially quicker than last year's—everyone was going a little slower on 10 April, possibly because the circuit was slightly damp in places.

'It was more than slightly damp on race day, and all thoughts of fast times were forgotten. Despite my pole position I made a poor start—too much wheelspin—and got rather boxed-in on the inside of the corner, so that I was well behind the leaders at the end of the first lap. I managed to work my way up to third place, passing Flockhart's Ecurie Ecosse Lister-Jaguar and Brabham's Cooper Monaco in the process, but I could make no impression on Jim Russell and Roy Salvadori, whose Coopers finished first and second respectively. In the wet the car understeered a great deal, rear end adhesion being so good that the back end would not come round in the normal way, and attempts to un-stick it on the throttle only resulted in pushing the front end out even further.

'At Aintree, where I managed to do fourth fastest lap in the practice section for sports cars over 1,100 cc, the Fifteen still understeered and the handling seemed rather indefinite. After practice the amount of toe-in on the rear wheels was adjusted, and the car felt much better in the race, and from fourth place at the end of the first lap I managed to move up to second on lap three, in which position I stayed until the finish. I was unable to make a challenge to Salvadori, whose 2½ litre Cooper-Maserati finished nearly half a minute ahead of me, but I was not seriously threatened by Masten Gregory's Ecurie Ecosse Lister-Jaguar, which was 7.4 seconds behind at the end of the seventeen laps. There are few passing places at Aintree, particularly on the in field loop, where you have to gain at least three car's lengths between corners to get lined-up for the next bend, but I managed to pass both Bueb's and Gregory's Listers—which are faster than the Lotus on the straight—at Village Corner and to get just far enough ahead around Bechers to avoid being caught on the Railway Straight. But it was a near thing especially in the case of Gregory, who was right alongside me again just before Melling Crossing.

'By comparison with twenty gear changes per lap in last year's Formula Two car, which had the 1½ litre Coventry Climax engine and five-speed gearbox, I make only twelve changes to the lap in the Series Three Fifteen—due partly to the greater torque of the 2 litre engine and partly to the wider ratios of the four-speed box. Coming out of Tatts in second I change up into third and then top going past the pits, and stay in top (dropping to about 5,000 rpm) through Waterways. I go down to second for the right-hand at Anchor Crossing, up into third and down again for the left-handed Cottage Corner, using second for Country Corner (a left-hander) and third for Village Corner (a right-hander). On Valentines Way I get into top just before Bechers, go through Bechers in third and take top again by the gate just before the straight. Maximum revs in top are 6,500 (final drive ratio is 3.7 to 1) and I drop to third again for Melling Crossing and second for Tatts.

'My fastest lap was 2 min 6.6 sec, by comparison with Salvarodi's 2 min 5.4 sec (which is a new 2,000-3,000 cc class record) and Cliff Allison's 1,500-2,000 cc class record, set up in last year's 2 litre Fifteen with five-speed box—2 min 6.2 sec.

'From the driver's point of view the latest 2 litre Fifteen is a wonderful car—lots of steam low down, tremendous road holding, high maximum speed considering the engine size and an excellent gear change. I have never had any trouble with the five-speed box, but I know other people have; they couldn't have any difficulty with the BMC box, the change being absolutely conventional and particularly good "across the gate" between second and third. The driving position is comfortable, brakes work well and maintenance should be quite straightforward.'

As will be evident from what Graham wrote, there was new and formidable opposition in the 2,000 cc and 2,500 cc classes, in the form of the latest Cooper Monaco rear-engined sports car, derived from the team's Formula One cars, of which two examples were being entered by John Coombs. Roy Salvadori drove a car for Coombs with 2.5 litre Maserati engine and this was to be the dominant sports-racing car in British events during the year. In addition Coombs entered a Coventry-Climax-engined car for Jack Brabham. Except on very rare occasions, the big Jaguar-engined Listers and Tojeiros were now outclassed in British short-circuit events by the smaller, lighter Cooper and Lotus opposition. There were also now quite a number of 15s in private ownership and these scored a fair measure of success through the year in 1,500 cc events.

Early in the year with a Team Lotus 1,500 cc Alan Stacey won the sports car race up to 1,500 cc at the British Empire Trophy meeting at Oulton Park (the British Empire Trophy itself was now held as a Formula Two race). In the Aintree race to which Graham referred, Alan Stacey again drove his Team Lotus 1,500 cc car, but he retired because of an oil leak.

At the International Trophy meeting at Silverstone on 2 May, the 15s were out in force in the race for sports cars up to 3,000 cc. Graham Hill with the 2 litre Team Lotus car held second place behind Salvadori, but ahead of Stirling Moss with a works Aston Martin DBR1 on the first lap, moving up into the lead at the end of

Above Tom Dickson drove this 1,475 cc 15 into third place in the British Empire Trophy at Oulton Park in April 1959. The bonnet is non-standard and there appears to be an oil cooler jury-rigged in the cockpit. (T. C. March.)

Below With this 2 litre 15 Graham Hill led the sports car race at the International Trophy meeting at Silverstone in May 1959 until forced to retire by final drive problems. (T. C. March.)

Bottom Graham Hill braking heavily with his 2.5 litre 15 in the sports car race at Aintree in July 1959. He won the race from Alan Stacey at the wheel of another 15. (T. C. March.)

lap two and staying out in front until the Lotus expired with final drive problems. Alan Stacey with his Team Lotus 1,500 cc car had an incredible accident at Woodcote when the steering broke and the car went out of control into the retaining bank. Stacey was unhurt.

On 17 May the Grand Prix des Frontières was held at Chimay in Belgium and a total of twelve private Lotus cars were entered. Michael Taylor won the race with his private 15 from Douglas Graham with his similar car, registered 100 MDG. In Finland on 10 May a race meeting was held at Elaintahanajo and here David Piper drove his private 15 with 2 litre engine into second place behind the Cooper Monaco of Curt Lincoln, a local driver and of course later Jochen Rindt's father-in-law. At Oulton Park on 6 June the Hon Edward Greenall won two races in his private 15 running in 1,500 cc form. The following day David Piper with Keith Greene as co-driver, and the similar car of Tim Parnell/David Buxton with single cam engine enlarged to 1,530 cc ran in the Nürburgring 1,000 km race. Parnell/Buxton retired and Greene finished the last lap, holding the rear suspension together with his hand after the right-hand rear radius rod broke, but there was a Lotus victory in the 1,100 cc class; the Eleven of Campbell-Jones/Horridge was the class winner, despite strong opposition from the Lola of Broadley/Ashdown until it went off the road.

At Le Mans Team Lotus entered a 15 with 2,495 cc Coventry-Climax FPF engine driven by Graham Hill/Derek Jolly, in addition to two 17s, the fate of which is discussed in the next chapter. With Graham Hill at the wheel the 15 showed tremendous form in the opening laps, holding seventh place, but it soon started to jump out of fourth gear. A long time was spent in the pits trying to resolve the problem and eventually the car retired with a broken engine, in the ninth hour, the result of repeated over-revving when the car jumped out of gear.

On 28 June Graham Hill drove a Team Lotus 15 with 2,495 cc engine at Mallory Park and won the unlimited capacity sports car race, scoring an easy victory after Salvadori's Cooper-Maserati non-started as a result of a broken chassis and Salvadori was forced to drive a Cooper with 1,500 cc engine. At the British Grand Prix meeting at Aintree on 18 July two Team Lotus 15s were entered in the sports car race with 2.5 litre engine for Graham Hill and with 2 litre engine for Alan Stacey. Hill soon pulled out a good lead from Jack Brabham with Coombs' Cooper-Climax, and Stacey came through to take second place after Brabham spun his Cooper on the now streaming wet track in the heavy rain that fell during the latter stages of this race. On 26 July Stirling Moss drove the new 2 litre Maserati Tipo 60 to win in the 2,000 cc sports car race at Rouen, but the Team Lotus entries of Alan Stacey (2 litre engine) and Innes Ireland (1.5 litre) finished second and third. Another success for Graham Hill followed at Brands Hatch on August Bank Holiday Monday when he won the Kingsdown Trophy race for unlimited capacity cars with 2.5 litre 15. Admittedly, however, there was not much in the way of opposition once Hill had scrambled past Chris Bristow's Cooper. Hill won yet again at Brands Hatch on 29 August in the Farningham Trophy with the 2.5 litre 15 from David Piper with his private 15 with 2 litre engine and Alan Stacey finished third.

On 5 September the Tourist Trophy was held at Goodwood and there was a strong Lotus entry. A Team Lotus 15 with 1,960 cc engine and, because wheel

In the sports car race at the International Trophy meeting at Silverstone in May 1960 Michael Taylor (MT 100) and Tom Dickson (TOM 1) battle for third place. Taylor retired and Dickson went on to finish second to Salvadori's Cooper. (T. C. March.)

changes would be necessary in this race, centre-lock wire wheels was driven by Graham Hill/Alan Stacey, while David Piper's similar 1,960 cc car, co-driven by Bruce Halford, was also fitted with centre-lock wire wheels. Other 15s were driven by Michael Taylor/Martin and Tom Dickson/Ninian Sanderson. Although the results were dominated by Aston Martin, who clinched the Sports Car World Championship by trouncing the Ferrari team, the Lotus works entry ran well in the opening stages of the race. After holding fourth place initially, Hill was third overall at the end of the first hour, but Team Lotus pit work was not the slickest and a lot of time was lost whilst four new tyres were fitted and 25 gallons of fuel taken on board with the result that the 15 dropped well down the field. Further time was lost in the pits because of slipped ignition timing and this car was finally eliminated when Bristow (Porsche) and Stacey collided at St Mary's and both cars hit the bank. Piper crashed badly as a result of a burst tyre at Madgwick, Dickson's Lotus was eliminated by gearbox failure and Taylor's car was eliminated by gasket failure.

Throughout the two years during which Team Lotus had raced the 15s they had shown consistent performance, apart from early teething problems, in British short-distance events. However, as had been the case ever since the Elevens' fine results in 1956-57, their basic fragility and lack of endurance was such that they could achieve no success in long-distance events. The shortcomings were shortcomings as much of the Coventry Climax engines used, as of the Lotus chassis themselves.

Fifteens were raced by private owners in minor British events for several years to come, and perhaps the most interesting of these variants was 'Dizzy' Addicott's car powered by a Buick 3.5 litre V8 engine, registered DIZ 1. This was raced with

Doug Graham at the 1960 International Trophy at Silverstone. (T. C. March.)

considerable success by Addicott in club events in 1962, despite early problems with the rear-mounted gearbox. And it was something of a forerunner of the Group 7 sports-racing cars with American engines that were soon to be seen in British events in considerable numbers.

In June 1959 Lotus had moved to a brand-new factory at Cheshunt in Hertfordshire and here the Elite GT car was in production despite many early problems. The whole emphasis of Lotus activities was changing and in the future the company would concentrate on production cars and on Formula One more and more at the expense of the other categories of racing. The 15 and the single-seater Formula One and Formula Two cars raced by Lotus since 1957 were amongst the last of a dying breed, the front-engined competition car. During the years 1957-59 the rear-engined Cooper single seaters had become increasingly successful, with two Grand Prix wins in 1958 and outright victory in the Driver's World Championship in 1959 by Jack Brabham. The Cooper's basic simplicity and good-handling qualities revealed that all the technical complications that Chapman had employed to achieve a small frontal area with a front-engined car were not necessary and for 1960 Chapman switched to rear-engined cars.

Chapter 8

The 17, 1959

In 1959 Lotus Engineering introduced a successor to the Eleven, a car that was intended to be more compact, lighter, with smaller frontal area and even better handling, and was primarily the work of Len Terry who was now the Lotus Chief Designer.

In accordance with usual Lotus practice the chassis was a multi-tubular space-frame structure using light steel tubing of ⅝ in and ¾ in square and round 20 gauge steel. The propellor-shaft and the floor were stressed members, forming an integral part of the frame. The engine was carried on two rubber mountings at the front and a single rubber mounting attached to the gearbox at the rear.

At the front there was a completely new suspension of the strut-type. Each front wheel was located by a wide-based lower wishbone, with the tubular stub axle calliper mounting plate and steering arm all retained at the base of the strut by four bolts.

There was the familiar Chapman strut-type suspension at the rear, already seen on the single-seaters, the 15 and the Elite road car. Girling disc brakes with 9½ in discs were mounted front and rear, outboard at the front and inboard at the rear. The front and rear braking systems had independent master cylinders linked to the pedal by an adjustable balance bar. Lotus cast magnesium-alloy wheels were fitted as standard, but centre-lock wire wheels could be specified instead. There was new rack and pinion steering. The Coventry Climax FWA 1,098 cc engine in Stage Three tune developing 84 bhp at 6,800 rpm was the standard power unit (although the car was intended to be supplied with the Coventry Climax engine in 750 cc form when it became available and in fact had originally been conceived as a 750 cc car). The transmission consisted of a new hydraulically operated Borg & Beck single dry plate 7¼ in-clutch used with a new low-weight four-speed close-ratio gearbox in unit with the engine. The final drive was a hypoid unit with a choice of ratios and a ZF limited slip differential could be supplied at extra cost.

The body, principally the work of Len Terry, had a much smaller frontal area than the Eleven (the frontal area was said to be 9 sq ft) and it incorporated the high tail and very curved windscreen first used at Le Mans by Lotus in 1957. The 17 was 3 in shorter, 4½ in narrower, 3½ in lower at the scuttle and 7½ in lower overall than its predecessor. The aluminium-alloy fuel tank holding approximately 8 gallons was mounted in the tail of the car, as was the spare wheel. Although slightly wider tyres were used at the rear, wheel rim sizes front and rear were the same, on 15 in wheels.

The wheelbase was a mere 6 ft 10 in, front track 3 ft 6 in and rear track 3 ft 9 in. The weight less fuel was said to be 750 lb. In every dimension the new 17 was smaller and more compact than the Lola which, by way of example, had a wheelbase of 7 ft 1 in, front and rear track of 4 ft, and overall length of 11 ft 9 in. The Lola was of course also somewhat heavier.

The 1959 Racing Season

Purely on the basis of the successes of the Eleven, a number of private owners immediately ordered the 17 and cars were also raced by Team Lotus. Throughout the year, however, the 17 was plagued by handling problems, it was absolutely no match for the rival Lola-Climax which had first appeared in 1958, and whilst private owners struggled in disappointment with their cars, Lotus Engineering also struggled, without a great deal of success, to sort the 17 out.

The first car was due to be driven by Alan Stacey at the Goodwood meeting on Easter Monday but it had to be withdrawn because the handling was so terrible. The 17 was next entered at the International Aintree meeting on 18 April and whilst Stacey drove a Team Lotus car, Ian Walker was at the wheel of his own 17. On a very wet track Stacey set fastest lap, but throughout practice—and the race—Walker's car

This shot of the starting grid of the Rochester Trophy for 1,100 cc cars at Brands Hatch in August 1959 sums up this class of racing at that time. On the inside of the front row are the Lolas of Ashdown and Gammon with, alongside, Graham Hill at the wheel of a Team Lotus 17 and Mike McKee's Elva Mark V. (LAT.)

sounded very sick. Stacey joined the grid at the last moment for reasons explained later in this chapter and was forced to start from the back. On the first lap he came right through the field to hold second place behind Michael Taylor's Lola, but on only the third lap he retired with gearbox trouble. In the 1,100 cc sports car race at the International Silverstone meeting, again, the race was Lola-dominated and after holding sixth place initially, Stacey dropped back, eventually retiring with brake problems. At the Crystal Palace on the Whit Monday another new 17 appeared in the hands of Derek Randall and Stacey drove the Team Lotus car again. The 1,500 cc sports car race was run two heats and a final, but although Randall was third in his heat, neither he nor Stacey featured in the results of the final.

In the July 1959 issue of *Sports Car & Lotus Owner*, Alan Stacey narrated the testing and development of the 17: '. . . To start with let me first say that I believe it will be quicker than all its predecessors. To all the pessimists and members of the Lola fan club who suggest "It's too narrow", I would say "what is the fastest car round a corner?"—a '500' with a 3 ft 6 in track. The point is that, as cars are going increasingly quickly these days and reaching a higher state of development, there is little chance of an entirely new design being "right" straight off the drawing board.

'The need for a certain amount of modification became apparent in practice for the Goodwood Easter Monday meeting. I managed to record 1 min 40.2 sec despite atrocious handling qualities, but decided it would be unwise to race the car and treated practice as a testing session, which allowed me to make a few suggestions to the powers-that-be.

'The next meeting for which the 17 was entered was Aintree on 18 April, although I was busily engaged preparing the new 15 I was assured that all my suggestions concerning the roadholding of the 17 had been carried out.

'In practice I thought we had really got somewhere. It was wet, but I had little difficulty in recording fastest practice time. However, in a "free for all" practice session in the dry the increased cornering forces brought out the old oversteering tendencies. Nevertheless I decided to race the car, and although I lost my pole position on the grid due to some last minute carburettor trouble, starting from the back row, I managed to take the lead within two laps, when second gear went. Still, the car had shown its potential.

'Practice for the Silverstone International Trophy meeting revealed the same inherent trouble, and now I had got my 15 going quickly, I decided a sustained effort would have to be made on the 17. After two day's practice, with Mike Costin working full time on the 17, we discovered the cause of the disconcertingly sudden oversteer. Unfortunately, in the time available this could only be cured by adjustments giving a completely oversteering tendency. The race thus became a test again, but it did prove that the "twitch" had gone.

'At Silverstone, due partly to the not undeserved adverse publicity and lack of improvements we decided to do another day's testing at Silverstone. An early start was made and Colin and Mike brought the car and two mechanics with them, complete with an assortment of springs and anti-roll bars.

'The test began with a few laps warming up and making sure the faults encountered during the last race were still present, and sure enough the oversteer was still

The Lotus 17 entry of Keith Greene/Tony Marsh during the 1959 Goodwood Tourist Trophy.
(Geoffrey Goddard.)

pronounced. The first step taken to overcome this was resetting of the ride level. This was found to be very critical, and was definitely too high. Lowering it improved the handling immensely, but with a full load of fuel it was found that the rear of the car bottomed through Becketts.

'To prevent this, stronger rear springs were fitted. This, we knew, would bring back the oversteer, but it is the principle of such tests to try only one thing at a time. With the new springs fitted the car certainly oversteered but it was more gentle and easier to control. We had two ways of getting back to an understeering tendency, either by fitting a stronger roll bar or by stiffening up the front springs. As the car was not rolling excessively, stronger front springs were fitted, and as a result the car handled very well indeed. After 79 laps of the Grand Prix circuit throughout the day I got down to 1 min 49.5 sec—this with an engine that was 300 rpm down on Derek Randall's standard-engined 17. From this lap time it seems feasible to suggest that with a few more horses times of around 1 min 48 sec would be possible.

'In comparison with the 15 and Formula cars, the 17 now has a much more neutral steering, that is, less understeer. I believe it is quicker into a corner, and that with the increase in roadholding gained with the strut type rear end, it was essential to incorporate something similar at the front to maintain stability through the corner at the increased speed. This season all the quick cars using independent rear suspension seemed to suffer from understeer. I believe the 17 has the answer.

'After a quick check all round on the engine in an attempt to regain the lost horsepower, we took the car to the Crystal Palace for the Whit Monday meeting. Practice showed that the horses hadn't returned, but a time of 1 min 4 sec, under Keith Hall's 1,100 cc lap record, proved that the roadholding was now very good. During practice private timing showed that the 17 was easily the fastest up to 1,500 cc car, including Salvadori's Cooper Monaco and the Lolas, through the notorious Ramp Bend.

'On Sunday we rounded up the horses ready for Monday and for the first time we were feeling slightly confident. However in the first 25 yd of unofficial practice the crankshaft broke. Who said there's no luck in motor racing!

'Well, that's the story to date. We've proved that the 17 is the lightest 1,100 yet built and also that its roadholding is on a par with the best. Doesn't that mean it's the fastest?'

What Stacey did not claim in his article was that the oversteer had been cured and in fact the handling remained the problem for the 17 throughout the year. It was never a match for the rival Lola and never succeeded in beating the fastest cars of the rival marque.

At Le Mans two 17s with Coventry Climax FWMA 745 cc engines were entered by Team Lotus, but both were privately owned. Michael Taylor drove his car with Jonathan Sieff, but the car was plagued by distributor trouble and retired in the fifth hour of the race. The second 17 with similar power unit was owned by John Fisher and driven by Alan Stacey/Keith Greene. There is little doubt that this was the fastest 750 cc car ever to have raced at Le Mans, but it too was plagued by distributor problems which resulted in overheating. Under the race regulations water could not be taken on at intervals of less than thirteen laps, so Stacey was forced to park the car out on the circuit and walk back to the pits to collect water. The car eventually retired at half-distance with a blown cylinder head gasket.

During the remainder of the season Team Lotus fielded a 17 in a number of minor British events. At Mallory Park on 28 June Graham Hill drove the works car finishing third in the sports car race up to 1,200 cc, but the winner was Peter Arundell with a private 17. Graham Hill also drove one of the Le Mans 750 cc cars in the 2,000 cc sports car race at Rouen on 20 July but retired with steering trouble. Graham again drove a 1,098 cc 17 at Brands Hatch on August Bank Holiday Monday, finishing second in his heat of the Wrotham Trophy for 1,100 cc cars and third in the final behind the Lolas of Ashdown and Gammon. Alan Stacey was back at the wheel at the Crystal Palace meeting on 22 August, but again the 17 was absolutely no match for the Lolas. While Stacey won his heat from Peter Ashdown's Lola, he was beaten to third place in the final behind Gammon and Ashdown. By the International meeting at Brands Hatch on 29 August the 17 had been fitted with wishbone front suspension in an effort to improve its handling. Graham Hill was again at the wheel in the Rochester Trophy for 1.100 cc cars and Keith Greene drove his privately entered 17. It was evident that the handling was improved, but still the 17s were no match for the Lolas and Hill had to settle for third place behind Gammon and Ashdown. Greene finished sixth.

At the Tourist Trophy at Goodwood on 5 September there were two 17s entered in the name of Team Lotus, the works car driven by Innes Ireland/Jay Chamberlain and Keith Greene's car co-driven by Tony Marsh. However it was much the same story as before, the 1,100 cc class was dominated by the Lolas, the leading example of which driven by Ashdown/Ross finished sixth overall with other Lolas eighth and tenth. The Ireland/Chamberlain car retired with final drive problems, but Greene/Marsh finished eleventh.

Team Lotus continued to field their car during what little remained of the season and at Brands Hatch on 4 October Graham Hill won the 1,100 cc sports car race from the Elva of Mike McKee.

In the August 1959 issue of *Sports Car & Lotus Owner* David Phipps road tested the Lotus 17 and extracts are set out below:

'... The engine on the car I tried was "just as it came from the works" except for the fitting of twin-choke 38 mm Weber carburettors. The basically Austin A30 gearbox was fitted with the latest type of Lotus close-ratio gears.

'This latest "works" Seventeen is normally equipped with the lightweight bucket seat which provides very good lateral support—too good in fact, for my hips, so I arranged for the seat to be removed and replaced with a full-width seat back... The leather-rimmed steering wheel is set at just the right height and the long gear-lever projects to a point where the left-hand drops naturally upon it. Hidden away under the dashboard on the passenger side is a hand brake which, in customary Lotus fashion, works on a horizontal plane. Immediately to the driver's right, at the leading edge of the door sill, are the ignition/starter switch (operated by a key) the lights switch and the horn button. The latter is fitted mainly to comply with regulations, as it seems pretty obvious that anyone who has not heard the exhaust note is unlikely to hear the horn.

'Directly ahead of the driver is a tachometer, flanked by a combination oil pressure/water temperature gauge on the left and an ammeter on the right. All instruments are of Smiths manufacture.

'First impressions are that this is an extremely easy car to drive. The engine starts first time, the gear lever slips easily (with a surprisingly short travel) into bottom gear, and the hydraulic clutch takes up the drive smoothly but very firmly. Up to second and third, down to second again (the most suitable ratio for Cheshunt traffic)—it is just like driving a saloon car, a little noisier than most. Visibility is not impaired (as it will be, thanks to the CSI's new regulations, on next year's racing sports cars) by the windscreen, and the bonnet line falls smoothly away, with the relatively high front "wings" assisting accurate placing of the car for corners, or overtaking.

'...so we bumble along with the traffic stream , either in second or third, with the engine spluttering somewhat as the revs drop to around 2,000 but picking up smoothly and crisply at about 3,500, from which point the tachometer needle rushes round to 7,000 in second and third in the short distance needed to overtake a string of three lorries. This tremendous acceleration is a wonderful asset on the road, and once out of restricted areas the Seventeen is rarely held up by other traffic, almost always being able to slip by before the next corner or blind brow.

'The semi-open road after Hoddesdon becomes very much built up in Ware, but after this, on the undulations of A10 we get into top for the first time, and soar through Wadesmill and up the hill on the other side with the Seventeen imparting a tremendous feeling of security. Approaching Puckeridge at around 90 mph a firm application of the brake pedal (Girling discs with Ferodo pads) slowed the car to 20 in a few seconds and we thread our way through parked and parking vehicles to B1368.

'After the frustration of London and surburban traffic, the "road-through-villages" is like the entry to another world. It is by no means straight, or particularly fast, but provides a succession of fairly open sections on which one can obtain a very good impression of a car's real potential. Through the open bends before Barkway the Seventeen can be steered almost entirely with the throttle, and indeed, except for the sharp turning in Barley, the steering wheel rim is not moved more than three inches in fourteen miles. Together with the acceleration and "iron-hand-in velvet-glove" braking, this light and direct steering is another factor which makes a major contribution to safe high speed driving.

'Between Barley and Flint Cross some idea is gained of the Seventeen's potential in the way of straight-line speed. Then, turning right to A505, the open road really unfolds and, accelerating hard, the little car sweeps through the gentle left, right, left bends which proceed a two mile straight, coming out of the third "kink" at about 6,000 rpm in top, running rapidly up to 7,800 rpm (about 120 mph with the 4.9 to 1 "Brands Hatch" final drive ratio fitted) and holding this for about a mile before slowing for what turns out to be the mirage of a lorry shimmering over a slight rise. . .

'For this type of use the road-holding of the Seventeen can only be described as impeccable. Initial breakaway of the rear wheels can be induced quite easily, but it is obviously a wide margin between this condition and complete loss of adhesion. For normal cornering the steering characteristic is virtually neutral, with a slight tendency towards understeer, but "lifting-off" in a corner producing oversteer, the retarding influence of the engine having much the same effect as putting the brakes on.

'Despite the lack of upholstery (other than my own) I found the ride surprisingly comfortable, the relatively soft springs of the Seventeen smoothing out road surfaces which transmit all manner of jolts and jars into the more austere types of saloon cars. The propellor shaft tunnel became rather warm (something which might not have been evident with the bucket seat in use) but very little heat came through from the engine compartment, and on the whole I was much more comfortable than in certain current "luxury" sports cars.

'Thus, although it is first and foremost a racing car, there seems to be no reason why the Seventeen should not be used regularly on the road. The steering lock is adequate, full lighting equipment is provided, and with a Stage One rather than a Stage Three engine fitted the car would lose little in acceleration, and gain a great deal in terms of flexibility.'

Lotus Engineering discontinued the 17 at the end of the 1959 season, Keith Greene for example had built his own Gilby-Climax sports-racing car, Lola had yet another season of success with their Climax-powered cars, but the day of the front-engined sports-racing car was soon to be over. The 17 represented a bold attempt to build a car that was lighter, more compact, and with smaller frontal area than any of its rivals, but it also represented a rare Lotus failure.

Chapter 9

The 19, 1960-63

Chapman's fortunes had been built on the construction and racing of sports-racing cars, but by 1960 the situation had changed. Despite many problems, Lotus production was now concentrated on the Elite GT car with 1,216 cc Coventry-Climax engine. In competition work the team was concentrating more and more on single-seaters and Chapman had made a radical change in his approach to design and construction. For the latest Formula One and the new Formula Junior Lotus Chapman had switched to a rear-engined layout with the new 18.

The 18, whilst very different in layout from previous Lotus designs, followed closely Chapman's previous design and construction practice. The multi-tubular space-frame was constructed from 18 and 16 gauge ¾ in and 1 in mild steel tubes. It consisted of three sections. The fully triangulated forward section carried mountings for the front suspension, brake and clutch master cylinders, for the rack and pinion steering and for the pedals. Ahead of this there was a separate, lighter frame for mounting the water and oil radiators and oil tanks. To the rear of this frame was a fabricated sheet and tube frame used for mounting the instruments, steering column, gear lever, hand brake and switches. The scuttle panel was linked by triangulated tubular sections to the rear engine bulkhead. From this braced engine bulkhead ran two straight tubes, converging at the lower rear suspension pick-up points and there was a top frame of Y-shape that could be unbolted to permit removal of the engine and gearbox. At the front, Chapman adopted unequal-length double wishbones and inclined coil spring/damper units, a system tried out on the front-engined 16s in 1959. Because there was insufficient height at the rear to accommodate the familiar strut-type suspension, Chapman opted for a new layout based on double links. With this system, the transverse links were formed by the lower, tubular transverse links and the unsplined drive-shafts. Twin parallel radius rods on either side located the rear wheels longitudinally and there were again combined coil spring/damper units.

At the front 10½ in Girling disc brakes were mounted outboard and 9½ in Girling disc brakes were mounted inboard at the rear. A 22 gallon fuel tank was positioned over the driver's legs and there was an additional 9½ gallon tank behind the driver's seat on the right. Chapman retained the familiar bolt-on cast magnesium 'wobbly web' wheels, but these were now of wider rim-section at the rear. The power unit was the familiar 2,495 cc Coventry Climax FPF unit. There was a twin plate Borg and Beck clutch used with a Lotus five-speed gearbox/final drive unit. This gearbox was a direct development of the gearbox used on the Lotus 15 driven by Hill/Jolly at Le Mans in 1959. On the first car, to Formula Junior specification with Ford 105E-based engine, that ran at the Boxing Day Brands Hatch meeting in 1959, there was an aluminium body. However all subsequent cars had glass-fibre bodies built by Williams & Pritchard Ltd. In appearance the bodywork had a very square shape, but it had been designed to hug the mechanical components as closely as possible and frontal area was very small.

Chapman regarded the 18 as his first Formula One design and looked on its front-engine predecessors merely as Formula Two cars adopted for Formula One. Throughout 1960, despite the usual Lotus fragility and mechanical failings, the 18 enjoyed a tremendous run of success with wins by Innes Ireland in the Richmond Trophy at Goodwood and the International Trophy at Silverstone, a win by Stirling Moss with the Rob Walker-entered car at Monaco, a second place by Ireland at Zandvoort, and another second by Surtees in the British Grand Prix at Silverstone. Stirling Moss also won the Gold Cup race at Oulton Park, the Watkins Glen Formule Libre Race and the United States Grand Prix at Riverside. In addition the team won a string of Formula Two races when the cars were fitted with 1.5 litre FPF engines, and the 18 was also immensely successful in Formula Junior.

Directly developed from the 18 was the Lotus sports-racing derivative, the 19, which appeared in August 1960. The chassis was widened to make space for two seats in the cockpit, but otherwise was similar to the Formula One car. Likewise the suspension was similar front and rear, but featured rear radius rods of increased diameter as used on the Lotus 18 entered by Rob Walker. Other changes were that the rear disc brakes were mounted outboard to achieve better cooling both of the brakes themselves and of the gearbox. There were also separate hydraulic brake systems front and rear. Different engine mountings were used, the gearbox oil tank and the oil filter were mounted in the engine compartment, whilst only the engine oil was pumped through to the oil radiator in the nose, and the gearbox oil was kept in a separate system at the rear. The 2,495 cc Coventry Climax FPF engine was fitted with a starter motor and the Lotus five-speed gearbox incorporated a reverse gear. Fuel capacity was now 18 gallons, carried in two tanks on each side of the cockpit. The body was a very simple structure in glass fibre, with detachable one-piece nose and tail sections. The basic instrumentation of the Formula One car was retained with addition of an ammeter and the ignition/starter switch. The 19 featured a very wrap-round perspex windscreen and short cut-off tail so that it had more than a passing resemblance to the Cooper Monaco sports-racing car. As a result it was nicknamed the Lotus 'Monte Carlo', but in fact this name never really stuck and it has gone down in history as the 19.

At the Belgian Grand Prix at Spa-Francorchamps Stirling Moss had crashed badly in practice with the Rob Walker-entered 18 when the left-hand rear wheel had become detached at high speed. As a result he was out of racing for some while and his first reappearance at the wheel of a competition car was at Silverstone when he drove the 19. At this time the 19 was fitted with a Coventry Climax engine from one of Rob Walker's Cooper Formula One cars and during the test session there were problems with cooling. However these were overcome in time for Moss to drive 19 at Karlskoga on 7 August and on the Swedish circuit he won the 75 km sports car race from Joakim Bonnier's Maserati. Following this race Bonnier borrowed the 19 for an

Stirling Moss with this UDT-Laystall-entered Lotus 19 won the sports car race at the International Trophy meeting at Silverstone in May 1961. At this time the 19 was in its original, unmodified form. (T. C. March.)

attempt on the Swedish National record for the flying kilometre and broke the record with a speed of 157.5 mph. Apparently Bonnier had only 1,000 yards in which to work up to maximum speed and the record was set without him managing to get the car into fifth gear.

As a result of these encouraging first performances Chapman decided to go ahead with a limited production run of twelve examples of the 19. It was stated at the time that six cars would be sold in the United Kingdom and a further six would be sold overseas. One of the reasons for limiting production was the comparative shortage of 2,495 cc engines. Ultimately nine of the original production batch of twelve cars were exported to the United States, whilst three were delivered in the United Kingdom to the UDT-Laystall Team to race in British events. It does seem however that total production was in fact slightly greater than twelve cars.

The 19 from a different angle—again the sports car race at Silverstone in May 1961, but the driver is Cliff Allison who finished third. (T. C. March.)

By October only two of these cars had been completed, and the second car was delivered to Frank and Philip Arciero, who ran a constructors' contractors business in the United States, and had bought the second car to be driven by Dan Gurney. Both cars ran in the Times-Mirror Riverside Grand Prix at Riverside Raceway in California on 16 October. Initially Moss led from Gurney, but then Gurney went into the lead. Moss retired on lap ten because of final drive failure and Gurney ultimately retired because of cylinder head gasket failure. The 19 driven by Moss in this race was later also sold to the Arciero brothers.

Throughout the 1961 season the three UDT-Laystall cars dominated British sports car events, with little in the way of opposition except for Roy Salvadori at the wheel of the latest Cooper Monaco entered by John Coombs. These light green cars, distinguished by the high perspex windscreens necessary to comply with the latest regulations and by a tartan strip across the nose, first appeared at Oulton Park on 15 April. Henry Taylor, Graham Hill and Cliff Allison took the first three places in the twenty-lap sports car race, completely unopposed. On 22 April at Aintree the 19s were in action again and in this seventeen-lap race run on a damp track driven by Stirling Moss, Henry Taylor and Cliff Allison they took the first three places. It was much the same story at the International Trophy meeting at Silverstone on 6 May; Moss won the 25-lap race with his 19, but Salvadori managed to finish second ahead of Allison and Taylor finished fifth, but in this race his car was fitted with a 1,475 cc Climax engine and he of course won the 1,500 cc class. This pattern of domination broke at the Crystal Palace on Whit Monday where all three 19s retired in the Green Helmet Trophy and two of the cars were eliminated by a wheel falling off, whilst the third was eliminated by final drive failure. The problem had been the centre-lock wire wheels fitted for the cars to compete in the Nürburgring 1,000 km race the following weekend. As a result of these problems the UDT-Laystall cars non-started in the German endurance race. On August Bank Holiday Monday Henry Taylor, driving for the first time after a crash in the British Grand Prix, ran at Aintree with a UDT-Laystall 19 powered by a 2 litre engine finishing second in his heat and second also in the fifteen-lap final of the unlimited capacity sports car race.

One of the main problems faced by UDT-Laystall was a lack of unlimited capacity sports car races in the United Kingdom and accordingly the 19s were shipped to the United States to tackle the races over there in the autumn of 1961. On 22 October Moss won the Pacific Grand Prix at Laguna Seca from Dan Gurney with the Arciero brothers' 19, with a Cooper driven by Jack Brabham in third place. At the Nassau Speed week in the Bahamas Moss drove a 19 for Team Rosebud in the Governor's Trophy which was run as a five-lap qualifying heat and a 25-lap final. In the heat Moss was eliminated by a broken rear upright. Gurney also ran in this event but the aim of several of the drivers was to use the race as merely a test for the main race on the Sunday, the Nassau Trophy, and did not run in the final. Moss repaired his 19 with borrowed parts and it was ready in time for the Sunday race in which four 19s competed. Moss led the race until a rear wishbone broke and Gurney won with the Arciero brothers' car. Also in 1961 Moss had won at Mosport Park in Canada on 24 June with a 19, the race being decided on the results of the two heats, and had finished third in the Canadian Grand Prix at Mosport on 10 September; in this race his 19, fitted with a Colotti gearbox, suffered transmission problems and Canadian Pete Ryan had won the race with his 19.

During 1962 the success of the 19s continued. In February Dan Gurney won the Daytona 3 Hours race for sports and GT cars at 104.10 mph, but it was a lucky victory because the 19s engine broke on the last lap and Gurney crossed the finishing line to take the chequered flag on the starter motor. On 7 April Innes Ireland won the fifteen-lap unlimited capacity sports car race at Oulton Park with the UDT-Laystall 19 from a Cooper Monaco driven by Blumer. For 1962 the UDT cars featured centre-lock wire wheels and cutaway rear wheel arches. It was an easy victory in the face of little opposition and Ireland won by a margin of over 20 seconds. Ireland won again at Goodwood on Easter Monday in the Sussex Trophy for sports and GT cars, beating Mike Parkes's Ferrari 250 GTO. Ireland's third victory of the season with this car followed at Aintree on 28 April when he again beat Blumer into second place. His fourth victory of the season followed in the sports car race at the International Silverstone Meeting and again Blumer with his Cooper Monaco took second place. In July Graham Hill drove a UDT-Laystall 19 to a fine win in the Archie Scott-Brown Memorial Trophy at Snetterton and on a drying track achieved the first 100 mph

Innes Ireland on his way to a win in the sports car race at the Gold Cup meeting at Oulton Park on 1 September 1962. By this time the rear wheel arches of the 19 had been cut away, centre-lock wire wheels were fitted and there was a lower windscreen. (T. C. March.)

sports car lap of Snetterton. On August Bank Holiday Monday the Guards International Trophy was held at Brands Hatch and although the race was won by Mike Parkes with a Tipo 246 Ferrari, Innes Ireland brought his UDT-Laystall 19 across the line in second place.

In North America the Lotus 19s were still enjoying substantial success. There were two lucrative races held on the Mosport Park circuit in Canada; the Canadian Grand Prix held over 246 miles and the Players 200 over a distance of 196 miles, both of which were won by Masten Gregory with UDT-Laystall 19. In the North West Grand Prix at Pacific Raceway Gurney won with the Arciero-entered 19, Lloyd Ruby finished second in the Pacific Grand Prix at Laguna Seca and Gregory finished third in the Riverside Grand Prix at Riverside Raceway, California. Gurney with the Arciero car also won the World's Fair Grand Prix at Pacific Raceway, with Gregory in second place, and a string of successes during the year was rounded off by Innes Ireland's win with Team Rosebud's 19 in the 252 mile Nassau Trophy in the Bahamas at the end of the year. In 1963 much of the emphasis of Lotus efforts in sports car racing was on the 23 and 23B cars, described in the next chapter, but the 19s

Still racing in 1966, the Lotus 19 of J. Scott Davies with 2,750 cc Climax engine in the sports car race at the International Trophy meeting in May. No 8 is the Ferrari 250LM of Peter Clarke. (T. C. March.)

soldiered on, now with most examples in the United States, and Dan Gurney at the wheel of the one-off 19B with Ford 4.7-litre V-8 engine. At the North West Grand Prix at Kent in Washington State Innes Ireland crashed heavily in practice with the Team Rosebud 19 suffering injuries to the legs and hips which put him out of racing for the remainder of the year. In the United Kingdom Innes Ireland had raced a 19 for what was now the British Racing partnership formerly UDT-Laystall (but the British races were dominated by Roy Salvadori at the wheel of the latest Cooper Monaco. In addition a 19 was being raced with success in Australia by Frank Matich. By 1964 Gurney's Ford-powered 19B had been joined in America by other American-powered 19s, including a Chevrolet-engined Lotus 19 raced by Bobby Unser and a similar car raced by Jerry Grant.

The 19 had not been a significant car in Lotus history, but it had proved an inexpensive car to develop, it enjoyed an exceedingly profitable racing career and it was still winning races in its fifth year.

Chapter 10

The 23, 1962-63

Following the failure of the 17 in 1959, sports car racing in the 1,100 cc category was dominated by the Climax-powered Lolas until the end of 1961. At the Racing Car Show in January 1962 Lotus exhibited the new 23, a car based very closely on the 1961 Formula Junior Lotus 20 which had dominated its class, but incorporating the modifications made to that design for 1962 when it was known as the 22. As on the original 18 rear-engined Lotus single-seater, the chassis was a multi-tubular space-frame constructed in three bays and fully triangulated. It was of course widened on the sports car to accommodate two seats and generally it was a much stiffer chassis than the Formula Junior chassis. The front bulkhead provided the mounting points for the front suspension, steering rack, battery, pedals and cross-flow radiator (which featured an integral oil cooler). At the scuttle the bulkhead, formed by two tubular rectangles linked by sheet steel, located the steering column, seats, gear level, instruments, and switches. The engine bulkhead mounted the rear radius arms and the 9 gallon fuel tank. The top left and bottom right longitudinal chassis members doubled as water pipes linking the engine and the radiator. The top right and bottom left longitudinal members acted as oil pipes. At the front the suspension was similar to that of the 1961 Formula Junior car and was by unequal-length double wishbones and coil spring/damper units. For the rear suspension Lotus adopted the layout used on the 1961 Formula One car, the 21, with upper lateral links, wide-based lower lateral links, parallel radius arms and coil spring/damper units. The 9½ in Girling disc brakes were mounted outboard at the front and rear.

The power unit in the ordinary way was the Cosworth-developed Ford 1,098 cc engine, developing 100 bhp at 7,500 rpm, although the Cosworth in 997 cc or 1,470 cc engines were available as optional alternatives. Transmission was by a four-speed close-ratio gearbox/final drive unit based on either Renault or Volkswagen components and there was a modified Ford clutch.

Lotus fitted their familiar 'wobbly-web' four-stud cast magnesium wheels in 13 in size. Steering was by rack-and-pinion. The glass-fibre bodywork complied with the latest sports car racing regulations in relation to windscreen height, luggage space (which was provided alongside the engine), ground clearance and turning circle. The overall length of the 23 was 11 ft 8 in, the width was 4 ft 11½ in and the height to the top of the windscreen was 2 ft 3 in. Weight was 880 lb.

Early in 1962 John Blunsden testing an early 23 for *Sports Car* and his report was published in the March issue:

'Quite a time has passed since Colin Chapman's cars have played an important role in small-capacity sports car racing, but there is little doubt that, with the new type 23, Lotus comes back into the picture in a convincing way.

'Conforming to a pattern which was first demonstrated on the new Elva, and which is likely to be copied by other manufacturers in the near future, the new sports Lotus is based, as far as is practicable, on the current Junior. The Lotus goes further than the Elva in this respect, the engine and transmission units being common to both cars. . .

'Unlike the Junior, the type 23 has the Cosworth-Ford 1,097 cc engine mounted vertically in the frame, coupled to either a Renault or VW four-speed gearbox and final-drive unit. The prototype car, which was used for the test at Goodwood, featured the Renault box, and this puts the gear positions of the central lever in the "upside down" layout, with first and second on the right-hand side of the neutral gate and third and top to the left of the gate. First and third gears are forward, second and top back, as on a conventional layout.

'Although the central location of the lever has called for quite a complicated gear linkage, including two universal joints and three guides, the change retains a positive action, and despite the gate being fairly wide and the lever movement moderately long, only a light touch is called for.

'The gearing of the Renault box offers a ratio of 2.92, 1.81, 1.36 and 1.11 to 1, with a 4.37 to 1 final drive as standard. This gives a slightly closer box than the VW, but it is obvious that, due to the generous rev range offered by the engine, either box, despite only four speeds, will be more than adequate for all normal requirements.

'I understand that the use of the VW transmission has called for a minor redesign of the rubber couplings, which are fitted between the Lotus-designed side plates of the gearbox and the drive shafts. These couplings, which were first used by Lotus early last year on the Type 21 Formula cars, helped to remove some of the stresses from the transmission, and act as shock dampers in the power line itself. Whether it is due to these rubber units, or to the suspension geometry and tyre performance I would hesitate to suggest, but the Type 23 undoubtedly puts a lot of its engine power through the back wheels and on to the track, while gear changes at near maximum engine revs can be made with nearIturbine smoothness.

'Front suspension, with double wishbones and steeply inclined, coil-spring-damper units, based on that of the Mark 19 Monte Carlo, while the rear suspension with lower wishbones, parallel radius arms, inclined coil-damper units, and single upper transverse arms acting as lateral radius rods, is the same as used on the new Junior, and follows the pattern of last year's Formula 1 cars; new magnesium alloy hub castings are used at the rear.

'The spring stiffness and damper settings are slightly harder on the Type 23 than on the Type 22, and in fact are the same as used on last year's Junior. This gives the sports car quite a soft, but by no means spongy ride, although there is some body lean when indulging in spirited cornering, the twin anti-roll bars. . . ensure that the chassis movement does not get out of hand.

The cornering power of this car is such that most drivers will find themselves cornering on a geometrical line, coupled in the case of a car set up as tested, with a modest amount of understeer. An attempt to break away the rear of the car at Lavant Corner produced only a mild slide on a dry surface, which was killed by a small steering correction.

'I gained the impression that with the engine right in the "meaty" part of the power range a skilful driver would be able to sustain a slightly oversteering drift in classic style as an aid to cornering. . .

'Although already well used, the Cosworth-Ford engine, which is given a minimum pass-out figure of 95 horsepower at 7,400 rpm, had a usable rev range from about 3,000 rpm upwards, and an effective one from the 5,000 rpm mark up to the recommended maximum of 7,800 rpm. In other words there was ample "overlap" between the available gear ratios. Top sufficed from past the pits, through Madgwick and Fordwater, then third was used for St Mary's and Lavant, with top coming up almost immediately afterwards. Third came into use again for Woodcote and second for the chicane. . .

'It goes without saying that the brakes of the Type 23 are tremendous; I left the braking point for Woodcote later on every lap, and still found I could have gone even deeper into the bend before cutting off. . .

'Unlike the Junior the Type 23 calls for no contortions when climbing in or out although there is a frame diagonal ready to catch the right knee of unwary tall drivers. Once in position, there is complete freedom of movement for the feet, and the pedal layout should suit most people, although the stiffness of the accelerator pedal may be more than some drivers would like.

'The foam rubber padded and vynide trimmed glass-fibre seats are based on those used in the Lotus 21, and have high shoulder supports to hold the driver firmly through the bends. There is considerable wind protection from the three-piece screen, which blends in neatly with the rear bodywork instead of being an obvious appendage.

'There is a slight lip immediately above the instruments, which comprised a 9,000 rpm rev counter, flanked by an oil pressure gauge on the right and an ammeter on the left, with a water temperature gauge further over to the left. I understand that on future models the ammeter and thermometer are being transposed. The test car was also fitted with an oil temperature gauge, which was mounted in one of the flanged openings in the cockpit diaphragm, on the right-hand side. The ignition-starter switch is in the centre of the facia, and the minor hand controls, for lights etc, are of the now familiar tumbler pattern.

'The only serious criticism of the Type 23 was the level of exhaust noise which was transmitted into the cockpit. The reason for this, it seems, is that the exhaust pipe length was such that some of the gasses were being deflected by the rear panel of the car, which was acting as a type of echo chamber. An extra inch or so on the pipe will overcome this. The nearside cockpit door came unfastened during the test, and touched the ground as it trailed, but this was a prototype car, remember, and the fault is unlikely to be repeated on production versions.

'One or two minor modifications are being carried out as production gets under way, including the replacement of the wedge-shape tank behind the seats by a longitudinal tank on the near side, filling the space between the chassis frame and the outer skin of the glass-fibre bodywork. A supplementary right-hand tank will be available as an extra.

'There is no doubt whatever, that the Lotus 23 will be playing a leading role in the rejuvenated 1,100 cc sports-racing class this season, and although opinions seem to be divided on whether a Climax FWA or a production-type pushrod engine should be used for this class, the Lotus in its present form is unlikely to be an easy car to beat.'

Demand by private entrants for the new 23 was substantial and the cars were raced throughout the year with considerable success. In addition there were certain works entries made during the year, two of which created a very considerable impression, but for completely different reasons. At the Nürburgring 1,000 km race in May a 23 was entered by the Essex Racing Team but in reality was a works entry under the supervision of Mike Costin. This 23, to be driven by Jim Clark/Trevor Taylor, was fitted with the prototype Lotus twin-cam engine developed by Harry Mundy with a capacity of 1,498 cc and based on the new Ford 116E block. At this time this Ford engine had not even been announced in standard production form, as it was due to power the Ford Classic which was not revealed until July. Accordingly the block fitted to the car in Germany was claimed to be the smaller 109E block, although in fact the inscription 116E appeared clearly on the side of the engine. This car was also fitted with a Hewland five-speed gearbox which became standard on later 23s.

When the car arrived at the circuit it was not even completed and it missed practice on the Thursday. On the Saturday Clark lapped with the 23 in 9 min 48.9 sec, the fastest in the 2 litre sports car class and seventh fastest overall. Only 15 minutes before the race was started on the Sunday, rain began to fall and by the start the 14.17 mile circuit was completely wet. At the Le Mans start Clark was first to his car, but he fumbled his getaway and McLaren led through the South Turn in his Essex Racing Team-entered Aston Martin; then Clark forged ahead and by the end of the first lap had pulled out a lead over the entire field of 27 seconds. By the end of the second lap he had increased this lead to 47 seconds and by the end of lap four his lead was 78 seconds. As the race progressed so Clark extended his lead and after eight laps he was 2 minutes in front of the rest of the field. Now the circuit began to dry out and Mairesse with a 4 litre Ferrari came through to challenge for the lead, and by the end of lap eleven Clark's lead had been reduced to 42 seconds. Apart from the fact that circuit conditions now favoured the bigger cars, the exhaust pipe of the 23 had broken, fumes were being swept into the cockpit and Clark began to feel unwell. On the next lap Clark, badly affected by fumes, was unable to control a slide at the Kesselchen and the 23 slid into the ditch and out of the race. It was a disappointing end to a magnificent performance, but a very clear demonstration of the potential of the new Ford-based twin-cam engine and the 23 chassis. In this race the standard 23 entered by Ian Walker Racing and driven by Peter Ashdown/Bruce Johnstone won the class for sports cars up to 1,000 cc. A second Walker-entered car driven by Paul Hawkins/Peter Ryan set fastest lap in the class in 10 min 26.6 sec, whereas Clark's fastest lap with the new car was 9 min 46.3 sec (86.94 mph).

The second outing for a works-entered 23 in 1962 was at Le Mans where a 23 with 997 cc twin-cam engine was entered for Jim Clark/Trevor Taylor by Lotus Engineering Company Ltd. A second 23 in this race was the car entered by UDT-

Laystall Racing Team with 745 cc Coventry-Climax FWMC engine to be driven by Les Leston/Tony Shelly. However at the French classic race the 23s were in immediate problems with the scrutineers. The scrutineers rejected the cars because the front wheels had four-stud fixing and the rear wheels six-stud. The basis of the complaint was that the spare wheel could replace a wheel on one axle only. Accordingly Chapman immediately had the rear wheels modified to a four-stud fixing. The officials then refused absolutely to examine the cars, pointing out that they had already been rejected and adding the rider that since the wheels had originally been designed for a six-stud fixing, modifications to four-stud made the 23s unsafe. Chapman protested vehemently, Dean Delamont of the RAC flew over to argue with the officials but they were not prepared to listen to any arguments. It was only too obvious that the Automobile Club de L'Ouest were not interested in reasonable arguments and behind their attitude was the desire to protect interests of the French entrants René Bonnet and Panhard in the Index of Performance. Although Chapman announced originally that Lotus would take legal proceedings against the organizing club, later saner counsels prevailed and Chapman contented himself with the statement that he would never again enter the Le Mans race.

At Clermont-Ferrand on 15 July two 23s were entered in the GT and sports car race. Paul Hawkins retired the Ian Walker-entered car with gearbox trouble, but Alan Rees, who took over the works twin-cam 23, after Peter Arundell had crashed in the Formula Junior race, finished second to the winning Ferrari, despite never having sat in the car before he went out to the grid.

On 29 September Jim Clarke drove a 23 entered by the Essex Racing Team with 1,500 cc push-rod engine in the *Autosport* Three Hours Race at Snetterton but was plagued by gearbox trouble. He stalled the car on the grid, sat there whilst the rest of the field streamed past and joined the race trying desperately to make up ground. By lap seven he was in second place, but then spun off as a result of a loose fuel filler cap allowing petrol to spray on to the rear tyres. He set off again after the leaders and by lap thirty was ahead of the field. As Clark's gearbox trouble became worse and worse and the 23 slowed more and more, the Ferrari of Parkes went into the lead. Eventually Clark stopped at the start/finish line and pushed the car across when the chequered flag fell, too far behind to feature in the results. In the Paris 1,000 km race at Montlhéry on 21 October the 23 that had been entered by the UDT-Laystall Racing Team at Le Mans, but now fitted with a 997 cc twin-cam engine, was driven by José Rosinki/Bernard Consten. The French pair drove a steady race to finish eleventh overall and win the 1,000 cc sports class.

Of the many 23s raced in British events during the year, the most successful were the two Ian Walker-entered cars and Mike Beckwith's car sponsored by car dealers Normand Ltd. During the year this car fitted with Cosworth-developed wet-sump 1,100 cc engine and four-speed Renault gearbox, scored a total of twenty class and outright wins, five second places, one third place and two fourth places. In addition Beckwith set class lap records at Snetterton, Goodwood, Oulton Park, Castle Combe and Silverstone.

Above left *The 23 made its mark in the 1962 Nürburgring 1,000 km race; Jim Clark led the opening laps of this race with the car entered by the Essex Racing Team and powered by the new twin-cam 1,500 cc engine.* (LAT.)

Right *Colin Chapman talks things over with Jim Clark.* (Geoffrey Goddard.)

For 1963 the 23 featured a strengthened and more rigid chassis and was now fitted as standard with the 1,594 cc Lotus-Ford twin-cam engine and Hewland five-speed gearbox. In this form it was known as the 23B. Throughout the year the most successful team was the Normand Racing Team which fielded three 23Bs for Mike Beckwith, Tony Hegbourne and, when his Formula One and other commitments permitted, Jim Clark. At Oulton Park on 6 April Clark won the 102 mile sports car race with a Normand 23 from Beckwith's Normand car in second place and other

Jim Clark at the wheel of a Lotus 23 at the Gold Cup meeting at Oulton Park on 1 September 1962. This car was fitted with a new body after a crash in practice and after problems sorting out the gears at the start of the race Clark came through to finish second to Innes Ireland in a Lotus 19. (T. C. March.)

23s driven by Bloor and Keith Greene third and fourth. At the Crystal Palace on Whit Monday Clark won the 36-lap Crystal Palace Trophy after Salvadori's Cooper Monaco retired with transmission trouble, setting a class lap record of 85.37 mph, with other 23s driven by Beckwith, Greene, and Bloor in second, third and fourth places. Clark also won the *Autosport* Three Hours Race at Snetterton on 28 September from the Ferrari 250GTO of Mike Parkes. In all the Normand Racing Team made nearly fifty starts during the year, and took fifteen first places and eight lap records. In club racing Jack Pearce with a 23B scored a whole string of successes.

The best continental result was in the Nurburgring 500 km race in which Fritz Baumann finished second to the Fiat-Abarth of Pilette/Herrmann. In Scandinavia Josefsson won races at both Karlskoga and Roskilde in Denmark, while Scheiber won at Zeltweg in Austria. It was in Austria that Toni Fischaber raced a 23B powered by a

At Oulton Park in September 1963 are Jim Clark (above), who finished second to Salvadori's Cooper Monaco, and Paul Hawkins (below) who finished eighth and won the 1,150 cc class with a Lotus 23B. (T. C. March.)

1.8 litre BMW engine and in Italy Cesare Topetti raced a 23 powered by a Giannini engine with considerable success.

Although the Ian Walker team concentrated on racing sports Brabhams in 1963, it had retained a 23 and Graham Hill drove this in the Canadian Grand Prix on the Mosport circuit near Toronto on 28 September. Hill had chosen to race the Lotus because the Brabham which he had intended to drive had been crashed heavily by Frank Gardner at Oulton Park on 21 September and though completely rebuilt in the space of less than a week, was handling far from well. This 246 mile race was won by Pedro Rodriguez at the wheel of a Ferrari 250P, but Hill took second place, 1 minute 39 seconds in arrear. A week later Hill drove Winklemann Racing's 2 litre Climax-powered 23 in the North West Grand Prix at Kent, Washington, but retired because of transmission problems. At the Riverside Grand Prix at Riverside Raceway in California on 13 October Clark drove a new 23B borrowed from the local Lotus dealer who was about to deliver it to a customer in place of the Arciero brothers' 23 with 2.7-litre Climax engine which was not running well enough to qualify as a starter. Clark finished fifth overall and won the 2 litre class. Graham Hill drove Walker's 23B at both Riverside and at Laguna Seca, but retired in both events. However in the Pacific Grand Prix at Laguna Seca Tim Mayer with an ex-Normand 23 won the 2 litre class (finishing sixth overall) and he also finished third overall in the 252 mile Nassau Trophy race in the Bahamas. Another success by a 23 in 1963 was Peter Warr's win with a 1,650 cc push-rod Ford-engined 23 in the Japanese Grand Prix at Suzuka from Arthur Owen and Mike Knight, both also at the wheel of 23s.

The 23 remained in production until 1966 and a total of 131 cars were built, including the original 23s. The cars continued to enjoy many successes in minor events and in 1964 Peter Gethin, later a member of the BRM works team, won the Guards Sports Car Championship with his 23. In 1965 there were also a number of interesting variants of the 23 theme.

Perhaps the most eccentric of these was a 23 fitted with an engine formed by six Ariel Arrow motor cycle engines. forming a twelve-cylinder two-stroke engine of 1,482 cc. The engines were each inclined outwards at 45°, so that the angle between the cylinders was 90°. Each engine had a straight-toothed pinion on its main shaft which engaged with a similar pinion on a shaft running down the centre of the engine . The gears were enclosed in housings and the shaft had a flywheel on the end which carried the single dry-plate clutch and drove the two distributors for the electronic ignition system by toothed belts. Transmission was by a Hewland five-speed gearbox. This engine made an incredible noise and it was extremely difficult to identify whether the engine was running on all twelve cylinders and, if it was not, which cylinders were not working. To settle this difficulty a system of thermocouplers was used whereby lamps on the instrument panel indicated if any of the exhaust branches were not maintaining working temperature. The engine was the work of R. V. Marchant and the Lotus was driven by Bill Hill. It was known as the Rotorvic. It was tested at Snetterton, but there is no record of it having been raced.

Another interesting variant was the Lotus-Brabham-BMW raced by Chris Williams. It featured a strengthened Lotus 23 chassis and suspension, Brabham

McArthur with a 1.6 litre 23B leads Youlten's Lola in the sports car race at the Silverstone meeting in May 1964. (T. C. March.)

wheels and disc brakes and 2 litre BMW engine. R. Harvey-Bailey had built up a 23 with a 2 litre V8 Climax engine by former Team Elite Manager Cyril Embrey. This used an ex Bowmaker-Yeoman Formula One engine enlarged to two litres by Alan Smith. The engine ran on four Weber carburettors, although the constructors were planning to fit fuel injection. The chassis incorporated Lotus 19 components, Formula One-type Girling disc brakes were fitted and the body was widened and the chassis modified to take the engine.

In 1966 the Lotus 23 was still winning and Ken Crook took a victory in the Guards Championship. Another successful development of the 23 was the car built by Vegantune with a 1 litre BRM Formula Two engine, driven by Tommy Weber. John Markey also developed a 23 in enclosed form as a Group 6 Prototype, fully complying with the international regulations.

The 23 was the last successful sports-racing car built by Lotus and it came close to recapturing much of the mystique and brilliance the Lotus had displayed in the 1950s. However, Lotus ambitions were more and more closely focused on Formula One and production cars. The emphasis had shifted as the company had grown.

Chapter 11

The 30 and 40, 1964-65

During the early 1960s there was strong growth in interest in Group 7 sports car racing, mainly with cars powered by big push-rod American engines. The trend had started by the installation of American V8s in such cars as the Lotus 19, Bruce McLaren stimulated the trend when be bought Roger Penske's Zerex Special and raced it with an Oldsmobile engine, the first McLaren proper appeared in the autumn of 1964 and Lola joined in with the T70 in 1965. However, Colin Chapman was one of the first to see the potential for this class of car and the Lotus 30 was one of the earliest of the type to be built—but also one of the least successful.

Chapman had conceived a backbone-type chassis, similar to that used on the Lotus Elan, and although chief designer Len Terry was convinced that this was a thoroughly bad idea for a big sports-racing car, both from the point of view of stiffness and construction problems, Chapman was the boss and inevitably he had his way. A deep box-section girder, flanged and baffled for stiffness and panelled in 20 gauge mild steel sheet, formed the backbone of the chassis. Although this girder-section was 12 in deep, it was only 6 in wide at the top and 9½ in wide at the bottom. At the front of the backbone a transverse box-section mounted the front suspension, while at the rear extensions from the main backbone forked outwards to mount the engine.

At the front Chapman used unequal-length double wishbones and coil spring/damper units and at the rear there were upper wishbones, reversed lower wishbones, lower radius rods that passed through slots in the forked members and coil spring/damper units. Within the backbone structure there was housed a 13 gallon rubberized fuel tank, but there was provision for additional 9 gallon tanks to be mounted within the door sills. There was a one-piece glass-fibre bodyshell straddling the backbone of the chassis. The wheels, similar to Lotus Indianapolis designs, were 13 in and there were Girling 11 in disc brakes. There were twin radiators mounted in the nose behind the twin air intakes.

Because of his connections with the American Ford company through collaboration over the Indianapolis Lotus entries, Chapman had little difficulty in obtaining Ford V8 engines at a very favourable price. Lotus bought the standard 4,727 cc V8s (289 cubic in) in the so-called Hi-Performance form in which power output was about 271 bhp. Lotus carried out their own modifications to the engine, including the fitting of four downdraught Weber carburettors and as raced the Ford engine developed about 350 bhp. Transmission was by a ZF five-speed all-synchromesh gearbox and final drive.

Two views of Jim Clark with the Lotus 30 Series 2 in the 1965 Tourist Trophy at Oulton Park.
(T. C. March.)

The wheelbase was 7 ft 10½ in, front and rear track 4 ft 5 in and overall length 13 ft 9 in. The weight was around 1,550 lb. In component form Lotus offered the 30 for a mere £3,495 and this was clearly not an economic proposition. The chassis was expensive to manufacture and necessitated the purchase of special equipment and the ZF trans-axles were also an expensive item. During the production run of the 30 in 1964 a total of 21 cars were built.

In April 1964 the 30 was first entered by Ian Walker-Team Lotus and driven by Jim Clark at the '200' meeting at Aintree. The car was not completed when it arrived and there was an immense amount of work to be done in the paddock. Clark was forced to practise with John Coundley's Lotus 19 and as a result he started from the back of the grid. Despite brake and gearbox problems (after the race Clark admitted that he was never quite sure what gear he was in) he came through the field to finish second to Bruce McLaren at the wheel of the latest Cooper Monaco.

The 30 was next entered at the International Trophy meeting at Silverstone, but failed to make the start because of problems with the Tecalemit-Jackson fuel injection that was now fitted. One success was achieved and at Mallory Park on 16 May Clark won the sports car race from Roy Pierpoint's Attila Mk3-Ford. At the Martini meeting at Silverstone the car was driven by Trevor Taylor, but was put out of the running by clutch problems. Subsequently this car was destroyed in a practice crash with Tony Hegbourne at the wheel at Brands Hatch and the Walker team, already suffering a number of other problems, withdrew from racing.

The 30 next appeared at the Guards Trophy at Brands Hatch on August Bank Holiday with Jim Clark at the wheel. It was slow in practice, failed to move off the line at the start because fuel was vapourizing in the fuel pump and covered only nine laps—during which time it made five pit stops! The race was won by McLaren's Cooper-Zerex-Oldsmobile. On 29 August Clark was again at the wheel of the 30, in the Tourist Trophy at Goodwood. Although the car was still plagued by overheating problems Clark was second fastest in practice at 1 min 23.8 sec (McLaren took pole position with a time of 1 min 23.2 sec), he took the lead on lap sixteen, lost it during a routine pit stop, regained it from Graham Hill's Ferrari and then stopped again at the pits. After this second routine pit stop there was difficulty in restarting the car and eventually Clark, his lead of over a lap now diminished to third place a minute behind Hill, rejoined the race to chase after the leaders. Another pit stop for attention to the suspension followed (a wishbone pin had fallen out of the nearside front), once more the car was difficult to start, the battery had to be changed and Clark rejoined the race to finish twelfth. It had in fact been a very encouraging performance, for the Lotus had averaged 98.84 mph for the first 75 laps including the pit stop (180 miles) and at the chequered flag had covered 271 miles, albeit 17 laps in arrear of the winner.

On 26 September Clark drove the 30 on its first American outing in the 250 mile Canadian Grand Prix at Mosport Park. The 30 was plagued by overheating both in practice and the race; it stalled at the start, causing a four-car pile-up and was out of the race after only a few laps. Clark next appeared with the 30 in the *Los Angeles Times* Grand Prix at Riverside Raceway in California and, despite the fact that the car was still suffering overheating problems, he managed to finish third in this 200 mile

Left *Conference in the pits—Clark and Chapman discuss the shortcomings of the Lotus 30 Series 2 at the Tourist Trophy in 1965. (T. C. March.)*

Right *Jack Sears at the wheel of the Team Lotus-entered 30 Series 2 in the sports car race at Silverstone in May 1965. He finished third. (T. C. March.)*

Below right *Bob Bondurant at the wheel of the Willment-entered Lotus 30 Series 2 at the Grand Prix meeting at Silverstone in July 1965. He was disqualified for receiving a push-start after the engine had failed to fire. (T. C. March.)*

race behind Parnelli-Jones (Cooper) and Penske (Chaparral). Next came the Monterey Grand Prix at Laguna Seca where Clark's 30, now acquired by Bob Challman, Lotus distributor on the West Coast, was driven by Billy Krause who finished fourth in the first heat. The winner of both heats was Penske (Chaparral). Krause retired early in the second heat.

In the meanwhile David Prophet, the first British private owner of a 30, took his car to South Africa for a series of races, starting with the Rand Nine Hours Event, but he achieved no success apart from a win in the Rhodesian Grand Prix and his car needed a new chassis on its return to the United Kingdom.

Early racing outings with the 30 had only too quickly revealed its many shortcomings. Lack of stiffness in the chassis had soon revealed itself and after the first three cars had been completed all subsequent 30s had considerably stiffened chassis with 18 gauge panelling. For 1965 Lotus introduced the 30 Series 2. The chassis was much revised. At the rear the bridge bolted between the forks of the chassis and mounting the gearbox, which meant that the rear suspension had to be removed before the transmision could be worked on, was dispensed with. Repiping of the radiator system was believed to have cured the overheating and 10¼ in ventilated Girling disc brakes were now fitted front and rear. On the cars entered by the works larger 15 in wheels were fitted. There was new bodywork with an upswept tail spoiler and a roll-over bar was fitted to comply with American regulations. Tecalemit-Jackson fuel injection was now standard and power output had been boosted to 360 bhp. Among buyers of the Series 2, of which twelve were built, were the JCB Excavator Company whose car was driven by Trevor Taylor (the first car was written off in testing with Peter Sadler at the wheel and Lotus were glad to supply a replacement), the Willment organization and John Dean.

It soon became obvious that the 30 was no match for the new McLarens and Lolas. Apart from the fact that the iron block Ford engine in the 30 was very much on the heavy side, the opposition's Chevrolet and Oldsmobile engines had more litres and more power. Some success was, however, achieved. On 20 March Jim Clark won the rain-soaked Senior Service '200' race at Silverstone that was stopped short after

Above *John Dean's Lotus 30 at Silverstone in July 1965. Dean retired with mechanical problems.* (T. C. March.)

Below *The infamous Lotus 40 with Jim Clark at the wheel at Brands Hatch in August 1965. (LAT.)*

eighteen laps and Clark also won the Lavant Cup at Goodwood on Easter Monday. In the Tourist Trophy, now held as a Group 7 race at Oulton Park, Clark drove in practice a 30 fitted with a new 5.3 litre engine, an attempt to match the power of the 30's rivals, but this blew up in a spectacular fashion and he started the race with a 4.7 litre unit installed. Clark led the first two-hour heat, but was forced to stop at the pits because of a loose rear wishbone, rejoining to finish sixteenth. In the second heat Clark fought his way through from the back of the grid, spinning at Esso bend, and leading McLaren until the 30's gearbox broke.

At the International Trophy meeting at Silverstone Jack Sears drove the Team Lotus 30 (Clark was of course committed to the Formula One event) and finished third behind McLaren and High Dibley (Lola). At Mallory Park in June Frank Gardner with the red Willment car won the second heat of the Guards Trophy, but as he had retired in the first heat because of a sheared fuel pump drive, he was out of the results on aggregate. At the Grand Prix meeting at Silverstone Trevor Taylor with the JCB entry finished second in the sports car race behind Coundley's McLaren, but the works McLaren and the Team Surtees Lola did not run because of lack of starting money and there were only fifteen runners, mainly mediocre. During practice for the Martini meeting at Silverstone the JCB car caught fire and Trevor Taylor had a very lucky escape. The highest Lotus finisher in the Martini race was David Prophet in fifth place with his Series 1 car.

In a desperate effort to retrieve the situation Lotus hastily produced the 40 with strengthened chassis, minor suspension modifications, the 5.3 litre engine and the much beefier Hewland LG500 transmission; the body was modified so that the two huge 'stack' exhaust megaphones could rear upwards through the engine cover. The new car made its debut in the Austrian Grand Prix at Zeltweg on 22 August driven by Mike Spence. Spence took pole position in practice and led until eliminated by engine overheating. On August Bank Holiday Monday the 40, now apparently fitted with a 5,754 cc engine claimed to develop 500 bhp (that was highly improbable), was driven in the Guards Trophy at Brands Hatch by Jim Clark. The race was run in two heats; in the first Clark spun twice before retiring with broken gear linkage and in the second heat he suffered brake problems and was apparently eliminated by final drive failure. *Autosport*, rather understating the position, commented, 'Obviously this design will have to be further modified before long.'

Clark was scheduled to drive a 40 in the North West Grand Prix at Kent, Washington, but failed to appear, allegedly because the car had been damaged during testing in England. He did however appear at Riverside, where a second 40 was entered for Richie Ginther, and a new 40 painted pale blue had been delivered to Holmann & Moody for A. J. Foyt to drive. Clark finished second, Ginther retired, describing the 40 as 'the 30 with ten more mistakes', and Foyt's car was wrecked in practice when it crashed with Bob Tattersall at the wheel.

Already Chapman had decided to abandon the 40, only too well aware of its many shortcomings and, apart from anything else, lack of trade support had meant that Group 7 racing came to an end in Britain in 1965. The 40 was the last sports-racing car to be built by Lotus.

Appendix 1

Contemporary Lotus Road Tests

The Lotus, *Autosport* 2 October 1953

AUTOSPORT, OCTOBER 2, 1953

JOHN BOLSTER

TESTS

THE

LOTUS

HEY PRESTO!: "Magician" John Bolster demonstrates the lightness of the Lotus frame; weight is 55 lb. bare, 90 lb. with panels and brackets.

AT the Crystal Palace on 19th September, we beheld an astonishing sight. During a sports car race, in which some of the "hottest" 1½-litre machines in the country were engaged, a vehicle propelled by a *side-valve* Ford 10 engine, linered down to 1,100 c.c., proved itself capable of fighting it out with the best. This was what a contemporary described as, "the preposterously fast Lotus," and it was the talk of the paddock afterwards.

Naturally, I was duly impressed with these goings-on, as seen from my commentator's box, and so it came to pass that I arranged to borrow this little projectile for a week of varied motoring. I had observed that, in the very skilled hands of Colin Chapman, the Lotus appeared to possess the most phenomenal road-holding, braking and cornering power. What I wanted to know was whether it would do the same sort of thing for me, or if it were all much more difficult than it looked.

At this point, it might be as well to digress and give a brief explanation of the Lotus set-up. In the first place, it must be made clear that the Lotus Engineering Co., Ltd., of 7 Tottenham Lane, Hornsey, N.8, do not supply complete cars. Their main product is a space-type, multi-tube frame, to which you fit your own machinery. They will carry out certain modifications to your components for you, but it is up to you to acquire such things as engine, axles and wheels, either new or second-hand, in the open market. The thing has been found to work out more satisfactorily that way, from every point of view, and it avoids the interference with production and skyrocketing costs that the incorporation of customers' own ideas usually

entails. In other words, Colin Chapman will sell you a chassis frame for £110 and tell you how to make the best use of it, but he won't complete your car for you or furnish a kit of parts.

The Lotus chassis is extremely rigid and very light, which are the main essentials of any sports car frame. It weighs 55 lb., bare, or 90 lb. complete with all mounting brackets and stressed panels. A standardized bonnet, mudguards and floor tunnel are available from a neighbouring coachbuilder, and when these are added the total weight is 120 lb. A Ford Eight or 10 rear axle is normally used, though the torque tube and propeller shaft must be shortened. Similarly, a Ford front axle is employed, and is converted to swing-axle i.f.s. by dividing the main beam and the track rod, and modifying the radius arms. Messrs. Lotus will do all this for £15 10s., and they will shorten your prop. shaft and torque tube for £2 10s. and £3 10s. respectively. I have no room to go into further details, but suffice it to say that all the necessary parts are easily available, and no welding or machining are called for in assembly.

Such proprietary power units as the M.G., the Ford Consul, or, of course, the ubiquitous Ford 10, will "drop straight in", so to speak. To give some idea of the expense involved, a Ford 10-powered car, complete with hood, screen and full equipment, could be built, with all new material, for about £425. Naturally, such things as engine tuning and close ratio gears would be added to choice.

"My" Lotus had a Ford 10 engine which had been warmed up as far as the "1,172 Formula" allows. It had an aluminium cylinder head, raised compression ratio, larger inlet valves than standard, and double valve springs. It had twin S.U. carburetters mounted on a flexible induction system, to avoid frothing of the fuel

★

WEATHERPROOF: With hood up, the Lotus occupants are well protected from the elements, while headroom is adequate.

★

AUTOSPORT, OCTOBER 2, 1953

from vibration. Two separate exhaust manifolds paired cylinders 1 and 4, 2 and 3, as is correct practice.

The three-speed Ford gearbox was converted to close ratios by the use of Buckler C-type gears. A remote control was mounted on top of the propeller shaft tunnel, which was of considerable height, due to the general low build. The rear axle had been fitted with a 4.7 to 1 final drive.

On the road, the performance just didn't make sense! I have driven many Ford 10-engined cars—in fact I own one myself—but this was an entirely different experience. At the very bottom end, it had not perhaps quite the "stepaway" of the standard job, and the tick-over was a little lumpy. Once on the move, however, the little thing screamed away at apparently unlimited revs. I would say that the unit peaked around 6,000 r.p.m., but the owner told me that I could exceed "seven thou." if I felt like it. As that would be equivalent to 84 m.p.h. in second gear, it will be realized that this is quite a car!

The total weight of only 8½ cwts. gives the willing power unit every chance to show its paces. The acceleration is even better than the figures in the data panel indicate, for the very high bottom gear makes considerable slipping of the clutch essential on get-away. However, that component seemed to have no objection to such rough treatment, in spite of the many standing starts that are entailed when taking the average of a number of runs in both directions. The mean maximum speed was 88 m.p.h., and I frequently exceeded 90 m.p.h. under favourable conditions. After all that, I had to have another look under the bonnet and, yes, it really was a side-valve.

In close-ratio form, the Ford gearbox gave a very easy change between top and second, the synchromesh operating well. First speed was a little less easy to engage, and one had to judge the relative speeds fairly accurately if noiseless meshing of the pinions was to be secured. By pressing the lever to the right, the shift from bottom to second went through in one quick, clean movement.

The suspension was fairly firm without being in any way harsh, and the ride was level and free from pitching. The springing was by helical springs all round, with telescopic hydraulic dampers. At the rear, lateral location of the axle was by a Panhard rod, and alternative holes were provided in its brackets, so that the roll centre could be raised or lowered to choice. In front, the divided axle automatically gave a high roll centre, and certainly the machine remained on an even keel while cornering.

To begin with, the steering felt a little unusual. The Burman box gave light operation and a moderate degree of caster return action but, at low speeds only, one felt that there was a slight tendency to wander. As soon as one became used to the general "feel" of the car, that tendency entirely disappeared, and one was free to enjoy the very exceptional cornering powers provided. This car has just enough under-steer for stability, and no more. What is so uncanny is the exemplary behaviour of the rear end. Thus, although a corner may be taken with the back wheels definitely sliding, a complete breakaway does not occur. Once one has learned that the machine will not "swop ends", the curves may be swerved with a very great degree of abandon indeed.

The standard Ford brakes are comparatively enormous, having regard to the weight to be stopped. More elaborate equipment is available, but I would

POWER PACK: The Ford 10 engine in the car tested had an aluminium head, twin carburetters and other "mods".

regard the present arrangement as entirely adequate for any type of competition. The brakes may be applied at maximum speed without inducing any deviation or patter; that comes from the positive location of the axles.

The very low seating position was comfortable, and the steering wheel was ideally placed for "doing a Farina". At the outset, the pedal department seemed rather full of feet, but I soon became accustomed to the fairly narrow space. The weather protection, with hood and side flaps in position, was much better than one would expect, even though a slight defect in the body allowed some water to enter my right shoe during heavy rain.

As Mr. Chapman has no intention at present of invading the Rolls-Royce and Bristol market, he has given a little less attention than those two manufacturers to sound deadening and exhaust silencing. In consequence, particularly at peak revs. with the hood up, one can definitely hear the machinery at work, to put it mildly. Let us remember, though, that I took over the car exactly as it was raced at Crystal Palace, apart from the replacement of the hood and screen, and for touring purposes one could easily fit larger silencers.

I feel that the Lotus is the best attempt yet to provide the enthusiast with a competition car at a price he can afford to pay. In essentials, it is just as sound an engineering job as the most expensive sports car, and the economy is only brought about by the clever adaptation of mass-produced components. Its excellent handling qualities ensure not only that the driver is safe and enjoyable motoring, but that he will automatically receive the right sort of training, with nothing to unlearn if he graduates to big-time racing. It is a fine little road car, too, and lots of fun to drive.

SPECIFICATION AND PERFORMANCE DATA

Car Tested: Lotus Sports two-seater (for price, etc., see text).

Engine: Four cylinders, 61.5 x 92.5 mm. (1,099 c.c.). Side-valves. 8½ to 1 compression ratio. Approx. 40 b.h.p. at 6,000 r.p.m. Twin horizontal 1¼-in. S.U. carburetters. Lucas coil and distributor.

Transmission: Single plate clutch. Three-speed gearbox with central remote control, ratios 4.7, 6.2 and 10.8 to 1. Torque tube transmission and spiral bevel final drive.

Chassis: Multi-tubular construction with stressed-skin panels. Swing axle i.f.s. and conventional beam rear axle. Helical springs front and rear surrounding Woodhead Monroe telescopic dampers. Front swing axles located by radius arms, and rear axle positioned by torque tube and Panhard rod. Cable operated Girling brakes, 10 x 1¼ in. 4.50 x 15 in. front tyres and 5.25 x 15 in. rear tyres on bolt-on disc wheels.

Equipment: 6-volt lighting and starting. Speedometer, revolution counter, ammeter, oil and water temperature and oil pressure gauges.

Dimensions: Wheelbase, 7 ft. 3½ ins. Track, front, 4 ft. 1 in., rear, 3 ft. 9 ins. Weight, as tested, 8½ cwts.

Performance: Maximum speed 88 m.p.h. Speeds in gears, 2nd 75 m.p.h., 1st 40 m.p.h. Acceleration, 0-50 m.p.h. 9½ secs., 0-60 m.p.h. 12⅜ secs., 0-70 m.p.h. 16⅜ secs.

Fuel Consumption: 40 m.p.g.

Lotus Mark 8, *Autosport* 19 November 1954

AUTOSPORT, NOVEMBER 19, 1954

HAVING WONDERFUL TIME: The Lotus, writes the author, "obviously enjoyed some rapid laps of the Brands Hatch road circuit". One suspects Bolster found the experience enjoyable also.

with two 1¼ in. S.U. carburetters. The connecting rods are special, but the crankshaft is standard. This unit develops around 85 b.h.p. at 6,200 r.p.m.

It is not the maximum b.h.p. which first impresses the driver, however, but the astonishing torque of the engine in the middle ranges. Right from 1,800 r.p.m. upwards it pulls strongly, and top

JOHN BOLSTER TESTS
THE LOTUS Mk. VIII

Low Weight and Efficient Aerodynamics Give Over 120 m.p.h. from 85 b.h.p. in Competition-Proved 1½-litre Sports Car

EVERYBODY who takes the slightest interest in motor racing knows Colin Chapman's streamlined Lotus. This phenomenally successful 1½-litre sports-racing car has had a most spectacular season, in which victories and record laps have abounded. Perhaps its defeat of a formidable German car at Silverstone was its greatest triumph, but even more valuable data was gained on those occasions when things did not go so well.

As a result of the concentrated experience that this car has provided, an improved version is now in steady production. It was the hard-worked prototype, however, that I took over recently for a busy week of varied motoring. It carried me to various social occasions in London's West End (perhaps you saw it parked outside the "Steering Wheel"). It was used for long, fast journeys, it was put through its paces against the watch, and it obviously enjoyed some rapid laps of the Brands Hatch road circuit. Before discussing these activities, however, let us take a brief look at the design of the car.

The basis of the machine is a rigid, multi-tubular chassis. The front wheels pivot on swing axles, which are supported on helical springs embracing telescopic dampers. At the rear the final drive gear housing is solidly mounted on the frame, and carries the brakes, which obtain their cooling air from an aperture in the undershield. Behind this assembly is the de Dion tube, which has fore and aft location by parallel trailing arms, and is positioned laterally by a central sliding block. The axle is hung on bell cranks, which compress a single helical spring. This layout gives no roll stiffness, but in production cars a modified arrangement does provide some roll resistance. The front end geometry has also been slightly amended to correspond, and new tubular half shafts eradicate a previous weakness.

The body is one of the most important features. It is scientifically streamlined as a result of a mathematical design approach, followed by wind tunnel tests and the photography of woollen tufts during actual racing. It has a wide but shallow air entry and two large stabilizing fins above and behind the enclosed back wheels. There is ample room for the two occupants and some luggage space, but the passenger's seat is normally covered during racing. This body can also be fitted to the Mark VI chassis.

Various engines may be installed in the Lotus by the owner, including 2-litre Bristol, 1½-litre Connaught, Turner, and M.G., and the 1,100 c.c. Coventry Climax. The Climax-engined car is also sold complete for £1,150, though purchase tax must then be added to this figure. I hope to test the 1,100 c.c. car later on, but as the present test refers to the M.G. version, a short description of this power unit is indicated.

The block is a standard one, bored and fitted with cast iron liners for strength, with Cromard liners therein. In this slightly laborious fashion the 66.5 mm. bore is increased to 72 mm., and the ex-1¼-litre engine approaches 1½ litres. There are no water passages through the gasket, these being external. The head is a light alloy Laystall-Lucas, with special Lotus valve gear and a racing camshaft. It gives a compression ratio of 9 to 1 and its enlarged ports are mated

gear may be engaged at quite low speeds, the half-ton car accelerating strongly on this ratio. Any premium grade fuel may be used, without a sign of pinking, though running-on does sometimes occur when switching off. The engine revs freely, and I went up to 6,000 r.p.m. on the gears during the performance tests. While timing the maximum speed, the rev. counter remained steady at about 6,500 r.p.m. so a slightly higher gear ratio might increase the already excellent figure.

The streamlining must be very efficient, for to exceed 120 m.p.h. on 85 b.h.p. is a phenomenal achievement. Another virtue of this body shape is its directional stability. In spite of the extremely light weight and short wheelbase, I have never driven any car which was steadier at two miles a minute. One simply sits back in comfort, well protected by the high body sides, and the machine rides absolutely level, ironing out the bumps in a most praiseworthy manner. At high speeds some engine vibration can be felt, which is probably "telephoned" down the propeller shaft to the chassis-mounted differential.

At lower speeds the "streamliner" is at

CLOSE CONFINES beneath the Lotus bonnet, showing the very low and forward-mounted radiator, the long helical springs of the front suspension, and the increased-bore, 1½-litre-type M.G. engine of 1,467 c.c.

first less easy to handle than the earlier Lotus cars. I think that this is probably due to the unusually light steering, with very little caster return action. At all events, I soon became accustomed to the handling, and the initial tendency to wander disappeared. The controls are all well placed, the steering wheel is arranged for the modern straight-arm technique, and the aerodynamic body does not impede the driver's view.

The acceleration is tremendous, even in the upper speed ranges. The time of 15.5 secs. for the standing quarter-mile deserves special emphasis, and it was only made possible by the virtual absence of wheelspin. Not only does the de Dion axle confer its usual advantages, but the petrol tank, battery and spare wheel all lie behind the beam. This puts the weight where it is wanted for maximum traction.

From a racing point of view, such a getaway is very valuable, for a lead snatched on the starting grid may be decisive in a hard-fought race. It also pays dividends after sharp corners, for full throttle may be applied far earlier than with a conventional rear axle.

The well-known M.G. gearbox gives an easy change, and the ratios suit the Lotus very well. The clutch has a short pedal travel and is most positive in action, which makes it far more suitable for

ACCELERATION GRAPH OF THE 1½-LITRE LOTUS MK. VIII

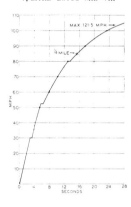

only became really noisy at full throttle, and I never had occasion to change a sparking plug. Nevertheless, it is as an extremely potent competition machine that most people will buy this car, and for this purpose it really has all the essentials. One does feel that this is a scientifically designed vehicle, and not the "lucky accident" that some sports cars really are.

Above all, I am completely converted to the fully aerodynamic type of body. It gives so much extra speed, and such improved stability that one would be foolish to ignore its advantages except on the very slowest circuits. It certainly gives the brakes a harder task, but these proved quite adequate on the car under review, though requiring fairly heavy pedal pressure. The new larger drums of the production cars should be a worthwhile improvement.

The Mark VIII Lotus is a sports-racing car that must be seriously considered by anybody who is in the market for a competition machine. Whatever engine he may choose, he can be certain that this chassis and body will give it every chance to distinguish itself. I shall remember its incredible steadiness at maximum speed, and the ease with which it can be taken round appreciable curves at over 100 m.p.h., for a long time.

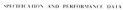

SPECIFICATION AND PERFORMANCE DATA

Car Tested: Lotus Mark VIII Sports 2-seater. Price (component form, without engine), £500.

Engine: Four cylinders. 72 mm. x 90 mm. (1,467 c.c.). Pushrod-operated valves in light alloy head. 85 b.h.p. at 6,200 r.p.m. 9 to 1 compression ratio. Twin 1⅛ in. SU carburetters. Lucas coil and distributor.

Transmission: Borg and Beck racing clutch. Four-speed gearbox with central remote control and synchromesh on upper three gears, ratios 4.1, 5.5, 8.0, and 13.8 to 1. Open Hardy Spicer propeller shaft to chassis-mounted final bevel and differential unit. Articulated shafts to rear hubs.

Chassis: Multi-tubular space frame. Independent front suspension by swing axles, helical springs, and telescopic dampers. Rear suspension by de Dion axle, bell cranks, single helical spring, and piston-type dampers. Lockheed hydraulic brakes in Al-fin drums, 2¾ in front, inboard mounted at rear, 9 ins. x 1¾ ins. (11 ins. x 2¼ ins. on production cars). 4.50-15 ins. front, 5.25-15 ins. rear tyres on bolt-on wire wheels (knock-on hubs for production cars).

Equipment: 12-volt lighting and starting, speedometer, revolution counter, oil pressure and temperature, water temperature, and fuel gauges.

Dimensions: Wheelbase, 7 ft. 3½ ins.; track, front 4 ft. 0½ ins., rear 3 ft. 11½ ins. Overall length, 11 ft.; weight, 10½ cwt.

Performance: Maximum speed, 121.5 m.p.h. Speeds in gears: 3rd 80 m.p.h., 2nd 52 m.p.h., 1st 30 m.p.h. Standing quarter mile, 15.5 secs. Acceleration: 0-50 m.p.h., 5.4 secs.; 0-60 m.p.h., 8 secs.; 0-70 m.p.h., 10.4 secs.; 0-80 m.p.h., 13 secs.; 0-90 m.p.h., 17.4 secs.; 0-100 m.p.h., 23.8 secs.

Fuel consumption: 30 m.p.g. (approx.).

RECIPE for fast cornering: "The controls are all well placed, the steering wheel is arranged for the modern straight-arm technique, and the aerodynamic body does not impede the driver's view".

competition work than the usual M.G. article.

An interesting detail is the headlamp mounting. The lamps fold away beneath the bonnet during the day, and when they are erected at night they have the advantage of being higher than is normally the case with small streamlined cars. Although they are not large, they give a good light, and I exceeded 100 m.p.h. in the dark with their aid.

I found the Lotus quite tractable as a town and shopping car. The exhaust

★

RETRACTABLE: (Right) The small but adequately powerful headlights on the Lotus fold away beneath the bonnet when not in use.

Lotus Mark 9, *Autosport* 18 November 1955

630

A YEAR ago, I tested the then prototype aerodynamic Lotus. At that time, the machine had only been seen in the hands of its progenitor, Colin Chapman. Since then, the thing has been rationalized, finalized and delivered to quite a number of lucky customers. Having come in at the beginning, as it were, I was naturally agog to try the current version.

I was thus extremely elated when Colin offered me the loan of *both* the works cars. One of these has a highly tuned M.G. engine, in which respect it resembles the car I borrowed last year. This is the well-known 1¼-litre unit, "stretched" to nearly 1½-litres. The long stroke and pushrod valve operation limit the ultimate performance, but the exceptional torque in the middle range of

JOHN BOLSTER TESTS

THE LOTUS MARK IX

with both M.G. and Coventry Climax power units

revolutions is invaluable when maximum acceleration is required. About 85 b.h.p. is developed at 5,800 r.p.m.

The other car has the Coventry Climax engine, an "over-square" 1,100 c.c. light alloy job, with a single overhead camshaft. When Colin Chapman took the Brands Hatch sports car record, the engine was standard, but it now has a special camshaft giving additional overlap. In this form, it produces 81 b.h.p. at 6,700 r.p.m.

Apart from the difference in power units, the two cars are virtually identical. Both engines are attached to M.G. gearboxes of the early "J" series, without synchromesh. Customers' cars normally have the later type of box, but a few pounds of weight are saved if one is willing to forgo the alleged advantages of a simplified gear change. The final drive is a spiral bevel, for which various ratios are available. It transmits its power, through articulated half shafts, to the tubular hub assemblies that carry the knock-on wheels.

The real basis of the Lotus is a triangulated space frame of welded-up tubular construction. The independent front suspension is by swing axles, and at the rear there is a de Dion axle. Suspension is by helical springs and telescopic dampers all round. The brakes are Girling 9 ins. discs, inboard mounted at the rear. The Lotus aerodynamic body is too well known to need description.

On the road, the performance figures of the two cars were very similar, and yet the difference in handling was surprisingly large. Pulling a 3.66 to 1 gear, the M.G. version registered 128.6 m.p.h., whereas the Climax did 127.7 m.p.h. The latter unit had a 3.9 to 1 rear end and the rev. counter showed just about 6,500 r.p.m. continuously during the timed runs. There was a slight side wind blowing throughout the test period, and it is possible that under ideal weather conditions one could attain peak revs and "bust" 130 m.p.h.

It will be seen, from the graph, that the 1,100 c.c. car was fractionally quicker in the lower part of the acceleration

range. Both machines are commendably free from wheelspin, having regard to their very high performance, but the smaller one is fractionally the better in this respect. It is lighter by some ¼ cwt. than the M.G.-powered model, and consequently there is better traction, because the weight is taken off the forward end of the chassis.

Once third gear has been engaged, cubic capacity tells. The high torque of the M.G. engine pays dividends, and the 1½-litre car takes the lead. That is not the whole story, however. The difference in weight distribution naturally affects the handling characteristics, and whereas the heavier car understeers, the lighter one is just about neutral in response.

The steering of the Lotus is a typical feature. It is very light and high-geared, with little caster action, and there is no lost motion at all. A driver who had only handled the "soggier" type of modern saloon would at first find himself putting on too much helm and swerving involuntarily. After a time, he would find that, left alone, the car tended to run straight, and then he would suddenly realize what he had been missing.

The Lotus, particularly in its Climax-engined form, has phenomenally high cornering power. I was extremely happy to take it very fast through the curves of a road circuit, and there are no peculiarities to learn. I would, however, require a good deal more practice before I was certain that the ultimate limit was being attained. The whole cornering process is so effortless, with no rolling, bouncing, or tyre scream to give an air of urgency to the proceedings, that only experience gives warning that one is going from the improbable to the impossible. I know a particular corner which I habitually negotiate at just on 100 m.p.h. in the better class of sports car. The Lotus Climax took it first try at better than 110 m.p.h. You see what I mean!

The Girling disc brakes are very

POTENT PACKAGE: The Coventry Climax unit is mounted well back in the tubular frame; the body is readily removable. In the heading picture the M.G.-engined car is on the right—but who could tell?

AUTOSPORT, NOVEMBER 18, 1955

Specification and Performance Data

Cars Tested: Lotus Mark IX Sports-racing two-seaters. Price (component form without engine and gearbox), £850.

Lotus M.G.

Engine: Four cylinders, 72 mm. x 90 mm. (1,467 c.c.). Pushrod operated valves in light alloy head, 85 b.h.p. at 5,800 r.p.m. 9.5 to 1 compression ratio. Twin S.U. carburetters. Lucas coil and distributor.

Transmission: Borg and Beck racing clutch. Four-speed gearbox with central remote control, ratios 3.66, 4.87, 7.10 and 12.25 to 1. Open Hardy Spicer propeller shaft to chassis-mounted spiral bevel and differential unit. Articulated shafts to rear hubs.

Chassis: Multi-tubular space frame. Independent front suspension by swing axles. Rear suspension by de Dion axle. Helical springs and telescopic dampers all round. Girling 9 ins. disc brakes. Racing type wire wheels with knock-on hub caps, fitted 4.50 x 15 ins. front, 5.25 x 15 ins. rear tyres.

Equipment: 12-volt lighting and starting, ammeter, revolution counter, oil pressure and temperature and water temperature gauges.

Dimensions: Wheelbase, 7 ft. 3½ ins.; track, front 4 ft. 0½ in., rear 3 ft. 11½ ins.; overall length, 11 ft. 8 ins.; weight, 9 cwt.

Performance: Maximum speed, 128.6 m.p.h. Speeds in gears: 3rd, 85 m.p.h.; 2nd, 53 m.p.h.; 1st, 32 m.p.h. Standing quarter mile, 15.4 secs. Acceleration: 0-30 m.p.h., 3.4 secs.; 0-50 m.p.h., 6.6 secs.; 0-60 m.p.h., 8.6 secs.; 0-80 m.p.h., 13.2 secs.; 0-100 m.p.h., 22.4 secs.

Fuel Consumption: Racing, 20 m.p.g.; Road, 30 m.p.g. (approx.).

Lotus Climax

Engine: Four cylinders 72.4 mm. x 66.6 mm. (1,097 c.c.). Single overhead camshaft operating valves in light alloy head, 81 b.h.p. at 6,700 r.p.m. 9.8 to 1 compression ratio. Twin S.U. carburetters. Lucas coil and distributor.

Transmission: As above, except ratios 3.9, 5.27, 7.64 and 13.07 to 1.

Chassis: As above.

Equipment: As above.

Dimensions: As above, except weight 8 cwt. 1 qr.

Performance: Maximum speed, 127.7 m.p.h. Speeds in gears: 3rd, 95 m.p.h.; 2nd, 60 m.p.h.; 1st, 36 m.p.h. Standing quarter mile, 15.8 secs. Acceleration: 0-30 m.p.h., 3.2 secs.; 0-50 m.p.h., 6.2 secs.; 0-60 m.p.h., 7.8 secs.; 0-80 m.p.h., 14.6 secs.; 0-100 m.p.h., 23.6 secs.

Fuel Consumption: As above.

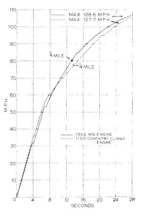

Acceleration Graph

powerful, but entirely smooth and constant in action. Some earlier discs were inclined to be fierce and noisy at low speeds, but the Lotus equipment has absolutely perfect manners. There is, in fact, no particular in which a drum brake would be superior and, of course, the complete elimination of fading is an advantage that needs no emphasis.

As already related, the two cars tested were fitted with "crash" boxes. I must say that, for this type of machine, the absence of synchromesh is, if anything, an advantage. All the half forgotten tricks of one's youth can again be employed, and the ratios can be snatched just as fast as hand can move the lever. The Borg and Beck racing clutches gripped instantly after every shift, but they were not too fierce for gentle use in traffic.

Speaking of traffic, I had occasion to drive both cars in London, though this is scarcely a normal procedure for sports-racing machines. I had no trouble with oiled plugs, though both engines were fairly "lumpy" at the lowest speeds. In standard trim, the Coventry Climax is a very flexible engine, but the special camshaft deletes all power below 2,500

r.p.m. On the open road, the phenomenal acceleration and powerful brakes render the Lotus a very safe car. One can frustrate the knavish tricks of even the British Sunday Driver, and 100 m.p.h. cruising is normal on the more deserted stretches.

Regarding the Lotus as a competition car, which is after all its *metier*, one cannot but be impressed by the excellent accessibility. A normal bonnet panel is removed for routine maintenance, but the rest of the body is secured by aircraft-type fasteners, and a virtually bare chassis can be achieved in a few minutes. There is no need to emphasize the advantage of being able to strip the car down in this way between races. It makes possible a thorough check-over under ideal conditions, and all chassis parts can be as carefully maintained as the engine.

Compared with last year's car, the body is greatly improved; the vibration of the panels at high engine revolutions has been noticeably reduced. The general sensation is that one is sitting in a solidly constructed vehicle, and there seems no reason why the body should not stand up well to a hectic competition career. Retractable headlamps of a simple

but effective type remain a typical feature.

For the rest, there has been much cleaning up of details, and the knock-on racing wheels add greatly to the appearance as well as being stronger than the original bolt-on type. The rear suspension with zero roll resistance has been replaced by a more normal layout, and the front roll resistance has been increased to match. As a result, cornering is even more effortless than before.

The racing successes of the Lotus need no underlining from me. However, I now have a fuller understanding of how they have been achieved. Particularly in the case of the Climax-engined car, one finds a machine which is so well balanced that all the power can be used nearly all the time; and, on the rare occasions when this is not so, those Girling discs give straight-line braking as powerful as it is dependable.

ABINGDON PRODUCT: A 1,250 c.c. M.G. unit, bored out to nearly 1½ litres, is fitted to 9 EHX and develops some 85 b.h.p.

HEAT EXCHANGER (above) on the Climax car effects a balance between the temperatures of lubricating oil and cooling water.

The works Mark 9, *Motor Sport* January 1956

EMPHASIS ON SPORTS CARS—

ROAD IMPRESSIONS OF THE WORKS Mk. IX LOTUS

DISTINCTIVE

APPEARANCE

characterises the aerodynamic Mk. IX Lotus, a 1,100-c.c. sports/racing car of outstanding performance and controllability.

THERE is no need to underline the excellent performance, one might write "circuit-performance," of Colin Chapman's Mk. IX aerodynamic Lotus, for its race successes at various club meetings and its splendid showing, while it was running, at Le Mans and in the T.T., speak nearly as loudly as the little car's exhaust note! Moreover, enthusiasts who went to last year's Earls Court Motor Show were able to examine the appetising components which Chapman offers to "specials"-builders on his stand in the main hall—such covetable fare as divided-axle i.f.s., de Dion back-end, a lightweight tubular space-frame with low-drag radiator and other factors enabling it to wear a two-seater sports body of reasonable aerodynamic form.

I write of this Lotus in the singular because this article is concerned with the actual Le Mans/T.T. car, Mk. IX/87, which is the property of Peter Jopp and is driven in races by its designer/creator, Colin Chapman. In fact, of course, the small firm of Lotus Engineering Ltd., at 7, Tottenham Lane, Hornsey, London, N.8, has been "mass-producing" these advanced little cars for some time—"mass-producing," that is, for a concern of this modest size, making what are essentially specialised sports/racing cars—Lotus supply the chassis frame and components in various combinations at prices which they will quote gladly if you apply to them.

This particular Lotus, when MOTOR SPORT had it for test in November, had led a particularly hard life. Apart from doing a very appreciable proportion of Le Mans and the T.T.—at Le Mans the car was disqualified and in the T.T. it was leading on Index of Performance until an oil-pipe broke, causing it to lose the 1,100-c.c. class to a Cooper-Climax by a mere five seconds—it had been driven in various lesser races and used by two other motor journals for assessment purposes, besides which, on November 16th, just before we went to Hornsey to take it over, XPE 6 had been tried out at Brands Hatch circuit by a dozen different drivers, who collectively drove it at racing speed for more than 240 laps (or over 300 miles), six of them unofficially approaching or equalling the absolute sports-car lap record for this course. Reg. Bicknell clocked 61.2 sec., Alan Brown 61.6, Ivor Bueb and Graham Hill both got round in 61.7, George Wicken recorded 62.8 and Dennis Taylor 62.9 sec., while Ken Tyrrell, D. Boshier-Jones, F. Hobart-Smith, John Brown and Chapman himself all "had a go," the last-named modestly refraining from quoting his lap times. And all this without a proper overhaul since it was registered early in June.

Not surprisingly, after such high-speed usage, the Lotus was becoming rather weary during our spell with it, and we experienced a few minor bothers, such as a "flat" battery due to a "shorting" electrical lead, a flat tyre, failure of the rev.-counter drive (which mystified us for a time by rotating its drive-gearbox until the latter chafed against the base of the distributor, cutting out the ignition), and breakage of a dynamo support bracket. It takes more than this to mar the joy of driving a Lotus and, anyway, the car wasn't built to run in a Mille Miglia and is probably more at home going to Silverstone or Brands Hatch in a van, accompanied by a plentiful supply of tools, than being put to work as a long-distance road-express.

Certainly this low, tail-finned two-seater places emphasis on "racing" rather than "sports" and is today's equivalent of the Grand Prix Bugatti or Amilcar Six of earlier times—so that lack of a spare wheel, an exhaust note more obvious than that of a Grand Prix car, and a driving position calling for helmet and goggles, are all part of the fun.

The battery is a small 12-volt affair, sharing the tail with a six-gallon fuel tank which would have to be removed to extract it, the snap-action filler of this tank had to be wired down, no speedometer graces the dash, and for the benefit of those who have never examined a Lotus I add that before the single headlamp could be used the bonnet panel had to be lifted and the lamp prised upwards into the night; obviously, there were no hood or sidescreens!

Yet if these remarks paint the T.T. Lotus as a stark sports/racing car, as you would doubtless expect it to be, the Coventry-Climax engine is happily devoid of temperament, whether poodling through towns or shooting the car up to 85 m.p.h. along the meanest straights, the Lodge HLNP plugs uncomplaining, consuming normal Esso Extra petrol, lubricating itself with Essolube 30 and, incidentally, remaining commendably free from oil leaks. Moreover, with the not-unduly-fierce camshaft which produces 81 b.h.p. at 6,700 r.p.m. on a compression ratio of 9.5 to 1, this clever little 72.4 by 66.6-mm. (1,097 c.c.) engine proved able to run up to 7,000 r.p.m. in the indirect gears in the normal course of business, Harry Mundy, who had a large hand in its design, telling us that something around 400 r.p.m. beyond this wouldn't really stress things too far. And 7,000 r.p.m. in third is equal to no less than 87½ m.p.h. on the low axle ratio!

On this "sprint" ratio of 4.5 to 1 the Lotus-Climax is well able to reach 85 m.p.h. between corners on the average rolling English road, and on our test circuit, under not very favourable conditions, achieved 100 m.p.h. at the end of a stretch where far larger-engined sports cars do not often exceed this figure. Given time to work right up to it the maximum should be approx. 108 m.p.h., while with a high axle ratio (3.9 to 1) installed, speeds in the region of 130 m.p.h. are encompassed.

The handling qualities of the car are interesting. The driving position suits persons of medium height, although even then the pedals seem rather distant and not amenable to easy heel-and-toe gear changes. The position is essentially arms-straight to the pleasing (if slippery) three-spoke, 15-in., leather-rimmed steering wheel and, as has been hinted at, a gale of wind sweeps round the driver's head, although the flatter screen before the passenger gives him or her quite good protection.

On first acquaintance there are two surprises. First, the comparatively hard suspension; secondly, the high-geared steering. The former intrudes only over bad surfaces taken at modest speeds i.e., up to 65/70 m.p.h.; above this speed the ride smooths out and bad roads have less effect on the car. The Lotus rack-and-pinion steering, however, is geared like that of a "chain-gang" Frazer-Nash, asking barely 1¼ turns lock-to-lock, with a reasonable turning circle. The result is that in cornering the wheel is scarcely moved and certainly it is impossible to steer into skids in the cus-

THE WORKS.— A very useful feature of the Lotus is the manner in which the various components are rendered accessible by removing the quickly-detachable body panels.

tomary enthusiastic manner — just a flick and the car is under control. It is fatal to grip the wheel tightly or the Lotus proceeds in a series of swerves, yet kick-back from the divided-axle i.f.s. precludes letting the wheel go free, the technique over bumps being to let the rim play through one's fingers. Incidentally, castor-action is virtually nil.

The cornering characteristics of the Lotus-Climax are of the kind that win races. There is a tendency to understeer which never becomes embarrassing; indeed, the action is virtually neutral, while the de Dion rear-end enables the power to be turned on early out of slippery corners, for both wheels spin together and the car keeps to the intended course. If it doesn't, the aforesaid flick of the taut yet light steering is all that is required.

Everyone who tried the Lotus was impressed with its excellent acceleration for a 1,100-c.c. machine, aided by reasonable spacing of the gear ratios in the M.G. J2 box — for want of a substitute. Chapman uses secondhand, but overhauled, M.G. J2 boxes, substituting for the cast-iron bell-housing a light-alloy one, drilled with lightening holes — what a tribute to the quality in pre-war M.G. cars ! A standing-start ¼-mile, essayed two-up, without fireworks, and without practice, occupied a mere 16½ seconds. While driving over our measured ½-mile we took pains to check the engine/road speed relationship, 1,000 r.p.m. being equal to 15.8 m.p.h. in top gear and 12.5 m.p.h. in third gear.

The enjoyment of this excellent and progressive acceleration is somewhat marred by the force required to change gear, the remote lever being set high up, so that the action is that of lifting rather than moving from one position to the next; using strength, the swapping of cogs is a rapid action, but how tiring in a long race . . . The central hand-brake lever is also too long and moves through too great an arc for convenience, and it cannot be dismissed as merely a parking adjunct, for on a car which likes the revs, maintained for a brisk get-away, it is useful to approach road junctions holding the car back temporarily by hand.

The Borg and Beck racing-type clutch is either in or out and heavy to operate, but showed no general tendency to overheat, save when changing rapidly into top after 7,000 r.p.m. had registered in third gear.

The brakes — 9-in. Girling disc — deserve a paragraph to themselves, for in all ordinary circumstances of fast road motoring nothing more was called for than just resting the foot on the pedal; in an emergency-stop they were of exceptional power, to wearing flats on the Dunlops on a dry road or converting the car into a toboggan in the wet ! They gave a real sense of security and gain 100 per cent. full marks. Twin master-cylinders and fluid reservoirs are used, one for the front and one for the back brakes.

In appearance XPE 6 is exciting, for the well-known aerodynamic form was offset by racing number discs and night-racing recognition lamps. Of more practical interest is the extreme ease with which the body can be removed completely from the chassis. During our times of trouble we took off the one-piece bonnet, front wings and scuttle in a matter of minutes, when almost all the machinery is accessible. Genuine Dzus fasteners facilitate this useful operation. This body, which has ample accommodation laterally and fore-and-aft for two adults, is in a very thin-gauge light alloy and is the work of Williams and Pritchard.

The general specification of the Lotus-Climax Mk. IX is well known but for those who like details, let us run over the general layout and construction. The multi-tubular space-frame has swing-axle front suspension, formed from a divided Ford axle beam, liberally drilled, with long radius-arms, suspension being by coil-spring-cum-damper units. At the back similar suspension units are employed with the de Dion rear-end, where the disc brakes are mounted inboard. Centre-lock wire wheels are used, those on the car tested being shod with 4.50-15 Dunlop racing tyres at the front, 5.25-15 at the back.

Right in the nose of the car is the small ducted radiator, from which a long pipe on the near side runs to a tiny water-system header tank under the scuttle, the water return pipe leaving the back of the head on the off side, and a pump on the near-side front of the engine encouraging circulation. This pump is belt-driven in conjunction with the dynamo on the off side, which is a normal Lucas dynamo with an extension driving a Smith's 5-in. rev.-counter reading to 8,000 r.p.m. Normal Lucas coil ignition is used, the sparking plugs being inclined in the off side of the cylinder head.

Above the radiator is a water/lubricant heat-exchanger. Two 1½-in. H4 S.U. carburetters are used, which have ram-pipes projecting into an air-box on the near side of the car, and on the same side four separate exhaust pipes feed into a single larger-bore pipe which ends flush with the side of the car. The oil-filler is accessible on the off side of the engine and there is a breather in the camshaft cover adjacent to the interesting(!) Godiva emblem which forms the Coventry-Climax trademark. A Purolator oil-filter lives outside the frame behind the near-side front wheel and fuel is fed from the tail tank by a single electric petrol pump, also situated outside the engine compartment nearer the scuttle. The steering column incorporates a universal joint, voltage regulation is through the latest Lucas RB310 unit, and stop-lamps, as required for night racing, are actuated by the brake pedal.

The dash is pretty fully occupied with accommodating two fuse-boxes, aircraft-type switches for panel lighting, the triple rear lamps, the side lamps, the two retractable Lucas headlamps (only one being fitted when we had the car), the recognition lamps, ignition and fuel pump, the aforesaid rev.-counter, and three small Jaeger dials indicating water temperature (normally 65/70 deg. C.), dynamo charge, and oil pressure (normally 40 lb./sq. in.), the last-named being a combined oil pressure/water-temperature dial, with the latter function deleted. The steering-wheel spokes rather blank the essential dials. In addition, there are : a dynamo master-switch, a switch for cutting out the lamps circuit during daylight racing, a dipper for the non-existent headlamp, and a pull-out starter switch, as well as a Tapley performance meter, horn button and central mirror. Incidentally, no fuel gauge or reserve tap was fitted. The fuel range wasn't great, but for long-distance racing an auxiliary pannier tank is carried on the near side.

The interior of the cockpit is devoid of trimmings, but the shallow seats are not uncomfortable and the driver is kept nicely in place by the propeller-shaft tunnel, which is not upholstered. In the tail, under a Dzus-fastened panel, repose the tightly-packed fuel tank and lightweight battery, and when a spare wheel has to be carried this is somehow inserted in front of them and secured by a length

WHAT MAKES IT GO ?—Perhaps the most impressive part of the Mk. IX Lotus which we tested was the Coventry-Climax single-o.h.c. engine. It would run happily down to 1,000 r.p.m. in top gear or rev. to 7,000 r.p.m. quite unconcernedly, as occasion demanded.

SPLENDID ANCHORS.—No praise is too great for the Girling 9-in. disc brakes fitted to the works Lotus. Note also the coil-spring front suspension unit.

PURPOSEFUL.—A three-quarter rear-view of the tail-finned Lotus, in this instance the car used by Colin Chapman in the T.T. and at Le Mans.

of rubber cord. Lift forward the wafer-thin seat squab and the mysteries of de Dion back-end and inboard disc brakes are immediately apparent !

This starkness notwithstanding, the remarkable TWA Coventry-Climax engine commenced readily and did not run-on after terminating hard spells of motoring, we never had to look at a plug, and carburation is commendably clean over the 1,000/7,000 r.p.m. speed range, the car running without snatch at the former speed in top gear, *i.e.*, at less than 16 m.p.h., and pulling away without hesitation. Moreover, it refused to boil, even in London traffic. The useful range from the aspect of power is from about 3,000 to 6,700 r.p.m.

The splendid performance of this 1,100-c.c. sports/racing car and the excellent understeer handling which enable it to do so well in races also render it a very fast road car. In the hands of a colleague it averaged more than 63 m.p.h., two up, over 195 miles of main-road motoring with Saturday traffic to contend with, 6,700 r.p.m. being the genuine top-gear maximum along the Salisbury straights, equal to nearly 106 m.p.h. This run included averaging 68 m.p.h. between

Winchester and Petersfield and 78 m.p.h. from Andover to Lobscombe Corner, which gives some idea of the potentialities of the Lotus as a road car. Moreover, at these high speeds the consumption of Esso Extra worked out at about 24 m.p.g., so that, driven more like a mere sports car, this Lotus-Climax would obviously return economy figures comparable to those expected of a small saloon. Understandably, the engine consumed a lot of oil. The weight is 9 cwt. 1 qtr. 21 lb.*, without passengers, but ready for the road with approximately two gallons of fuel.

The basic soundness of Chapman's design and the excellence of the Coventry-Climax engine add up to a fascinating small competition car, able to challenge many machines far larger than itself.—W. B.

---

* As this weight does not tally with those quoted in other reports, we would emphasise that MOTOR SPORT always uses the same weigh-bridge—the County Council of Middlesex Public Weighbridge at Brentford.

London Motor Club's Gloucester Trial (Dec. 3rd)

THE thirty-seventh Gloucester Trial was held on December 3rd at Birdlip, Glos. This well-known reliability trial consists of a road section of about thirty miles and a trials section involving the ascent of various hills and mudbanks.

Competitors were split up into odd and even number groups, the route being so arranged that neither group had long to wait before commencing the special tests, which began from a track in the valley of a wood, the seven observed sections being marked out on the inclines on either side. The first section consisted of a straight hill; the second, third and fourth were straight with turns or bends half-way; the fifth was similar, after the cars had negotiated a mild form of watersplash before it; the sixth, a steep, straight climb with a bend at the finish; and the seventh involved traversing several banks and ditches.

Amongst the successful gentry at Hill One were A. Erskine in a Ford and T. Harrison (Harford III), who made good, steady climbs. E. Reynolds failed with his Dellow owing to the use of too many revs., and N. Carr (Trafford) also failed to complete the last two sections, much water and steam emitting from his radiator.

Hill Two again saw Harrison make a fair climb, Carr making to section four. On Hill Three Harrison did some aviating but just failed to reach the summit. Hill Five was a stiff one for most people, Cotton (Cotton Special) and Lawson (M. & L.) having fair luck, as did R. N. Stallard (Ford) and T. Bellm in a smart Dellow. E. Chandler in the Chandler Special made another good attempt, but H. Smart (B.S.T. II) was less successful. B. Dees, in a smart and very clean P.A.B. Special with aluminium painted chassis and large folding windscreen, reached the summit with assistance but got stuck in the puddle at the bottom before joining the main track, a branch having lodged between the spokes of his rear wheel. R. Davis, driving the only Austin Seven-engined car, was one of the last to ascend the hill but failed to get very far, the mauve-coloured car was well turned out, however, being fitted with hydraulic brakes (by Lotus Engineering, Ltd.), Stromberg carburetter, high-compression head, large sump and pressurised Nippy crankshaft.

Hill Six proved to be an easy one, few cars failing to reach the top; Cotton, Lawson, Hollingworth (Oliver), Faulkner (Paul Special). Highwood (Exspence) and Corbishley (C.C.S. IV) being seen to make clear climbs, as did Chappell in his Cannotton with punctured tyre and Dadswell (Sanford) after starting troubles at the bottom.

The final test, Hill Seven, proved to be the most interesting to watch, drivers forcing their " Bucking Broncos " over mounds of earth and rubble. " Mike " Lawson gave a spectacular showing of how to do the thing properly by completing all six sections without stopping ; a very enterprising spectacle, accompanied by much cheering on the part of the spectators. Nearly all other competitors had to try some of the obstacles more than once. Hopkinson. Appleton (Cannon Eight) and Needham (Needham Special) completed the course, along with Ackerley (Ford) and Broadhead (J.C.B.), who stopped for breathers in between. T. Harrison cleared section three after examining the lie of the land with his passenger, and finally reached section six and cleared it. Imhof (Imhof Special) cleared point two, and reached point six after several attempts at the steep bank at point three. Reynolds (Dellow) inspected the layout also but failed at point two, when he motored off down the main track. the car sounding like a Ford V8 owing to a broken exhaust system. F. Harrison (F.H. Mk. IV) went in for tree felling and cleared point one only, as did Cotton's steaming Cotton Special, trailing some of the undergrowth behind it.

So ended a very interesting few hours of inexpensive motor sport, the special tests being well chosen and the cars well finished and carefully driven.—I. G.

Results :

Gloucester Cup : B. Dees (P.A.B. Special).
Thomas Cup : E. Chandler (Chandler Special).
Committee Cup : P. Highwood (Exspence).
First-Class Awards : G. Newman (Cannon Seven), R. Chappell (Cannotton), J. Jenkins (Austin) and T. Harrison (Harford III).
Team Award : I. Appleton, B. Dees and E. Chandler (175 points).

The low-drag Mark 9, *The Motor* 1 February 1956

February 1, 1956   11   *THE MOTOR*

FLAT OUT on the Belgian motor road, the Lotus shows its paces in the quiet conditions early on a winter Sunday morning.

49 MILES PER GALLON AT A MILE A MINUTE!

JOSEPH LOWREY, B.Sc.(Eng.) Reports on Some Tests of the Low-drag 1,100 c.c. Lotus Mk IX Two-Seater

JUST about nine years ago, I was a fairly regular competitor in sprints and occasional races for 1,100 c.c. sports cars. Using the same H.R.G. which had been my business conveyance all through the war years, and with an honest maximum speed not far above 70 m.p.h. on a too-high axle ratio, I was quite often able to collect "place" awards. My! How times have changed!

Just how much standards of performance in races for small sports cars have advanced was clearly illustrated recently, when I was given the chance to drive an 1,100 c.c. Lotus, a car which has been very near to big successes repeatedly in a busy, but unlucky, summer of racing. It is a car which many people have driven in many different circumstances, but which has survived a lot of fast miles on most of Europe's racing circuits amazingly well. Despite winter conditions, a sparse set of instruments, and the realization that to try to fit a "fifth wheel" behind such a light and well-streamlined car would seriously reduce its performance, we decided to apply "Road Test Report" methods to finding out as much as possible about just what sort of performance a modern 1,100 c.c. sports racing car really has.

As handed over to us, the Lotus had the same Coventry Climax engine with which it had been raced in the Tourist Trophy (and led on handicap until an oil pipe broke), much used since but still sound in wind and limb except for an unidentified fault (probably a tired valve spring) which snuffed out the power rather suddenly at about 500 r.p.m. beyond the speed giving maximum power. The long-range tank on the left side had been removed, leaving some six gallons of fuel in a rear tank. Rear axle gears of 4.22/1 ratio were in use, alternatives also

available and used on fast or slow courses being 3.89/1 and 4.55/1. The one big divergence from racing trim comprised a full-width windscreen giving protection for a passenger, whereas in racing the car has usually had only a small curved windscreen to protect the driver and has had the passenger-carrying half of the cockpit covered over.

Built in a very small works in North London from which an astonishing number of replicas are now being dispatched to America, the Lotus Mark IX is one of a line of cars which record a fascinating story. After scoring notable successes in Trials with a car of Austin 7 ancestry which incorporated some strictly personal ideas on wheel adhesion, Colin Chapman turned to racing under the "750 Formula" which, by compelling use of the side-valve Austin 7 cylinder block and other parts, was supposed to provide inexpensive racing. Having read Ricardo's classic textbook on The Internal Combustion Engine as an early edition (before the best parts

LOTUS MK. IX SPECIFICATION

Engine dimensions			Chassis details		
Cylinders	...	4	Brakes	...	9-in. Girling disc
Bore	...	72.39 mm.	Suspension: Front	...	Coil springs and divided axle
Stroke	...	66.6 mm.			
Cubic capacity	...	1,098 c.c.	Rear	...	Coil springs and de Dion axle tube
Piston area	...	25.4 sq. in.			
Valves	...	Single o.h. camshaft	Shock absorbers	...	Girling telescopic
Compression ratio	...	9.75/1	Wheel type	...	Centre-lock wire
Engine performance			Tyre size	...	5.25—15 rear
Max. power	...	72 b.h.p.			4.50—15 front
at	...	6,000 r.p.m.	Steering gear	...	Rack and pinion
B.H.P. per sq. in. piston area	...	2.83			
Piston speed at max. power	...	2,620	**Dimensions**		
			Wheelbase	...	7 ft. 3½ in.
Engine details			Track: Front	...	4 ft. 0½ in.
Carburetters	...	2 S.U., 1½ in	Rear	...	3 ft. 11½ in.
Fuel pump	...	S.U. electric	Overall length	...	11 ft. 7½ in.
Transmission			Overall width	...	4 ft. 8 in.
Clutch	...	7½ in. s.d.p. Borg and Beck	Overall height at scuttle	...	2 ft. 3 in.
			Unladen kerb weight	...	9½ cwt.
Gear ratios:			Front/rear weight distribution	...	51/49
Top (s/m)	...	4.22			
		(Optional 4.55 or 3.89)			
3rd (s/m)	...	5.7	**Gearing**		
2nd (s/m)	...	8.24	Top gear m.p.h. per 1,000 r.p.m.	...	17.2
1st	...	14.4			
Rev.	...	14.4	Top gear m.p.h. per 1,000 ft/min. piston speed	...	39.3
Prop. shaft	...	Open			
Final drive	...	9/38			
		(optional 9/41 or 9/35)			

THE MOTOR

MECHANICS of the Lotus shown in the left-hand picture include the half-blanked aircraft pattern radiator, an oil cooler, front suspension by coil springs and a divided axle, disc brakes, multiple tube "fuselage," Coventry Climax engine and rear mounted coolant header tank. One headlamp is also shown folded back below the bonnet line.

PRACTICAL trials with wool tufts aided development of the Lotus body lines, seen (right) broken by a raised headlamp and a windscreen of full-width type. Dzus fasteners secure the front section of the body, which is quickly removable for major servicing jobs."

49 MILES PER GALLON

were deleted as out of date), Chapman found means of splitting siamesed inlet ports into two small but shapely halves, going on to evolve a car which, when a mechanical failure called for hurried removal of a piston and connecting rod, still lapped Silverstone on three cylinders faster than could most of its rivals on four.

Having proved himself as an engine tuner, Chapman (who was then employed on design of light alloy structures) concentrated for a while on chassis design, and evolved a "space frame" of multiple small-diameter steel tubes, incorporating Ford 10 components wherever possible but leaving room for any of several engines such as the M.G. Since then, the Lotus frame and the components to fit it have both developed steadily, but the next advance came with the evolution of an aerodynamic body, much of the design and practical testing being done by Frank Costin in his spare time from work as an aircraft aerodynamicist.

Ready-made Power

Whereas in Italy various engines are built almost purely for racing, and in Germany the Porsche engineers have developed so far beyond the Volkswagen design with which they started that no significant mechanical component of the VW is now used, in Britain the small teams which build super-sports cars for racing have not in the post-war years usually built their own engines from scratch. Almost always they have preferred to build lighter, more controllable and better streamlined cars around tuned versions of existing power units. Recently, however, their work was mightily encouraged when Coventry Climax Engines, Ltd., announced a lightweight engine designed for use in portable fire pumps, a single overhead camshaft engine but one which incorporated many lessons which Wally Hassan had learned while developing the XK120 Jaguar. Like their rivals in various classes, the designers of the Cooper and the Buckler, the Lotus team have made very good use of the Coventry Climax 1,098 c.c. power unit during the past season.

As loaned to us for test, the Lotus had this engine, fed by two S.U. carburetters on Y branch pipes, and with an abbreviated exhaust system unobstructed by any perceptible silencing. It had the usual divided-axle independent front suspension, a de Dion rear axle located by long radius arms and a Panhard rod, and four Girling sus-

pension units comprising flexible coil springs encircling extremely firm telescopic dampers. Mated to the engine was an M.G. gearbox of TC type, and Girling disc brakes were mounted outboard on the front hubs, inboard on the sprung differential unit at the back. Lightweight knock-off wire wheels completed the picture.

Collecting the Lotus from Hornsey and heading into central London, the first impression was inevitably made by the exhaust note which, to say the least, makes other "audible warning of approach" superfluous! The next impression was of delight, however, at discovering that

LOTUS MK. IX PERFORMANCE

Fuel Consumption at Steady Speeds (with passenger)	Acceleration through Gears (from a rest, no passenger)		
		Driver "X"	Driver "Y"
65.0 m.p.g. at steady 30 m.p.h	0-30 m.p.h	3.2 sec	3.2 sec
61.0 m.p.g. at steady 40 m.p.h	0-40 m.p.h	4.5 sec	4.5 sec
55.5 m.p.g. at steady 50 m.p.h	0-50 m.p.h	6.1 sec	6.0 sec
49.0 m.p.g. at steady 60 m.p.h	0-60 m.p.h	8.2 sec	7.9 sec
43.5 m.p.g. at steady 70 m.p.h	0-70 m.p.h	10.8 sec	10.2 sec
38.0 m.p.g. at steady 80 m.p.h	0-80 m.p.h	13.9 sec	13.3 sec
33.0 m.p.g. at steady 90 m.p.h	0-90 m.p.h	18.0 sec	17.6 sec
	0-100 m.p.h	25.0 sec	25.8 sec
Acceleration in Gears (no passenger)	Standing ¼ mile	16.6 sec	16.1 sec

	Top gear	Third Gear
30-50 m.p.h	7.7 sec	4.7 sec
40-60 m.p.h	7.6 sec	4.8 sec
50-70 m.p.h	7.6 sec	5.2 sec
60-80 m.p.h	8.0 sec	6.1 sec
70-90 m.p.h	9.7 sec	—
80-100 m.p.h	14.9 sec	—

Maximum Speed (no passenger)
See text—approx. 113 m.p.h. mean.

dawdling through city traffic as un-noisily as possible at 1,000-2,000 r.p.m. (usually in top gear) did not provoke this well-worn racing engine into the slightest trace of overheating, plug oiling or other temperamental behaviour.

Our objective with the Lotus was not London, however, but the familiar Jabbeke motor road in Belgium where hard facts about the performance of this remarkable little car could be discovered. The objective was duly attained, after the negotiation of such hazards as rain, fog, pavé, and a Dover policeman who was unconvinced of the legality of far-inboard sidelamps or a much-sloped front number plate.

Obviously, alas, what everyone wants to know about this (or almost any other) car is the answer to the "What'll she do, Mister?" query. Ignoring fog delays, let it be put on record that driver X wearing a leather helmet recorded 111 m.p.h. upwind and 115 m.p.h. downwind, a mean of 113 m.p.h. at an indicated 6,200 r.p.m. Driver Y, with more height to project above the

AT A MILE A MINUTE! -   -   - Contd.

windscreen and using a bulkier crash helmet to keep his ears warm, was approximately 2 m.p.h. and 100 r.p.m. slower each way. In both cases, the car was running solo, but with full-width screen and open cockpit, tyre pressures having been set cold to 28 and 35 lb., front and rear, the r.p.m. figure suggesting that Colin Chapman made a very accurate choice of rear axle ratio.

Magnificent as the Coventry Climax engine is in its combination of smoothness and economy with high performance, there are limits to the power which can be expected from a simple 1,100 c.c. unit which proved very un-fussy as to what (premium) brand of pump fuel was fed to it. High top speeds have to come from low wind

production car Road Tested during the past two years have been 100 lb. for the M.G. "A" 2-seater with hard tyres and raised hood, 105 lb. for the Renault 750 saloon, 106 lb. for the Standard 10 saloon, 107 lb. for the Volkswagen and the Doretti 2-seater.

Alongside low wind resistance, the other big contribution to high performance on a limited amount of power is light weight. Exaggerated claims are sometimes made, but carrying a spare wheel and with its modest petrol tank full the Lotus scaled 9¾ cwt. at the L.C.C. Weights and Measures Office, so that with a low fuel level, but complete with its spare wheel and tyre, it would weigh 9½ cwt. In this latter trim, the front rear weight distribution would be 51 49, the driver's added weight coming towards the rear with the car in use. Whilst lower figures have been claimed, a kerb weight of 9½ cwt. means a lot

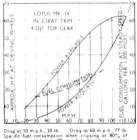

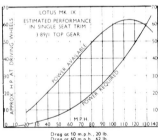

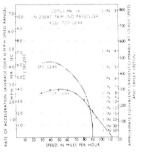

Drag at 10 m.p.h., 20 lb.   Drag at 60 m.p.h., 77 lb.
Specific fuel consumption when cruising at 80% of maximum speed (i.e. 90 m.p.h.), based on power delivered to rear wheels, 0.63 pints/b.h.p./hr.

Drag at 10 m.p.h., 20 lb.
Drag at 60 m.p.h., 62 lb.

and rolling resistances, and despite the handicap of being unable to supplement sparse instrumentation without spoiling performance, curiosity impelled me to attempt some measurements of what the drag of the Lotus really is. I would make no claim of dead accuracy for my drag figures, but the averaged experimental points plot much more tidily on graphs than might have been expected (some of the timing had to be done from a second car holding close formation behind the Lotus), and no major inconsistencies are shown up by cross-checking results.

As the graph shows, then, my estimate of the power needed to propel the Lotus at 100 m.p.h. in touring trim is approximately 45 b.h.p. at the road wheels, corresponding to a drag figure of 168 lb., and the drag at 60 m.p.h. is only about 77 lb. In contrast, the lowest 60 m.p.h. drag figures which we have estimated for any

of care over quite innumerable details as well as over fundamentals of the design.

How much faster will this 1,100 c.c. Lotus go in racing trim? One pointer is that when a single Lucas foglamp of 5½-in. diameter was in position on top of the bonnet instead of retracted back out of sight on a hinged mounting there was an apparent top speed loss of at least 5 m.p.h. Set well forward, this lamp is no doubt in a "better" strategic position for spoiling the streamlining than is the windscreen, but the full-width screen and uncovered passenger space would account for a substantial loss of top speed. Drivers report that at Le Mans this car was reaching 6,800 r.p.m. down the straight, which with the 3.89/1 final drive gears then used and with 5.25-15 rear tyres would represent appreciably over 130 m.p.h. There seems to be no reason to doubt this speed, on the basis of which it is possible to re-draw power and

February 1, 1956

IMPERFECT weather is one of the worries of winter testing, fog thick enough to make ordinary traffic use headlamps in daylight providing the background for tests at up to 70 m.p.h. on double-carriageway road.

49 MILES PER GALLON AT A MILE A MINUTE! - - - - Contd.

drag curves for racing trim and the high-ratio axle. The 10 m.p.h. drag will not change appreciably from its "touring" figure of 20 lb., but the 60 m.p.h. drag seems likely to be roughly 62 lb. total instead of 77 lb., and the 100 m.p.h. drag approximately 118 lb. instead of 168 lb.!

One immediate product of these low drag figures is a most remarkable economy of fuel. The Coventry Climax engine was tuned for performance, with carburetter settings rich enough to permit starts from cold without choking. But, running the car two-up at steady cruising speeds, petrol almost refused to disappear from the glass burette of our test outfit, figures of note being 65 miles per gallon at a steady 30 m.p.h., 49 miles per gallon at a steady 60 m.p.h., and 33 miles per gallon at a steady 90 m.p.h. Shortly after I had recorded these figures, the body stylist of a leading British factory in conversation about his latest product, asked me: "Do you really think streamlining matters?" On the spur of the moment, a polite answer eluded me, but perhaps when the car concerned turns up for Road Test its fuel consumption at 60 m.p.h. will provide one!

As a car on the road, of course, the Lotus is impressive in the extreme. From rest to 70 m.p.h., without a passenger, driver X recorded 10.8 sec., and driver Y 10.2 sec., on a damp road in each case. For comparison, the 3½-litre Jaguar C-type took 10.1 sec. from rest to 70 m.p.h. (carrying a passenger) when tested in the autumn of 1952, and the 5½-litre Cadillac-Allard (also with passenger) took 10.2 sec. early in 1951. The proximity of the Lotus figures to those for much larger machines is, to say the least, striking.

Disc Braking

Doing without unwanted drag is all very well, but there come times when drag is needed aplenty. On the Lotus, 9-inch Girling disc brakes look after these occasions, and very well too. On a patchily wet road, the car could be braked from 100 m.p.h. to rest with the wheels just about locking throughout, with quite a moderate pedal pressure and without any fade or sideways pull—although there was an aroma of warmed brake lining in the air as the car came to rest! Wet never seemed to affect the braking system, the behaviour of which was a good omen for disc-braked production cars some day.

With high performance and ultra low weight, the road-worthiness of the Lotus could hardly be taken for granted —especially as earlier models, whilst outstandingly good on corners, were apt to hop about a bit on the straight. In actual fact, this Mk. IX Lotus was amazingly well behaved in very varied conditions, completely stable right up to its maximum speed on a smooth surface. Interestingly, being rather big for the cockpit of the test model, I found I could cruise down smooth sections of the Autostrade hands-off for as far as I liked, steering quite precisely with

one knee pressed gently against the leather-over-rubber rim of the lightweight steering wheel.

Handling Technique

On bumpy surfaces, driving at high speeds is less easy. The simple swinging half-axles of the I.F.S. allow the steering to kick somewhat, a stranger's reaction being to hang on tight—but to do this with quick rack-and-pinion steering the sensitivity of which stops only just short of oversteer, produces snaking. On corners, the Lotus adheres to the road in magnificent style, and whilst use of too much throttle can make the tail move outwards pretty smartly, the response to corrective action is equally brisk. This is, after all, a racing machine, and whilst there are cars which give the unskilled driver more warning when he approaches the limit of adhesion on a corner, this chassis appears to let a skilled driver go that much nearer to the limit yet still does not suddenly fly right out of control when pressed too hard.

Comfort? Colin Chapman's ideas on suspension run to very soft coil springs indeed, in conjunction with telescopic dampers so abnormally firm that when you step into the car it sinks oh so slowly to the accompaniment of a long sigh from the rear shockers. The result is not exactly a "Boulevard Ride," but the objective of keeping the wheels on the road is seemingly achieved, and many more conventional suspensions can give a much jerkier ride. In detail, of course, the much-raced car which we drove let muddy water pour on to the driver from above, below, in front and behind, also neatly splitting a new pair of waterproof golf trousers before many entrances and exits had been made. But, on a fair day, with goggles and a helmet to provide protection above the low windscreen, there was quite a lot of comfort, a nice feature being the lateral support provided by lightly padded frame tubes. With fog freezing into black ice on the road, life was less comfortable, but the de Dion rear axle still permitted astonishingly rapid acceleration.

Produced by a huge amount of intelligent enthusiasm and sheer hard work, the Lotus is now a production car with a useful export market. Its performance, by showing up the unnecessary weight and air resistance of many recent cars, is undoubtedly helping to "improve the breed" of more ordinary vehicles. Incidentally, the all-round achievements of a team of young men who started work with very limited resources provide some answer to those who say that present-day conditions make it impossible for a young man to gain the varied experience which can lead eventually to a top-level job. Remembering the chief engineers around the industry who once built their own cars and ran them in competitions, before going on to produce such vehicles as the model T Ford, the Morris Minor or the Javelin, it would be dangerous to predict for the marque the long future it deserves.

Lotus Eleven, *Autosport* 23 November 1956

JOHN BOLSTER TESTS THE **Club Sports Lotus**

Fully equipped for touring, this latest Lotus gives 102.2 m.p.h. and 35 m.p.g. from a Ford 10 engine

When one mentions the latest Lotus "Eleven", most people at once think of the 1,100 c.c. and 1½-litre Coventry-Climax-engined cars, that have been covering themselves with glory in all the more important sports car races. There is, however, a simpler and cheaper version with a Ford engine. It retains many of the features of its more exalted brethren, and may in fact be converted to a full Le Mans model by addition of the necessary components. However, it was as a Ford 10-engined car, with conventional rear axle, that I took over my umpteenth Lotus in London recently.

NO DE DION at the back end, but nevertheless the roadholding is very good indeed. Spare wheel stowage is of the simplest kind, and the 12-volt battery is also housed at the rear.

The chassis frame—a genuine "space" type—is constructed of round and square steel tubes. In front is the well-known Lotus swing axle system, but behind is a proprietary rear axle, instead of the de Dion layout of the more expensive models. Normal drum brakes are used in place of the racing discs. The beautifully streamlined body is identical to that of the "racers".

My car had a full-width screen, with wiper, and a detachable hood. I removed the screen and replaced it with a single perspex deflector when timing the maximum speed, but all the other tests were done with the big screen in place. In the tail was a spare wheel, and there was some useful extra space which could be reinforced for carrying impedimenta. There are two shallow doors, but it is best to unfasten the hood when entering, though it can be done without.

The engine of "my" car was a very ordinary "old-type" Ford 10. It had a Ford 8 cylinder head to raise the compression, and enlarged inlet ports and valves. There were twin S.U. carburetters and the export-type water pump. Apart from that, the unit appeared to be aggressively standard, which makes the speed recorded all the more astonishing. Of course, the Ford three-speed gearbox had Buckler close-ratio gears.

On taking my seat, I found that I had plenty of room, and I liked the driving position. First speed was very high, but the Ford engine simply played with the 7¼ cwt. car. (Yes, I weighed it!) Second was a fine gear for fast overtaking, and on top one cruised easily at 80 m.p.h.

At first I was not happy with the steering. It is very light and phenomenally "quick", so that it is all too easy to wobble, especially after hitting a bump. Eventually, I became fully accustomed to it, and was able to see that it has certain charms. Nevertheless, as a purely personal preference, I would like a little more movement on the wheel. The lock is somewhat restricted, as is usually the case with streamlined bodies, but it is perfectly adequate for normal everyday use on the road.

As the last few Lotuses I have driven were equipped with de Dion axles and inboard brakes, I was interested to try a similar car with an orthodox axle and hub-mounted drums. Of course, the unsprung weight is considerably greater, though the type of springing adopted saves many valuable pounds compared with semi-elliptics. Let me say at once that the roadholding is good for so light a car. Compared with the Le Mans Lotus, one notices the rear axle mostly when accelerating hard from a standing start or away from a bumpy corner. Then, there is more wheelspin, as one would expect. The drum brakes seem just as good as the discs, at least for this 102 m.p.h. version of the Lotus.

That 102.2 m.p.h. maximum speed really does need some comment. For a side-valve 1,172 c.c. Ford—and not by any means a "hot" one—it is beyond all praise. The body shape certainly looks right, and this speed proves that the drag must be phenomenally low. I regret that the road never got really dry during my "ownership" of this car, and so the acceleration figures, good as they are, could easily be improved on a summer's day. It is interesting that, in the first-ever Lotus road test in 1953, I recorded a maximum speed of 88 m.p.h. with an identical engine. Thus, the body alone is worth 14 m.p.h.!

The particular car that I have been driving has often been seen in competition, in the capable hands of Graham

AUTOSPORT, NOVEMBER 23, 1956　　　663

Hill. I, too, drove the little machine at racing speed on Brands Hatch, and found that it was very controllable on a wet track as well as being lots of fun on a relatively dry one. At first, one feels that slight and occasional wandering sensation on the straight, which is typical of front swing axles. One almost forgets this after a few laps, though, and lets the Lotus look after itself.

As a sports touring car, I sampled the vehicle under all conditions in town and country. Colin Chapman advised me to use 18 lb. tyre pressure all round for touring, and 28 lb. (front) and 26 lb. (rear) for racing. Being lazy, I forgot to let the tyres down after a dicing session, and found the ride still quite comfortable at low speeds. The seats are of the competition type, with a minimum of padding, but they are much less tiring on a fast journey than the rock and roll variety.

The headlamps, behind their perspex fairings, are surprisingly powerful, and one can keep up a good speed at night. A very great improvement in the matter of body panel vibration and internal noise in general has been made, compared with the earlier Lotus. The driver and passenger keep warm and dry, even without the hood, and I seldom wore my overcoat during the rigours of a British November. A minor point, easily rectified, concerned the tendency of water off the road to penetrate upwards through the intentional drain holes in the floor. Personally, I would use a couple of corks, but the scientific Mr. Chapman

WEATHER protection includes a full width windscreen with wiper and a neat detachable hood with a large rear window. These pictures and the one opposite were taken at Brands Hatch.

will no doubt design a one-way valve for future models!

It would be no exaggeration to say that the ultra-low streamlined appearance created a real furore. Crowds collected wherever I parked the car, and the interest it aroused was enormous. It has a genuine, functional beauty, absolutely without decoration, and I heard numerous complimentary references from passers-by. I only heard two criticisms. One was from an enormously

(Continued on page 679)

Specification and Performance Data

Car Tested: Lotus Eleven Sports two-seater.

Engine: Four cylinders, 63.5 mm. x 92.5 mm. (1,172 c.c.). Side valves. 40 b.h.p. at 6,000 r.p.m. Twin S.U. carburetters. Coil and distributor ignition.

Transmission: Single dry plate clutch. Three-speed gearbox with remote control, ratios 4.2, 5.6 and 9.9 to 1. Open propeller shaft to hypoid rear axle.

Chassis: Multi-tubular space frame with stressed light alloy shaft tunnel. Independent front suspension by swing axles with rack and pinion steering. Rear axle on parallel trailing arms, of which one is A-shaped for lateral location. Helical springs and telescopic dampers all round. Knock-on wire wheels fitted 4.50 x 15 ins. tyres (front), 5.00 x 15 ins. tyres (rear). Hydraulic

2LS brakes with twin master cylinders. 9 ins. cast iron drums (front), 8 ins. drums (rear).

Equipment: 12-volt lighting and starting. Rev. counter, ammeter, water temperature and oil pressure gauges.

Dimensions: Wheelbase, 7 ft. 1 in. Track (front), 3 ft. 10 ins.; (rear), 3 ft. 11 ins. Overall length, 11 ft. 2 ins.; width, 5 ft.; height to top of scuttle, 2 ft. 3 ins. Ground clearance, 5 ins. Weight, 7¼ cwt.

Performance: (Damp road) Maximum speed, 102.2 m.p.h. Speeds in gears, 2nd 80 m.p.h., 1st 45 m.p.h. Standing quarter mile, 18.4 secs. Acceleration: 0-30 m.p.h., 4 secs.; 0-50 m.p.h., 9 secs.; 0-60 m.p.h., 12.6 secs.; 0-80 m.p.h., 23.2 secs.

Fuel Consumption: 35 m.p.g. (approx.).

ACCELERATION GRAPH

FULLY ACCESSIBLE, thanks to the completely detachable bodywork, the engine is revealed as that faithful work-horse, the Ford 10, with basic twin-carburetter modifications.

FUNCTIONAL cockpit layout contains all the necessary instruments and a small duralumin steering wheel with sponge-rubber rim, leather covered. The gear-change for the Ford box is of the Dellow type.

Lotus Eleven Le Mans model, *Autocar* 30 November 1956

824

Autocar
ROAD
TESTS

No. 1616

LOTUS 11
Le Mans Model

The Le Mans model has a wrap-round Perspex windscreen, the side sections of which hinge out and downward with the doors (when these are used). The diminutive duct to the radiator is more than adequate, some blanking off being required for best results in normal road work

FOR an 1,100 c.c. two-seater to attain over 112 m.p.h. on a Continental motorway, to cover the standing quarter-mile in 17.9 sec and average well over 50 m.p.g. fuel consumption for normal running is unique in road testing experience of *The Autocar*, yet that was the achievement of the Lotus Eleven Le Mans. On checking records we find only six other cars which have matched or bettered the performance figures—though without approaching the consumption—and all were of over 2-litre capacity.

Some readers may not consider such a comparison to be entirely fair, because the Lotus is built primarily for competition. It is true that there is no luggage accommodation as such, that weather protection is limited and by family car standards there are no more than the bare essentials of trimming and comfort, but to obtain the ultimate in one or two directions invariably necessitates some sacrifices in others. The exhilarating speed and acceleration of this car more than offset its austere furnishings, for the kind of enthusiastic driver who is likely to be found in its cockpit.

There is no reason why the car should not on occasions be used for local shopping or, in fine weather, for taking the younger member of the family to school—and no reason, either, to suppose that the Lotus would be harmed by such employment, for it has all the normal components and an engine which is far from being temperamental. On the other hand a milkman does not usually buy a racehorse to draw his float, nor does an Esquimo choose a whippet.

In the form in which it was tested, the Le Mans Lotus is ready for the track or road course for which it is primarily intended, and according to the merits of the driver, could be expected to finish among the winners. Racing apart, it provides enjoyment and satisfaction in the role of diminutive highway express, and it is under these circumstances also that its exceptional fuel economy is appreciated.

One of the very few specialized manufacturers in Great Britain, the Lotus Engineering company, has built up an enviable reputation since its first trials cars were produced in 1947 and were followed in due course by the Mark III 750 c.c. sports-racers. The present production models have a space-type chassis frame, built up of 1in and ⅜in round and square section steel tubing. The thickness of the tubes—18 and 20 s.w.g.—is varied according to the load on the particular section of the chassis. The floor and propeller shaft tunnel are stressed light alloy members which form an integral part of the chassis frame.

The heart of this Lotus is the 1,098 c.c Coventry Climax engine. Various stages of tuning may be specified by a purchaser. That of the standard model produces 75 b.h.p. at 6,250 r.p.m.; Stage 2 tuning, as applied to the car tested, provides 83 b.h.p. at 6,800 r.p.m. The engine is carried on two rubber mountings at the front and a single one at the gear box, and in order to keep down the frontal area, it is tilted to the left at approximately 10 deg. from the vertical. The compression ratio is 9.8 to 1 and thus high octane fuel should be used, although the admixture of a small quantity

Clips on each side secure the hinged front and rear body sections. The front of the chassis or the rear suspension can be revealed in a moment and the centre section is also quick to remove

of normal premium on one occasion during the testing made no detectable difference to performance.

Whether the engine, which has no "choke," would start readily in very cold weather we were unable to determine, but at temperatures within a few degrees of freezing point there was no difficulty at all. A twist of the ignition key until the S.U. electric fuel pump had finished ticking, one or two exploratory dabs on the throttle pedal as the key was twisted further to energize the starter motor, and the engine came to life readily and was soon firing evenly on all four cylinders. At high r.p.m. the exhaust note is very noisy—more so to the occupants of the car than to those on the road around—but the engine can be warmed up at a steady speed without causing any annoyance to the neighbours. No fan is fitted, and only a few minutes running is required to reach a comfortable operating temperature.

The Climax is at its best at about 80 deg C and, for ordinary road use a radiator blind would be well worth fitting, so that this temperature could be maintained. In traffic it rises rapidly, but was never seen to boil. A short burst in top gear brings the needle down immediately, and with an outside air temperature of about 50 deg F the open road running temperature stayed at little more than 60

Accommodation for luggage is confined to the space within the doors and the sills at their bases. The handbrake lever may be seen tucked away under the facia. Tall passengers have some difficulty in getting in because of the intruding chassis space frame member. There is no speedometer; the central dial records engine r.p.m. only

The Climax engine is inclined to permit an extremely low bonnet level, but the raised wings are easily seen and placed by the driver. The wipers would appear to be unnecessary refinement as neither driver nor passenger normally looks through the screen. The very light aluminium body has no protection against bumps which may occur in parking manœuvres

deg C, in spite of blanking off nearly a quarter of the area of the small transverse radiator.

To complete the specification preliminaries, before turning to the handling, there is the matter of rear axle ratio. Several ratios are offered to suit the various requirements. The car under discussion had a 4.22 to 1 axle which is to be recommended for road work. Others to choice are 3.66, 3.89, 4.55, 4.89 and 5.125 to 1—a good range for high top speed through to maximum acceleration, and calculated to cater for most competition requirements.

Without sacrificing much of the performance a higher than 4.22 back axle gearing could be selected to give exceptional economy on long journeys. On the other hand in England, where maximum speed would seldom be required or attainable, many drivers would prefer to use a little more fuel in order to experience the really exhilarating acceleration, and to increase slightly the tractability in heavy traffic.

Using the 4.22 to 1 axle and driving hard with full use of the gears and r.p.m., a representative figure of 44 m.p.g. was recorded. Jogging along at 60 to 70 m.p.h. and changing to a higher gear at no more than 4,000 r.p.m., nearly 60 m.p.g. was obtained. Such a figure surely provides a lesson in what can be achieved by reducing drag to a minimum. Very light weight, high gearing, outstanding engine efficiency, combine with the exceptionally low frontal area and fine aerodynamic shape to permit such economy.

The recommended pressures for the tyres vary considerably according to the driving contemplated. For high-speed touring 20 and 25 lb sq in front and rear respectively gives plenty of adhesion and a comfortable ride. For high-speed runs on good road surfaces, the pressures should be raised

The Coventry Climax engine unit is inclined at 10 degrees. There is a hole in the bonnet top for the air intake, this air passing through a box to the twin S.U. carburettors. The radiator is mounted very low at the front, and the separate header tank against the bulkhead. There are twin S.U. petrol pumps, of which one only is normally used

S26

The light on the right hand rear wing is for illumination of racing numbers in competition. There is no weather protection other than the screen

LOTUS 11 LE MANS . . .

to 30 and 35 lb and the ride is appreciably harder. It is not surprising that on a car so light and with such high performance, unbalanced or wrongly selected pressures can have a marked effect on ride, stability and steering characteristics.

Until comparatively recently, the carriage of a passenger as well as driver has been the exception rather than the rule on the Lotus, and the readiness with which the suspension bottoms on rough roads indicates that a little more development and experience would be advantageous. The thin foam rubber used for the seats is adequate for this type of vehicle, but it would not be unreasonable to advocate a considerable improvement in draught and waterproofing of the floor and sides.

There is no point in commenting on space and cockpit equipment, for quite obviously the car has been tailored to provide sufficient room for a large, though not outsize man to be accommodated in each seat—and no more. By accommodated, however, we imply with sufficient freedom of movement for all limbs for control of the car on road or track with comfort and safety. As delivered, the car carries no more than the essential instruments and switches and a legal and performance requirement in lamps and horn. If this model of Lotus is purchased mainly for use on the roads, it is up to the owner to specify the additional equipment he desires. There is plenty of room on the panel for a cigar lighter. Also according to specification, a hood can be provided and the makers advertise the availability of a hard top on all models.

Delivered to us almost hot from an economy run of the previous weekend, the shapely and diminutive sports car created quite a stir as it crouched between enormous lorries and vans outside our London headquarters. And such was the timing of our Silver City flight to the Continent for performance measurements that driver and car had to move off at once and get acquainted on the way. By the time the traffic intricacies of the Elephant and Castle had been negotiated, we were already geting along very nicely, though top gear as yet was in reserve.

The clutch is the only control likely to disconcert the inexperienced driver. As with those on most other competition cars, it has powerful springs and a very short, effective travel, being in effect either in or out. After a little practice with more or fewer engine r.p.m. and acclimatizing the foot to feathering the clutch into engagement, a normal, if eager getaway can be accomplished. It is perhaps prudent in traffic to leave rather more than the usual space between Lotus nose and car ahead, because the natural getaway is deceptively rapid and there is more length of Lotus ahead of the driver than he may think.

Even during the warming-up period, the engine pulls without hesitation, and in traffic it is not necessary to use

high r.p.m. to obtain responsive running—2,000 to 2,500 r.p.m. in the appropriate gear is adequate for keeping in the stream. Low gear must be used for getaway, but second and third are then selected much as they would be with any other sports car. The satisfying but raucous exhaust note does not become really obtrusive until the higher r.p.m. are used.

The gear lever is short, high-mounted and close to the driver's hand on the wheel. Movements are very small indeed between the gears, and changes are very slick at all speeds. The only occasion when a slight pause was desirable was between third and top at high r.p.m.

On the open road the Lotus takes on a new character, and comes to life at the derestriction sign as if it had been dozing before. The acceleration is such that 80 m.p.h. comes up in a quarter of a mile, and 100 in little over half a minute.

For the believer the exhaust sounds crisp and delightful. Until one is used to it, upchange time as judged by sound comes at perhaps 5,500 r.p.m. but the pull continues and increases, and between 6,500 and 7,000 r.p.m.—the normal maximum—the note becomes true blue. At 7,000 the speed in third gear is 92 and in second 57 m.p.h. By fitting alternative intermediate gear ratios which can be specified, it is possible to have maximum speeds of 100 m.p.h. in third and 75 m.p.h. in second.

Against the howl of exhaust and wind it is impossible to single out mechanical noise, but there is probably none deserving of comment. At low speeds the whine of the back axle can be detected—but then the driver can also see the back axle and inboard disc brakes behind his seat if he lifts the flexible cover.

The speed and acceleration figures quoted in this account were all obtained with two people on board and the road test gear attached. Even on wet surfaces very little wheel spin was experienced on these tests. An easy top gear cruising speed was found to be about 80 m.p.h., with the engine turning at 4,500 r.p.m. During the performance measurements in Belgium the limit of 7,000 r.p.m. was observed in indirect gears, and the maximum speed of 112.5 was reached at 6,200 r.p.m. after a fairly long run. On dry roads and with one occupant, this maximum could certainly be improved. The full width curved screen gives only partial protection to the crew of two.

Driver control of the Le Mans Lotus is ideal. The seat is not adjustable, but the position is such that most drivers feel happy at the wheel. It will be noticed from the data sheet that there are only 1¼ turns of the steering wheel from lock to lock. This is, by all standards, high-geared, even though the lock itself is very restricted by the tight enclosure of the wheels, but the driver is not aware of undue sensitiveness or constant correction of the helm. The car is, in fact, very stable directionally, and a light floating grip on the wheel is best. With load and tyre pressures as mentioned, there is a tendency to understeer, but at all speeds a touch of throttle brings the car neatly round the sharpest of corners and if need be oversteer can be induced with power.

Although it is so light, the Lotus clings to the road in a remarkable manner. Readers who have seen the marque in action at racing circuits will not need to be told that it is one of the safest and most controllable cars built. A driver can cause or experience skids and then correct them as easily as can a man on skates. The response to movement of the steering wheel is instantaneous. On corners there is no roll at all, nor is there any tyre scream. For manœuvring, the steering wheel can be moved from lock to lock with one finger, yet it is not undesirably light at maximum speed.

The Girling disc brakes are more than adequate for the car's performance, and give the driver the greatest confidence in their dependability and stopping power. Pedal pressure required for stopping from high speed is substantial but not unreasonably so; unless the discs are cold there is no squeal. The car pulls up in a straight line and even under maximum braking conditions there is little tendency for the

The wrap-round screen deflects wind but not rain. Weather protection can be provided by hard top or hood

wheels to lock. The brake and accelerator pedals are arranged to permit heel/toe changes. Incidentally the parking brake lever is transversely mounted above the passenger's knees. It is, therefore, reasonably accessible to the driver's left hand.

Two penalties to be paid for the efficient shape of the vehicle which affect ordinary driving are low ground clearance and nearness of the driver to the road surface. Obstacles which the average vehicle would clear easily—bricks or branches in the road—need to be avoided in the Lotus because of its minimal clearance and light construction. At night, dipped head lights and auxiliary lights which would not ordinarily affect the driver of an oncoming vehicle are likely to dazzle the man at the wheel of the Lotus, whose eyes are 18in to 2ft below normal levels.

Provision is made for carrying a spare wheel beneath the tail fairing, and there is no reason why a light luggage grid

should not be mounted above it. Few cars can be more accessible than the Lotus, for by unclipping four springs the whole of the front and rear portions of the bodywork can be raised from the centre on hinges at the extremities to disclose engine, brakes, de Dion rear axle, front suspension, tanks and battery.

To summarize, drivers interested in high performance cars willingly sacrifice some of the comforts and other qualities of the conventional sports car to experience the pleasures of driving a car with urge and response like those of the Lotus. It is no great hardship to have to wear suitable clothing to keep out cold and wet if the weather is bad.

The manufacturers are to be congratulated on achieving an admirable compromise between track performance and road docility. The qualities of road holding, steering and braking required for racing place this car above most others so far as safety on the road is concerned.

LOTUS ELEVEN LE MANS MODEL

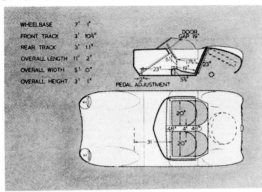

WHEELBASE	7' 1"
FRONT TRACK	3' 10¾"
REAR TRACK	3' 11"
OVERALL LENGTH	11' 2"
OVERALL WIDTH	5' 0"
OVERALL HEIGHT	3' 1"

Measurements in these ¼in to 1ft scale body diagrams are taken with the driving seat in the central position of fore and aft adjustment and with the seat cushions uncompressed

— DATA —

PRICE (basic), with two-seater body, £1,437. British purchase tax, £718. Total (in Great Britain), £2,155.

ENGINE: Capacity: 1,098 c.c. (66.9 cu in). Number of cylinders: 4. Bore and stroke: 72.4 × 66.6 mm (2.85 × 2.625 in). Valve gear: single overhead camshaft. Compression ratio: 9.8 to 1. B.H.P.: 83 at 6,800 r.p.m. (B.H.P. per ton laden 137.2). Torque: 74.5 lb ft at 4,400 r.p.m. M.P.H. per 1,000 r.p.m. on top gear, 18.00.

WEIGHT (with 5 gals fuel), 9.1 cwt (1,019 lb). Weight distribution (per cent): F, 53.9 R, 46.1. Laden as tested: 12.1 cwt (1,355 lb). Lb per c.c. (laden): 1.23.

BRAKES: Type: F & R, Girling disc. Method of operation: F, hydraulic; R, hydraulic. Disc dimensions: F, 9¼in diameter; R, 9¼in. diameter.

TYRES: 4.50—15in front; 5.00—15 rear. Pressure (lb per sq in): F, 20; R, 25 (normal). F, 30; R, 35 (for fast driving).

TANK CAPACITY: 18 Imperial gallons (not standard). Oil sump, 8 pints. Cooling system, 12 pints.

TURNING CIRCLE: 42ft (L and R). Steering wheel turns (lock to lock): 1¼.

DIMENSIONS: Wheelbase: 7ft 1in. Track: F, 3ft 10¾in; R, 3ft 11in. Length (overall): 11ft 2in. Height: 3ft 1in. Width: 5ft. Ground clearance: 5in.

ELECTRICAL SYSTEM: 12-volt; 31 ampère-hour battery. Head lights: Double dip; 48-48 watt bulbs.

SUSPENSION: Front, independent, coil springs, swing axle. Rear, de Dion, coil springs.

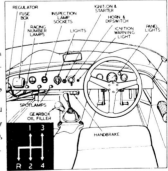

— PERFORMANCE —

ACCELERATION: From constant speeds. Speed Range Gear Ratios and Time in sec.

M.P.H.	4.22 to 1	5.79 to 1	9.32 to 1	15.30 to 1
10—30	—	—	5.1	2.8
20—40	—	—	4.0	—
30—50	—	—	3.8	—
40—60	—	6.8	—	—
50—70	12.6	6.8	—	—
60—80	11.9	7.1	—	—
70—90	14.0	8.3	—	—

From rest through gears to:

M.P.H.	sec.
30	4.0
50	7.9
60	10.9
70	15.7
80	19.2
90	25.6
100	38.9

Standing quarter mile, 17.9 sec.

SPEEDS ON GEARS:

Gear			M.P.H. (normal and max.)	K.P.H. (normal and max.)
Top	(mean)		111.75	179.8
	(best)		112.50	181.0
3rd	..	..	80—92	129—148
2nd	..	..	50—57	80—91
1st	..	..	28—34	45—55

SPEEDOMETER CORRECTION—(No speedometer fitted.)

TRACTIVE RESISTANCE: 21 lb per ton at 10 M.P.H.

TRACTIVE EFFORT:

	Pull (lb per ton)	Equivalent Gradient
Top	230	1 in 9.7
Third	340	1 in 6.5
Second	537	1 in 4.0

BRAKES:

Efficiency	Pedal Pressure (lb)
90 per cent	75
61 per cent	50
45 per cent	25

FUEL CONSUMPTION:
47.8 m.p.g. overall for 1,200 miles (5.9 litres per 100 km). Approximate normal range 44-58 m.p.g. (6.4-4.9 litres per 100 km). Fuel, premium grade.

WEATHER: Dull, cross breeze, damp concrete and tarmac. Air temperature 42 deg F. Acceleration figures are the means of several runs in opposite directions. Tractive effort and resistance obtained by Tapley meter. Model described in *The Autocar* of February 10, 1956.

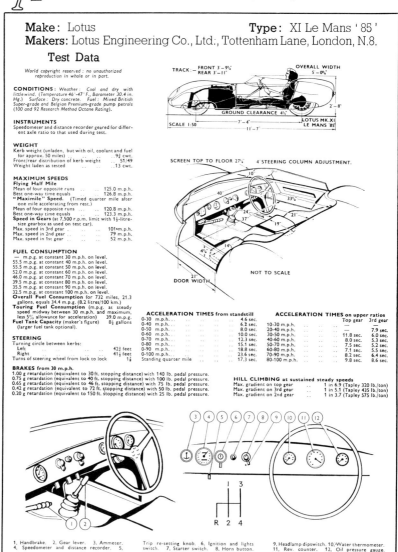

The **Motor** 786 *December 18, 1957*

The Motor Road Test No. 40/57 (Continental)—

Make: Lotus   **Type:** XI Le Mans '85'
Makers: Lotus Engineering Co., Ltd:, Tottenham Lane, London, N.8.

Test Data

World copyright reserved : no unauthorized reproduction in whole or in part.

CONDITIONS: Weather: Cool and dry with little wind. (Temperature 46°-47° F., Barometer 30.4 in. Hg.) Surface: Dry concrete. Fuel: Mixed British Super-grade and Belgian Premium-grade pump petrols (100 and 92 Research Method Octane Rating).

INSTRUMENTS
Speedometer and distance recorder geared for different axle ratio to that used during test.

WEIGHT
Kerb weight (unladen, but with oil, coolant and fuel for approx. 50 miles) .. .. 9¾ cwt.
Front/rear distribution of kerb weight .. 51/49
Weight laden as tested .. .. .. 13 cwt.

MAXIMUM SPEEDS
Flying Half Mile
Mean of four opposite runs .. .. 125.0 m.p.h.
Best one-way time equals .. .. 126.8 m.p.h.
"Maximile" Speed. (Timed quarter mile after one mile accelerating from rest.)
Mean of four opposite runs .. .. 120.8 m.p.h.
Best one-way time equals .. .. 123.3 m.p.h.
Speed in Gears (at 7,500 r.p.m. limit with 1½-litre-size gearbox as used on test car.)
Max. speed in 3rd gear .. .. 101 m.p.h.
Max. speed in 2nd gear .. .. 79 m.p.h.
Max. speed in 1st gear .. .. 52 m.p.h.

FUEL CONSUMPTION
— m.p.g. at constant 30 m.p.h. on level.
55.5 m.p.g. at constant 40 m.p.h. on level.
55.5 m.p.g. at constant 50 m.p.h. on level.
52.0 m.p.g. at constant 60 m.p.h. on level.
46.0 m.p.g. at constant 70 m.p.h. on level.
39.5 m.p.g. at constant 80 m.p.h. on level.
35.5 m.p.g. at constant 90 m.p.h. on level.
32.5 m.p.g. at constant 100 m.p.h. on level.
Overall Fuel Consumption for 732 miles, 21.3 gallons, equals 34.4 m.p.g. (8.2 litres/100 km.)
Touring Fuel Consumption (m.p.g. at steady speed midway between 30 m.p.h. and maximum, less 5% allowance for acceleration) 39.0 m.p.g.
Fuel Tank Capacity (maker's figure) 8¾ gallons (larger fuel tank optional).

STEERING
Turning circle between kerbs:
Left .. .. 42¾ feet
Right .. .. 41½ feet
Turns of steering wheel from lock to lock 1⅛

BRAKES from 30 m.p.h.
1.00 g retardation (equivalent to 30 ft. stopping distance) with 140 lb. pedal pressure.
0.75 g retardation (equivalent to 40 ft. stopping distance) with 100 lb. pedal pressure.
0.65 g retardation (equivalent to 46 ft. stopping distance) with 75 lb. pedal pressure.
0.42 g retardation (equivalent to 72 ft. stopping distance) with 50 lb. pedal pressure.
0.20 g retardation (equivalent to 150 ft. stopping distance) with 25 lb. pedal pressure.

ACCELERATION TIMES from standstill

0-30 m.p.h.	..	..	4.6 sec.
0-40 m.p.h.	..	..	6.2 sec.
0-50 m.p.h.	..	..	8.0 sec.
0-60 m.p.h.	..	..	10.0 sec.
0-70 m.p.h.	..	..	12.3 sec.
0-80 m.p.h.	..	..	15.1 sec.
0-90 m.p.h.	..	..	18.8 sec.
0-100 m.p.h.	..	..	23.6 sec.
Standing quarter mile	..	..	17.3 sec.

ACCELERATION TIMES on upper ratios

			Top gear	3rd gear
10-30 m.p.h.	..	..	—	—
20-40 m.p.h.	..	..	—	7.9 sec.
30-50 m.p.h.	..	..	11.8 sec.	6.0 sec.
40-60 m.p.h.	..	..	8.0 sec.	5.3 sec.
50-70 m.p.h.	..	..	7.5 sec.	5.2 sec.
60-80 m.p.h.	..	..	7.1 sec.	5.5 sec.
70-90 m.p.h.	..	..	8.2 sec.	6.4 sec.
80-100 m.p.h.	..	..	9.8 sec.	8.6 sec.

HILL CLIMBING at sustained steady speeds
Max. gradient on top gear .. 1 in 6.9 (Tapley 320 lb./ton)
Max. gradient on 3rd gear .. 1 in 5.1 (Tapley 435 lb./ton)
Max. gradient on 2nd gear .. 1 in 3.7 (Tapley 575 lb./ton)

TRACK:— FRONT 3'–9¼"
REAR 3'–11"
OVERALL WIDTH 5'–0½"
GROUND CLEARANCE 4½"
SCALE 1:50
7'–4"
11'–7"
2'–8"
LOTUS MK.XI LE MANS '85'

SCREEN TOP TO FLOOR 27¼" 4' STEERING COLUMN ADJUSTMENT.
NOT TO SCALE
DOOR WIDTH 21"

1, Handbrake. 2, Gear lever. 3, Ammeter. 4, Speedometer and distance recorder. 5, Trip re-setting knob. 6, Ignition and lights switch. 7, Starter switch. 8, Horn button. 9, Headlamp dipswitch. 10, Water thermometer. 11, Rev. counter. 12, Oil pressure gauge.

B16

Lotus Eleven Le Mans '85', *The Motor* 18 December 1957

————The LOTUS XI Le Mans "85"

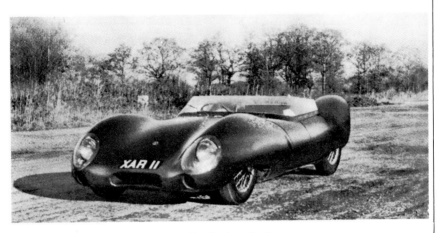

A Two-seater with Racing Performance
which can be Run on the Road

RECORDING a maximum speed of 125 m.p.h., as an average of timed two-way runs with a passenger as well as a driver being carried, the Lotus XI provides a vivid illustration of the huge gain in small sports car performance which has taken place during the past decade. Able to accelerate the same two-man load from a standstill to 100 m.p.h. in only 23.6 seconds, this car invites incredulity as to its modest 1,098 c.c. engine size, until almost equally miraculous fuel economy figures (which range from 32½ m.p.g. at a sustained 100 m.p.h. to 55½ m.p.g. at a steady 40 m.p.h. on the level) are also observed.

What sort of a car is it that Colin Chapman's brilliant team of young engineers and aerodynamicists has endowed with such astonishing acceleration, speed and economy of fuel? It is, in the form in which we drove it, a somewhat Spartan car in many respects, built to have the minimum weight and frontal area consistent with eligibility for the Le Mans 24-hour race and other sports-car fixtures. Our testing was carried out with a wrap-around windscreen of Perspex, a full-width screen but one so modest in height that a tall man is more comfortable wearing goggles and looking over it than crouching low to peer through its scratch-able transparency. No hood is provided, the two doors which open outwards on horizontal hinges do little to facilitate entry or exit from the car, and the frequently-raced test model did not claim to be proof against intrusion of water from the road into the cockpit on wet days. The bucket seats are sufficiently narrow and deep to make full jacket pockets an embarrassment, and the cockpit allows no spare width for a left foot beside the clutch pedal.

Spartan though it is by conventional standards, however, the Lotus XI with its background of success in long-distance races comes to be appreciated after a little while as an oddly comfortable car. Suitably clad and shod, a driver settles down to become very much at home behind the leather-covered steering wheel, with all the controls very conveniently at hand, and comfortably supported by the bucket seat, the curved rear wheel arch which forms a shoulder-rest on the right, and the high transmission tunnel which serves as an armrest on the left. Waste space around the passenger is even more scarce than around the driver, because of the handbrake, an unsymmetrical gearbox cover, some lateral frame tubes, and on the test car some all-too-accessible mountings of the electrical fuse and regulator boxes; yet a passenger also can learn to settle down and really enjoy being motored around with astonishing rapidity. Luggage space is scanty, there being room for a parcel above the enclosed spare wheel and for two more thin parcels just inside the doors, but as tested this was a car to carry its driver and either a passenger or some luggage, fast enough to win awards in racing yet able to run on the public roads without exciting the disapproval of the law. Available variations on the basic body include on the one hand a single-seat windscreen giving extra top speed, and on the other hand a glass windscreen giving two people slightly greater protection from the elements.

For experts on ordinary touring cars to assess the merits of the Lotus XI as a racing machine would be a foolish impertinence, and is unnecessary since results already achieved speak for themselves. Victories all over Europe and in America have confirmed that the speed and handling qualities of this model match one another. During 1957, a wishbone type of I.F.S. replaced the divided-axle layout used on earlier Lotus cars, and the result has been a great gain in ease of control at three-figure speeds on imperfect surfaces by drivers of no more than normal competence, without any offsetting loss of ultimate cornering power being evident.

Several engines can be used in this Lotus, from the 40 b.h.p. Ford 1,172 c.c. side-valve through 1,098 c.c. overhead-camshaft Coventry Climax engines in 75 b.h.p. and 84 b.h.p. forms to single-camshaft and twin-camshaft 1½-litre units of

In Brief

Price (including 84 b.h.p. engine as tested) **£1,690** plus purchase tax **£811** equals **£2,501.**
Price with 75 b.h.p. engine and normal axle (including purchase tax), **£1,937 7s. 0d**

Capacity	1,098 c.c.
Unladen kerb weight ...	9¾ cwt.
Acceleration:	
40-60 m.p.h. in top gear ...	8.0 sec.
0-50 m.p.h. through gears	8.0 sec.
Maximum top gear gradient	1 in 6.9
Maximum speed ...	...125.0 m.p.h.
"Maximile" speed ...	...120.8 m.p.h.
Touring fuel consumption ..	39.0 m.p.g.

Gearing: 17.1 m.p.h. in top gear at 1,000 r.p.m.; 39.1 m.p.h. at 1,000 ft./min. piston speed.

THE MOTOR   788   *December 18, 1957*

The LOTUS XI Le Mans

ACCESS to the Coventry Climax engine is easy when the body nose is hinged forward, details in view being the o.h.v. cover, twin S.U. carburetters with intake air box, ignition distributor and coil, hydraulic brake reservoir and rear-mounted coolant header tank.

limited availability developing up to 145 b.h.p. Our test car had the 1,098 c.c. Coventry Climax engine in stage 2 tune, developing 84 b.h.p. at 6,800 r.p.m. but giving less torque below 4,000 r.p.m. than does the 75 b.h.p. stage 1 engine. Wheel adhesion was improved because a ZF spin-limiting differential supplemented the de Dion rear axle layout on the test model, but this individual car's racing history penalized it to the extent of a 20-gallon petrol tank and extra-heavy gearbox as weight-increasing relics of past service with a 1½-litre engine and in long-distance races.

With only slight silencing of the exhaust and a fair amount of mechanical clatter, the stage 2 engine does not invite hard driving around towns. Numerous journeys in and out of central London at busy times showed a tendency for the coolant to heat up somewhat in traffic jams, and a firm clutch combined with splined rear wheel drive shafts, invited juddery starts from rest, but despite ragged carburation at low r.p.m. there was no plug-oiling or other serious temperament. Even when driven hard, the engine used very little oil. In the absence of choke controls, winter starting from cold required two hands to cover the carburetter intakes while the starter was operated, but the engine soon warmed up enough to pull normally.

In rural surroundings, the stage 2 engine begins to awaken at 3,000 r.p.m., develops its best torque at 5,000 r.p.m., and is still pulling very vigorously indeed at the suggested limit of 7,500 r.p.m. beyond which a risk of harmful contact between valves and pistons soon arises. The cry of a Lotus being driven at high r.p.m. and a wide throttle opening is decidedly audible, but less anti-social than it might be because a Lotus driven in this fashion disappears over the horizon and out of earshot in a brief space of time.

Eight different rear axle ratios are available for the car, covering a range from

SWINGING up the tail of the body reveals the battery and spare wheel, removal of the latter giving access to the de Dion rear axle assembly.

3.73/1 to 5.375/1, and our test was made with a 4.22/1 ratio with which almost exactly the maximum permitted r.p.m. were indicated at the timed maximum speed of 125 m.p.h. with full-width windscreen. For our usual standing-start acceleration tests with two people in the car, this axle ratio was too high to give best results, engagement of the clutch at even 5,000 r.p.m. being followed by a drop in r.p.m. to a figure at which there was momentary hesitation, and no wheelspin or clutchslip being evident. But, if a rest-to-30 m.p.h. time of 4.6 seconds and a standing ¼-mile time of 17.3 seconds do not represent the best that a Lotus can achieve in two-up trim (without a 1½-cwt. passenger, this 9¾-cwt. car becomes substantially livelier) such figures as rest-to-60 m.p.h. in 10.0 seconds and rest-to-100 m.p.h. in 23.6 seconds are remarkable for a car of any size and would until recently have seemed wildly impossible for an unsupercharged 1,100 c.c. car

carrying two people and using pump petrol. Most people will find that, in the lower gears, they have more power than they know how to use from this 1,100 c.c. Lotus, but once familiarity with the car is acquired the average speeds put up on away-from-towns cross-country running are astonishing, a reminder that the congested state of popular routes on summer week-ends has not eliminated all opportunities to go motoring for fun.

Perhaps partly because the coil springs had settled slightly (Lotus road-holding is based upon flexible springs controlled by exceptionally firm damper settings) the ground clearance of our test model was quite inconveniently small, especially below the disc-type inboard rear brakes but also below the sump and elsewhere, so that moderately rough going or the landing on a normal smooth road after crossing a hump-back bridge at just below take-off speed would produce grating sounds from beneath the car. On rough going, there

TAILORED to fit closely around driver and passenger are the individual seats. Wind protection is by a very low wrap-around Perspex screen, but the speedometer mounting illustrated is a temporary one for test purposes only. Fuel is normally carried alongside the passenger, the test car having a long-range tank in the scuttle.

"85"

LOW BUILD of the Lotus is emphasized in this rear view which shows how, by low mounting of the seats and some sacrifice of ground clearance, the body has been dropped well below the level of the mudguards.

was a considerable amount of rattle from the doors, wrap-around screen sections and elsewhere, the light-alloy body being functionally simple and without a scrap of superfluous weight, but ignoring this sound effect the riding comfort over most surfaces was good. The Lotus does, however, show up to best advantage (in both riding and handling qualities) on reasonably smooth roads.

Built so low to the ground and designed for racing, the car naturally corners without any perceptible roll or sidesway. The rack-and-pinion steering has comfortable self-centring action, yet is so precise and light that in ordinary road driving up to and beyond 100 m.p.h., it suffices to hold the wheel rim between the thumb and forefinger of one hand. Whereas earlier designs of Lotus chassis cornered well but needed handling with a very delicate touch in order to run truly straight at speed, this model can be placed precisely without conscious effort by the driver at speeds up to more than two miles a minute. Not pretending to be racing drivers, we confined our explorations of the ultimate limits of cornering speed to occasions when there was spare room for any resultant excitements, and whilst clumsy use of the power in a low gear on a very sharp corner could flick the tail outwards quite quickly, the handling qualities otherwise remained beautifully consistent right up to the cornering speed at which front and rear wheels were sliding outwards together. In fact, experiment confirmed our first impressions that, with consistently good cornering and an outstandingly quick response to any sudden change of plan by the driver, this car could safely be cornered at far more than normal speeds on the road.

Whilst a car weighing under 10 cwt. as it stands at the kerb does not demand great retarding forces from its braking system, a top speed of 125 m.p.h., and wind resistance so low as to let the car run very freely on the over-run, make good brakes extremely important on a car such as this. We did not have a chance to sample this Lotus in the wet, but past experience suggests that the Girling disc brakes would have been as reassuringly adequate in wet weather as they were on dry roads during this test. The pedal pressure needed actually to lock all four wheels is fairly high (there is no servo assistance) but the proportionality of braking response and the sustained firm feel of the pedal in repeated stops from high speeds give a driver great confidence. The handbrake did not earn commendation, but a hard pull to the last obtainable notch would in fact hold the car on gradients.

It is not to be expected that the Lotus XI will be bought as an economy car, but the astonishing m.p.g. figures which it can record are a testimony to its low air resistance and high engine efficiency. At any speed likely to be used outside towns, over the range from 50 m.p.h. to over 100 m.p.h., it would be difficult to find another car able to show equal economy of premium-grade petrol.

Built for the extremely specialized purpose of winning sports-car races, for which present-day requirements of roominess and weather protection are not very onerous, the Lotus XI Le Mans does not represent the average motorist's idea of an everyday car. But, it is a car which can provide extremely fast day or night travel on ordinary out-of-town roads, and can at the same time give immense enjoyment to suitably minded drivers and passengers. As an engineering tour-de-force, this race-proved two-seater of such astonishing speed and roadworthiness certainly suggests that the forthcoming coupé model from the same designers is likely to be worth waiting for.

Specification

Engine

Cylinders	4
Bore	72.4 mm.
Stroke	66.6 mm.
Cubic capacity	1,098 c.c.
Piston area	25.5 sq. in.
Valves	Single o.h. camshaft
Compression ratio	9.8/1
Carburetter	Two S.U.
Fuel pump	S.U. electrical
Ignition timing control	Centrifugal
Oil filter	Full-flow
Max. power (net)	84 b.h.p.
at	6,800 r.p.m.
Piston speed at max. b.h.p.	2,980 ft./min.

Transmission (With normal close-ratio gearbox: non-standard gearbox used on test car)

Clutch	7¼-in. single dry plate
Top gear (s/m)	4.22
3rd gear (s/m)	5.20
2nd gear (s/m)	7.05
1st gear	10.54
Reverse	10.54
Propeller shaft	Hardy Spicer open
Final drive	Hypoid bevel (choice of 8 ratios) on chassis
Top gear m.p.h. at 1,000 r.p.m.	17.1
Top gear m.p.h. at 1,000 ft./min. piston speed	39.1

Chassis

Brakes	Girling disc (outboard front, inboard rear) with hydraulic operation
Brake disc diameter	9½
Friction lining area	—
Suspension:	
Front	Independent by coil springs and wishbones, with anti-roll torsion bar
Rear	Coil springs and de Dion axle
Shock absorbers	Armstrong telescopic
Steering gear	Rack and pinion
Tyres	Dunlop racing 4.50—15 front, 5.00—15 rear

Coachwork and Equipment

Starting handle	No
Battery mounting	Behind seats
Jack	None
Jacking points: Lifting points at front and rear for use with quick-lift racing jacks.	
Standard tool kit	None
Exterior lights: 2 headlamp, 2 sidelamps, 2 tail lamps, 1 stop/number plate lamp.	
Number of electrical fuses	4
Direction indicators	None
Windscreen wipers.	Lucas electrical single-blade
Windscreen washers	None
Sun vizors	None
Instruments: Rev. counter, oil pressure gauge, ammeter, coolant thermometer (speedometer and oil thermometer optional).	
Warning lights	Dynamo charge
Locks:	
With ignition key	Ignition switch
With other keys	None
Glove lockers	None
Map pockets	Two in doors
Parcel shelves	Two inside doors
Ashtrays	None
Cigar lighters	None
Interior lights	Instrument lighting
Interior heater	None
Car radio	None
Extras available	As required
Upholstery material	Vynide
Floor covering	Carpet
Exterior colours standardized	Any colour as ordered
Alternative body styles: Full-width glass screen and hood, or single-person screen and metal cover for passenger seat, on same basic body.	

Maintenance

Sump	7 pints plus 1 pint in filter, S.A.E. 20/30 winter, S.A.E. 30/40 summer
Gearbox	2½ pints, S.A.E. 90 E.P. gear oil
Rear axle	1¾ pints, S.A.E. 90 hypoid gear oil
Steering gear lubricant	Graphite grease
Cooling system capacity	14 pints (1 drain tap)
Chassis lubrication	By grease gun every 1,000 miles to 21 points
Ignition timing	2°-6° b.t.d.c. static
Contact-breaker gap	0.015 in.
Sparking plug type	Lodge RL47
Sparking plug gap	0.022 in.
Valve timing: Inlet opens 30° b.t.d.c. and closes 60° a.b.d.c., exhaust opens 60° b.b.d.c. and closes 30° a.t.d.c.	
Tappet clearances (cold):	
Inlet and exhaust	0.006-0.008 in.
Front wheel toe-in	$\frac{3}{16}$ in.
Camber angle	½° to 1½°
Castor angle	5° to 7°
Steering swivel pin inclination	9°
Tyre pressures for road use:	
Front	18 lb.
Rear	22 lb.
(For very fast driving: Front 25 lb., Rear 30 lb.)	
Brake fluid	Wakefield
Battery type and capacity	12 v. 31 amp./hr. Exide lightweight

Appendix 2

Coventry Climax Engines

Without Coventry Climax the development of Lotus and of British motor racing generally would have been very different. Although the early Mark 6 and Mark 8 cars used Ford and MG engines, Chapman became dependent on Climax and every sports-racing car from the Mark 9 to the 19 (with the exception of the small number of Bristol-powered Mark 10s) were designed to use Climax engines and these were also used in every Lotus Formula One car from the first enlarged-capacity 12s through to the end of 1965.

Coventry Climax, run by Leonard Lee, was a long established manufacturer of fork-lift trucks and proprietary engines and did not build an engine for competition work until 1953. Chief engineer at Coventry Climax was Walter Hassan who had joined the company from Jaguar in 1950 and he was joined by Harry Munday who who had been working in an atmosphere of complete frustration on the develop ment of the supercharged V16 BRM. Because of the strong motor racing background of both Hassan and Mundy, Coventry Climax was asked by a number of British constructors to build an engine for the 2,500 cc Grand Prix Formula of 1954 onwards. Obviously the two designers were very enthusiastic and Lee sanctioned the project provided that there was no interference with the day-to-day work of the company. The result was the V8 FPE 2,477 cc unit (the FPE which meant 'Fire Pump Engine' was used purely to conceal the project from the opposition, suppliers and others whose interest was not to be encouraged). Although the new engine was successfully completed, it was never raced in its original form because Coventry Climax had been persuaded of the truth of the power output claims of some of the continental constructors. Whereas Coventry Climax wrongly believed that the 250 bhp of the FPE would have been uncompetitive, in 1954 it would have been a race-winner and its power comfortably exceeded that developed by the rival Maserati 250F and Ferrari 625/553 engines.

Instead Hassan and Mundy switched their attention to the FWA 1,098 cc single-cam engine which was derived from the FWP (Feather Weight Pump) fire-pump engine designed in 1951 and just happened to feature light-alloy construction and a single overhead camshaft cylinder head. The new FWA (Feather Weight Automotive) was first used by Kieft in 1954, it was fitted by Dickie Steed to his Lotus Mark 8 delivered in August 1954 and from 1955 onwards was standard 'wear' in the rear-engined Cooper sports-racing cars and the Lotus sports-racing car from the Mark 9 through to the 23, although of course most of the last-named were powered by Ford-

Cosworth engines. The FWA was used by a whole host of constructors big and small including Arnott (1955-57), Buckler, Beart-Rodger, Elva, Gilby, Halseylec (Eric Brandon's two cars built in 1955), Kinloch, Lester, Lola, Tojeiro and Victoria (Cedric Brierley's successful 'one-off').

From the FWA Coventry Climax developed the 1,460 cc FWB engine, a 'stop-gap' produced in small numbers in 1956 and used in the first Formula Two Coopers and in Lotus Elevens. Other variants were the FWC 744 cc engine used in the Index of Performance-winning Lotus at Le Mans in 1957 and the 1,216 cc FWE which was a production engine used in the Lotus Elite (of which 1,029 chassis units were built).

The next stage in development was the FPF 1,475 cc twin overhead camshaft engine that appeared in 1957 and, although by no means directly based on the original 1953 V8, incorporated the experience gained with that project, especially so far as valve gear was concerned. The FPF was primarily designed for the 1,500 cc Formula Two, but. as can be seen from the table, it was gradually enlarged to 2,495 cc, in which form it powered the Formula One Coopers and Lotus 16s and 18s of the 1959-60 era. A 2,750 cc engine was produced for Indianapolis (and used there in Brabham's Cooper in 1961) and there was also a 1,498 cc variant for the 1,500 cc Formula One of 1961 onwards until Coventry Climax's new V8 was ready.

Another line of development by Coventry Climax was the FWM series of engines (FWM meant Feather Weight Marine). The first of these engines was a 633 cc single-cam to be used in outboard-engined boats. From this were developed the FWMA and FWMC (the latter twin overhead camshaft) 745 cc units supplied to Lotus for use at Le Mans. The FWMA design was sold to the Rootes Group and was developed into the Hillman Imp engine.

For the 1,500 cc Formula One of 1961 onwards Lee had sanctioned the development of the 1,495 cc FWMV engine, incorporating some design features of the four-cylinder FWM engines. The V8 first appeared in Jack Brabham's Cooper at the Nürburgring in 1961 and was used by the British constructors from 1962 onwards. These engines were progressively developed during the life of the Formula and in 1965 versions with four-valve cylinder heads were supplied to Lotus (for Jim Clark) and Jack Brabham for use in his own cars. A final version of the V8 was a special 1,974 cc engine built by Coventry Climax (after they had officially withdrawn from racing) to power Jim Clark's Lotus 33 in the first year of the 3,000 cc Grand Prix Formula.

Jaguar took over Coventry Climax in 1963 and although Sit William Lyons allowed the racing programme to continue, it was decided that the company would pull out of racing altogether at the end of 1965. The announcement coincided with the appearance of Coventry Climax's last Formula One design, the very brilliant, very complex FWMW flat-16 of 1,495 cc that was never raced.

Coventry Climax Engines, 1953-66

FPE (1953)	2,477 cc V8 twin-cam (76.2 x 67.94 mm)	Developed for the 2,500 cc Formula One of 1954 onwards, but never raced. The engines were sold to Paul Emery in the 1960s and one, enlarged to 3 litres, powered the unsuccessful Shannon in the 1966 British Grand Prix.
FWA (1954 onwards)	1,098 cc single-cam (72.4 x 66.7 mm)	Extensively used in British 1,100 cc sports-racing cars. Stage 1: 72 bhp at 6,000 rpm Stage 2: 83 bhp at 6,800 rpm Stage 3: 84 bhp at 6,800 rpm
FWB (1956)	1,460 cc single-cam (76.2 x 80 mm)	Interim, enlarged version of the FWA used by Lotus in the Eleven and in the Formula Two Cooper.
FWC (1957)	744 cc single-cam (76.2 x 45.2 mm)	A 'one-off' engine built for use by Lotus at Le Mans. It won the Index of Performance and the 750 cc class.
FWE (1957 onwards)	1,216 cc single-cam (76.2 x 66.7 mm)	Production engine used by Lotus in the Elite.
FPF (1957 onwards)	1,475 cc twin-cam (81.2 x 71.1 mm	Developed primarily for Formula Two, the engine was also used by both Lotus and Cooper in sports-racing cars. Power output 142 bhp at 6,750 rpm.
FPF (1957 onwards)	1,960 cc twin-cam (86.4 x 83.8 mm)	Enlarged version of the FPF, originally for the Rob Walker and Cooper teams, but later used by Lotus in sports-racing cars.
FPF (1958)	2,015 cc twin-cam 87.5 x 83.8 mm)	Version of the FPF enlarged by Alf Francis for the Rob Walker team.
FPF (1958 onwards)	2,207 cc twin-cam (88.9 x 88.9 mm)	Works stretched version of the FPF produced in very small numbers and later used by Lotus in sports-racing cars. Power output 194 bhp at 6.250 rpm.
FPF (1959 onwards)	2,495 cc twin-cam (94.0 x 89.9 mm)	Definitive 1959-60 Formula One engine, later used by Lotus in sports-racing cars. Power output initially 220 bhp at 6,750 rpm, later 240 bhp at 6,750 rpm.
FPF (1961 onwards)	2,750 cc twin-cam	Developed for Indianapolis, 1961 and subsequently raced in Intercontinental events. Power output 251 bhp at 6,250 rpm.
FPF Mk II	1,498 cc twin-cam (81.8 x 71.1 mm)	Interim engine for the 1,500 cc Formula One of 1961 onwards.
FWMA (1958)	745 cc single-cam (64.3 x 57.2 mm)	Developed for Lotus to use at Le Mans, 1958, but plagued by problems.
FWMC (1961)	745 cc twin-cam (64.3 x 57.2 mm)	Used in the UDT-Laystall-entered Lotus Elite at Le Mans in 1961.

FWMV (1961 onwards)	1,495 cc twin-cam V8 (63.0 x 60.0 mm)	Formula One engine with power output of 186 bhp at 8,500 rpm.
FWMV (1963 onwards)	1,495 cc twin-cam V8 (67.94 x 51.66 mm)	Formula One engine with revised cylinder dimensions.
FWMV (1964 onwards)	1,497 cc twin-cam V8 (72.39 x 45.47 mm)	Formula One engine with further revised cylinder dimensions. The engines with four valves per cylinder loaned to Brabham and Lotus in 1965 developed 212 bhp at 10,300 rpm.
FWMV (1966)	1,974 cc twin-cam V8 (72.39 x 60.0 mm)	One-off version built for Lotus for 1966 Formula One. Power output 244 bhp at 8,900 rpm.
FWMW (1965)	1,495 cc twin-cam flat-16 1,495 cc (54.1 x 40.64 mm)	Never raced, but in testing in early form developed 209 bhp at 12,000 rpm.

Index